MENTALIZING
IN CHILD THERAPY

Developments in Psychoanalysis Series

Peter Fonagy, Mary Target, & Liz Allison (Series Editors)
Published and distributed by Karnac Books

Other title in the Series

Developmental Science and Psychoanalysis: Integration and Innovation. Celebrating the Renewal of the Collaboration of the Yale Child Study Center and the Anna Freud Centre in Promoting Psychoanalytic Developmental Research
  Edited by Linda Mayes, Peter Fonagy, & Mary Target

Orders
Tel: +44 (0)20 7431 1075; Fax: +44 (0)20 7435 9076
Email: shop@karnacbooks.com
www.karnacbooks.com

MENTALIZING IN CHILD THERAPY
Guidelines for Clinical Practitioners

Edited by
Annelies J. E. Verheugt-Pleiter,
Jolien Zevalkink, & Marcel G. J. Schmeets

Foreword by
Peter Fonagy

KARNAC

First published in 2008 by
Karnac Books
118 Finchley Road
London NW3 5HT

Dutch edition: *Mentaliseren in de kindertherapie*, copyright © 2005, Koninklijke Van
Gorcum BV, Assen, The Netherlands.

British Library Cataloguing in Publication Data

A C.I.P. for this book is available from the British Library

ISBN: 978-1-85575-581-9

Edited, designed, and produced by Communication Crafts

Printed in Great Britain

www.karnacbooks.com

CONTENTS

CHAPTER EIGHT

Intervention techniques: affect regulation

CHAPTER NINE

Intervention techniques: mentalization

ACKNOWLEDGEMENTS

Acknowledgements are in order. First of all, we would like to thank the children and their parents for their participation in the project. We are very grateful for their permission to make the video recordings and to use the therapy material. The personal details have naturally been anonymized. To identify the techniques or interventions that can be classified under mentalization-based psychotherapy, in 2002 a project group was set up, with the following members: Josée Haghedooren, Wietske van der Ree, Marja Rexwinkel, Arjen Schut, Froukje Slijper, and Annelies Verheugt-Pleiter—the latter also as project leader. They carried out the therapies, observed one another's treatments, identified the specific mentalization-based child therapy techniques, and discussed among themselves how to classify these techniques. The project was supervised by a supervisory committee consisting of Jolien Zevalkink, Annelies Verheugt-Pleiter, and Marcel Schmeets. The manuscript was given a thorough going over by Filip De Volder. Thanks are also due to Jan Stoker for his comments on a previous version of chapter 4, and to Gwen Marcelis for her comments on an earlier version of chapter 5. We want to thank all of them for their creative efforts and their enthusiasm in carrying out the project.

The English edition is an adaptation of the Dutch edition, which was published in 2005. A large part of the funding for the English translation was contributed by the "Psychoanalytische Fondsen" [Psychoanalytic Fund], and the editors would like to thank them for their generous financial contribution, which made the Dutch–English translation possible. The first two chapters were translated with the aid of the Frijling Prins Fonds and the Netherlands Psychoanalytic Institute. Finally, without the constructive support and trust of Peter Fonagy, we could not have made the language leap across the Channel.

The book was translated by Carol Stennis, a certified translator and member of the American Translators Association. The photographs were taken by Froukje Slijper.

Annelies J. E. Verheugt-Pleiter, Jolien Zevalkink,
& Marcel G. J. Schmeets

SERIES FOREWORD

Peter Fonagy, Mary Target, & Liz Allison

After the first hundred years of its history, psychoanalysis has matured into a serious, independent intellectual tradition, which has notably retained its capacity to challenge established truths in most areas of our culture. Above all, psychoanalytic ideas have given rise to an approach to the treatment of mental disorders and character problems—psychodynamic psychotherapy— which has become a thriving tradition in most countries, at least in the Western world.

The biological psychiatrist of today is called to task by psychoanalysis, much as was the specialist in nervous diseases of Freud's time, in turn-of-the-century Vienna. Today's cultural commentators, regardless of whether they are for or against psychoanalytic ideas, are obliged to pay attention to considerations of unconscious motivation, defences, the formative impact of early childhood experience, and the myriad other discoveries that psychoanalysts brought to twentieth-century culture. Twenty-first century thought implicitly incorporates much of what was discovered by psychoanalysis in the last century. Critics who try to pick holes in or even demolish the psychoanalytic edifice are often doing this from ramparts constructed on psychoanalytic foundations. A good example of this would be the recent attacks by some cognitive behaviour therapists on psychodynamic approaches. Vehement as these are, they have to give credit to psychoanalysis for its contribution to cognitive therapeutic theory and technique. These authors point to the advances they have made in relation to classical ideas but rarely acknowledge that the psychodynamic approach has also advanced. An unfortunate feature of such debates is that often attacks on psychoanalysis are addressed to where the discipline was 50 or even 75 years ago.

Both the epistemology and the conceptual and clinical claims of psychoanalysis are often passionately disputed. We see this as a sign that psychoanalysis may be unique in its capacity to challenge and provoke. Why should this be? Psychoanalysis is unrivalled in the depth of its questioning of human motivation, and whether its answers are right or wrong, the epistemology of psychoanalysis allows it to confront the most difficult problems of human experience. Paradoxically, our new understanding of the physical basis of our existence—our genes, nervous systems, and endocrine functioning—has, rather than finally displacing psychoanalysis, created a pressing need for a complementary discipline that considers the memories, desires, and meanings that are beginning to be recognized as influencing human adaptation even at the biological level. How else, other than through the study of subjective experience, will we understand the expression of the individual's biological destiny within the social environment?

It is not surprising, then, that psychoanalysis continues to attract some of the liveliest intellects in our culture. These individuals are by no means all psychoanalytic clinicians, or psychotherapists. They are distinguished scholars in an almost bewildering range of disciplines, from the study of mental disorders with their biological determinants to the disciplines of literature, art, philosophy, and history. There will always be a need to explicate the meaning of experience. Psychoanalysis, with its commitment to understanding subjectivity, is in a leading position to fulfil this intellectual and human task. We are not surprised at the upsurge of interest in psychoanalytic studies in universities in many countries. The books in this series will aim to address the same intellectual curiosity that has made these educational projects so successful.

The theme of our series is a focus on advances in psychoanalysis: hence our series title, "Developments in Psychoanalysis". In our view, while psychoanalysis has a glorious and rich history, it also has an exciting future, with dramatic changes and shifts as our understanding of the mind is informed by scientific, philosophical, and literary enquiry. Our commitment is to no specific orientation, to no particular professional group, but to the intellectual challenge to explore questions of meaning and interpretation systematically, and in a scholarly way. Nevertheless, we would be glad if this series particularly spoke to the psychotherapeutic community—to those individuals who use their own minds and humanity to help others in distress.

Our focus in this series is to communicate some of the intellectual excitement that we feel about the past, present, and future of psychoanalytic ideas, and which we enjoy seeing in our students each year. We hope that our work with the authors and editors in the series will help to make these ideas accessible to an even larger group of students, scholars, and practitioners worldwide.

University College London

ABOUT THE EDITORS AND CONTRIBUTORS

MARJA J. REXWINKEL is a clinical psychologist, psychoanalytic psychotherapist, and child psychoanalyst (IPA) at the Netherlands Psychoanalytic Institute (NPI) and in private practice. She has over twenty years of experience in working with children, adolescents, and some parents, and for the past decade she has specialized in parent–infant psychotherapy and has developed a special interest in attachment- and mentalization-based programmes. She heads the infant team at NPI. She has published articles on infant mental health and parent–infant psychotherapy. She participates in several training programmes. In addition, she is head of a two-year psychotherapy course organized by RINO that focuses on Infant Mental Health, in which infant observation is an important part of the training to become an Infant Mental Health specialist.

MARCEL G. J. SCHMEETS is a child psychiatrist and psychoanalyst (IPA) at the Netherlands Psychoanalytic Institute (NPI) and in private practice. He has over twenty years of experience in working with children and their parents. He heads the Child and Adolescent Department of NPI. At the present time he also chairs the board of the Dutch branch of the World Association for Infant Mental Health (WAIMH). His professional focus is on (the theory of) mentalizing, brain development, and infant mental health. He has published several articles on the integration of research findings from different disciplines, such as neurosciences, child development, and psychoanalysis. He participates in numerous training programmes.

FROUKJE M. E. SLIJPER is a psychoanalyst (IPA) and sexuologist (IASR). She works with adults, children, and adolescents in private practice and at the children's department of the Netherlands Psychoanalytical Institute (NPI). The first three decades of her professional career, she worked at the child and adolescent department of the ErasmusMC/ Sophia Children's Hospital in Rotterdam. Her PhD thesis (1983), entitled "Gender role Behavior in Girls with Congenital Adrenal Hyperplasia", has focused on the treatment of gender dysphoria and intersex problems. She has published many papers on these topics. Froukje Slijper has also published papers on psychoanalytic topics such as: "Psychoanalytic psychotherapy: Comparing classical interventions and mentalization based interventions" and "Enhancing parental skills by developing mentalization in parents". Together with Annelies Verheugt-Pleiter, she is a trainer in Mentalization-Based Child Therapy.

ANNELIES J. E. VERHEUGT-PLEITER is a clinical psychologist and a psychoanalyst (IPA) of adults and children at the Netherlands Psychoanalytic Institute (NPI) and in private practice. Her twenty years of experience also include working with adolescents and parents. She is a Training Analyst in the Dutch Psychoanalytic Society. As head of the department for Knowledge Transfer at the NPI, she is responsible for the development, implementation, and organization of the educational activities. As director of the project on Mentalization-Based Child Psychotherapy, she had been responsible for the categorization of the empirical observations. She has edited several books on psychoanalytic topics, such as *Psychanalyse anno nu* (2006), that consisted of 27 chapters in remembrance of Freud's 150 birthday. She has co-authored a paper on a clinical comparison of "Mentalization-Based Therapy and Transference Focused Psychotherapy" in *Psychoanalytic Psychotherapy*.

JOLIEN ZEVALKINK is a developmental psychologist and social anthropologist. She is a member of the Society for Psychotherapy Research. She heads the department for Research and Quality Assurance at the Netherlands Psychoanalytic Institute (NPI) and is currently teacher at the Radboud University Nijmegen. Her PhD dissertation (1997), entitled "Attachment in Indonesia: The Mother–Child Relationship in Context", has examined the quality of attachment relationships in economically deprived Sudanese–Indonesian families. At NPI, she has developed a routine outcome monitoring system that aims to follow the progress of children, adolescents, and adults before and during psychoanalytic treatment. The results are used both clinically, to discuss the individual patient's progress, and in research projects, to study the effectiveness of these treatments. She is particularly interested in bridging the gap between scientific research and clinical practice. She is the author of several papers in the field of developmental psychology and psychotherapy research and teaches in a wide range of training programmes.

FOREWORD

Peter Fonagy

The reader holds in his or her hands what we hope is the next chapter in the development of psychoanalytic techniques in individual therapy with children. Annelies J. E. Verheugt-Pleiter, Jolien Zevalkink, and Marcel G. J. Schmeets have put together an invaluable book that serves as the basis for training in individual child psychotherapy within the mentalization model. The model itself is quite simple. It assumes that many of the most important capacities associated with social cognition are programmed by evolution to be acquired in an interpersonal context, primarily a dyadic relationship between the infant and his or her attachment figure. With care and sensitivity, the therapeutic relationship between child therapist and patient can recreate elements of this generative intersubjective encounter with a healing function, in many respects regardless of the specific problem presented by the child. The experience of an interpersonal interchange in which the child can learn to see him/ herself as a psychological agent at the same time as seeing someone else working to create a picture of him or her as a psychological entity, the experience of another mind having his or her mind in mind, is crucial in reviving the capacity to perceive wishes and intentions in oneself and in others. The focus on the patient's mental function has always been at the heart of psychoanalytic and other psychodynamic treatments. Often as psychoanalytic clinicians we have been more concerned to discover what was hidden from us than what was presented to us and yet was not properly experienced by our patients. The issue in the kind of therapy that you will find in this book is less to do with rediscovering mental content that may once have been available but has become hidden, and more about helping the child to discover his or her capacity to be aware of the subtlety and complexity of his or her own and others' feelings, to place thought in between stimulus and action, to come to tolerate frustration, to be able to remember and recall experiences at will, to see the world with a minimum of self-serving distortion, to be able to apologize but also to be able to forgive.

The treatment strategy advanced in this book is innovative. The chapter by Annelies Verheugt-Pleiter describes the key elements of the approach, integrating the work of Efrain Bleiberg, Anne Hurry, Viviane Green, Anthony Bateman, Mary Target, and others to outline a model of working with the parents and the child in which the therapist adopts the stance of someone who does not assume that he or she know everything about the content of other minds but who models the process of trying to understand. The integration offered in the book brings together the work of my colleagues and myself on mentalization-based treatments with classical psychoanalytic work (Bion, Winnicott, Greenspan, Kernberg, Alvarez, and others). The treatment strategy that emerges creates a permissive framework for child psychotherapy that is firm in structure yet flexible in its focus, showing determination, conviction, and commitment and yet avoiding the pitfall of presuming to know and thus potentially foreclosing the child's budding capacity to think and feel for him/herself.

As the chapter by Rexwinkel and Verheugt-Pleiter beautifully describes, parents—and the family more generally—provide a key context for mentalization. Learning to understand misunderstanding and to repair misattunement are shown to be critical components of recruiting the parents to support the child.

The book is based on the systematic observation of therapy. Zevalkink elegantly describes the way in which study of theory and observation of interpersonal interaction can combine to generate a therapeutic approach based on identifiable techniques that can be spelt out, learned, focused on, disseminated, tested, and replicated.

Three chapters in this book present an invaluable set of insights into the ways in which child psychotherapy is probably often practiced and is probably most likely to be effective. Three key elements— attention regulation, affect regulation, and mentalization—are identified. Running across these three sets of treatment foci are common principles: a concern with the here and now, contact with the current mental state of the patient , ensuring the re-presentation of internal experience, a certain playfulness, and the engagement with process over content. Verheugt-Pleiter's manualization of techniques of working with attention in Chapter 7 is simple yet powerful. She describes, among others, the experience and causes of anxiety, making contact with the patient and retaining continuity of interaction, explicating interactions in mental state terms—techniques that are no doubt in common use in all therapies but are here clearly explicated and specified so that the reader can learn from examples of both what to do and how it should be done. Similarly, Chapter 8 on affect regulation gives clear advice on playing with boundaries, giving reality to the value of affect states, and guiding the development of a second-order representation of affect. Chapter 9 on mentalization techniques offers simple suggestions on how to comment on mental contents, where to focus interest in the child's subjective experience, and ways in which the therapist can engage with the child's mental processes and verbalize thoughts, feelings, and intentions. In a way this is the heart of the therapy, but the heart is also in the entire approach, the setting, the stages of therapy, the therapeutic relationship, usefully integrated by Slijper in Chapter 10.

This book is distinguished by three unique features: the simplicity and elegance of the links drawn between theory and practice, the full and realistic explication of the techniques recommended, and, finally, its orientation towards research and evaluation. The first of these attributes is a reflection of the creativity, scholarship, and intelligence of the authors. The second reflects clinical sensitivity, a wealth of clinical experience, and at times touching eloquence. The third attribute is perhaps the most unusual in the context of a clinical monograph. This is the first manual of child psychotherapy that is worthy of the name. It is clear, would be easy to replicate, and is applicable to a wide range of children. Unlike many treatment manuals that focus on a single group, this book encompasses a broad range of problems presented by children and families. I believe that there is an important place for these manuals, because children do not come with specific, easily classifiable problems: they arrive in our consulting rooms feeling themselves to be the problem. It is the assistance provided to therapists in understanding these young individuals and creating a healing relationship that makes this book such a precious contribution. Many therapists reading this book will acquire new ideas, develop new techniques, and be enabled to adopt fresh perspectives on cases that they are working with already. Others will find the book reassuring, and may find themselves saying "But this is what I do already!" This is the greatest compliment that they can pay to this effort at systematizing the common effective component of child psychotherapeutic technique.

MENTALIZING
IN CHILD THERAPY

CHAPTER ONE

Introduction

Marcel G. J. Schmeets, Annelies J. E. Verheugt-Pleiter,
Jolien Zevalkink

P sychoanalysis has always been in a process of development, and mentalization-based child therapy—previously known as developmental therapy—for the treatment of children whose development has come to a standstill is the latest branch on this tree of knowledge (Bateman & Fonagy, 2004; Hurry, 1998a). A combination of data from psychoanalysis, infant research, attachment research, and neurobiology was of decisive significance in reaching this point. It is becoming clear that neurobiological processes can be understood very well on the basis of psychoanalytic frameworks (Kaplan-Solms & Solms, 2000). These new insights into people's mental functioning also serve to foster collaboration, resulting in an integration of the more relationship-oriented and the more competence-oriented treatments. This book aims to fill a growing need in mental health care for children and young people for an integrated treatment—that is, one using several different modes of treatment simultaneously when the problems are complex. Treating complex problems in children with new psychoanalytic techniques is expected to add a new dimension to the practice of treatment, one that is interesting to cognitive behavioural therapists and psychoanalytically schooled psychotherapists alike. One step further, mental health care for children and adolescents may well draw benefits from the achievements of psychoanalysis, thus embedding psychoanalysis more firmly in the field of mental health care. To achieve this, not only will the various forms of psychotherapy need to be integrated, but the therapists as well (Bateman & Fonagy, 2004; Bleiberg, 2001).

The theory with respect to mentalization can be seen as a psychoanalytic model within developmental psychopathology. The field of work of developmental psychopathology focuses on the interaction between normal and atypical development: it emphasizes the use of a developmental framework in understanding psychological adaptation (Cicchetti & Cohen, 1995). Various theoretical models exist in this field. For their further development, theoretical models need feedback from both researchers and therapists who work with the children targeted in the model. Researchers may be able to demonstrate some relationships posited by the theory, although this may be more difficult in other parts of the model. Therapists may also find that some constructs are not workable in clinical practice. All these experiences can further refine the model. At the same time, a good theory ought to be a practical theory. The theoretical framework was formulated on the basis of extensive empirical attachment research (Bateman & Fonagy, 2004; Fonagy, 2001a). In this line of thinking, the present book can also not be regarded as an end point in itself. It describes a point in time in the development of therapeutic possibilities that can be achieved with mentalization-based child therapy.

In this chapter, starting from this theoretical framework, we focus on children who have difficulty to sense intuitively what they, and others, express in their actions. Essential mental processes do not operate properly in these children. More specifically, they are unable to see themselves and others as creatures with inner intentions. This means that they do not have a coherent inner world, and they are often driven by what happens to cross their path. We see these problems—as do Bateman and Fonagy (2004)—primarily as a disorder in the perception of the self as an active agent. Classical psychoanalytic therapy gives interpretations and suggestions about conflicts between wishes, fantasies, and reality, but this is only possible if a child is able to perceive these. In children with a serious disorder, the mental processes necessary for this are underdeveloped (Hurry, 1998a). We have come to refer to setting in motion the blocked mental processes as mentalization-based child therapy, on analogy with mentalization-based treatment for adults (Bateman & Fonagy, 2004). Mentali-zation-based child therapy comprises a number of techniques that address deficiencies in specific areas of psychological development (Cluckers, 1986; Hellendoorn, Groothoff, Mostert, & Harinck, 1992; Thoomes-Vreugdenhil, 2000; Verhofstadt-Denève, 1988). In terms of DSM–IV, such children are often diagnosed as having a Pervasive Development Disorder (PDD, PDD–NOS), Asperger's syndrome, or Disruptive Disorders such as attention-deficit/hyperactivity disorder (ADHD), oppositional–defiant behavioural disorder (ODD), or con-duct disorder (CD). In these children, the most important objective of treatment is to encourage the emergence of a coherent self, a sense of agency, and a capacity to postpone, modulate, and regulate emotional reactions (Tyson, 2005).

In normal development, in order for a child to develop a mentaliz-ing self-organization, it is of great importance for the child to explore the mental state of a sensitive caregiver. In the caregiver's mind, the child finds a picture of himself[1] as a being motivated by thoughts, feelings, and intentions. This refers not only to acquiring the capacity to read another person's mind, but also the integrative role played by such a capacity in a person's self-organization (Fonagy, Gergely, Jurist, & Target, 2002). A child who understands more about what might motivate others and can show some empathy for his own mo-tives will have greater flexibility in thinking and will be able to learn from incorrect assessments. This gives the child a fantastic resource to use in social life, in dealing with stress, and in building up a sense of self that will give direction to the child's actions. In many children this process has come to a standstill in certain areas because they did not feel they were seen, heard, or understood in their primary attach-ment relationship. These children have built up little in the way of an inner world, or they have a chaotic inner world that has internal-ized, for example, an overpowering, aggressive person, or a rejecting, depressive person. This can lead to rigid, controlling behaviour or to withdrawn, avoidant behaviour.

As we see it, mentalization-based child therapy leans heavily on systematic observation of the mentalizing techniques used in the

---

[1] For grammatical simplicity and comprehensibility the feminine pronoun has been used throughout the book for otherwise unidentified caregivers and therapists, and the masculine pronoun for children in general.

course of a therapy. The current book reports on a project in which these observations were carried out: the initial stages of six treatments were followed intensively, and the observing therapists wrote down interventions they had noted in each observed therapeutic session. The result is a unique data collection that has formed the basis for this manual. We have given the six children, who will often be quoted in this book, the following names: "Paul" (9 yrs), "Geert" (8 yrs), "Maartje" (7 yrs), "Ivo" (11 yrs), "Xander" (9 yrs), and "Eduard" (10 yrs). Observing treatments in their initial stages has had its disadvantages. For instance, in the middle stages of therapy, children might have exhibited different types of negative reactions from those included in the current observational system. In line with an earlier retrospective study of the predictors of results in child therapy (Fonagy & Target, 1996b), the children in our group also seemed to profit most from psychoanalytic treatment of a high frequency—an understandable result when we consider the seriousness of the disorder in personality development. In our ambulatory setting, we have therefore opted for fairly intensive treatment, with a frequency of two sessions per week. In the six cases described in this book, a higher frequency was not feasible in view of the parents' limited tolerance and the logistics problems in these families. The optimum frequency remains a point of discussion. If the frequency is high—that is, five sessions a week—the attachment system becomes activated to such a degree that anxiety can also mount. If the frequency is too low, the attachment system is not activated enough, yielding too little leverage for change. So far, our conclusion has been that two or three sessions a week is best.

In our six cases, parent guidance, which we always carry out parallel to child therapies, proved to be more intensive and of a different nature than when it accompanies regular psychoanalytic child therapy. On the one hand, this has to do with problems that the parents have. They are often people whose thinking is highly concrete and who spend little time reflecting on their children's intentions. If parents become better able to untangle complicated family interactions with the help of the parent counsellor, this is of great therapeutic value for them. They begin to feel more competent, and their ties with their children improve. On the other hand, it is also of great value for the treatment of the child. If parents gain a better picture of their children's thoughts or intentions—not only those of the child who is in therapy, but of their other children or the child's friends as well—then this helps them to deal with this and to coach their children better. If the situation at home becomes more reflective, then there is a greater chance that the mentalizing ability of the child will show improvement. We are in favour of an "integration of therapists", by which we mean that parent supervisor and child psychotherapist need to work together so that both of them can keep their focus on mentalization. Sometimes other care workers are also involved, or perhaps the child's teacher. Retaining a consistent focus on mentalization therefore demands consultation on a regular basis. Just as in the adult variant of mentalization-based treatment, practice has shown that therapist peer review meetings are a necessary and permanent aspect of such treatment. It is easy for schisms to occur between therapists, and they require mutual attunement. The better integrated the therapists, the safer the climate becomes for parents and children. There is a great deal to be said for the use of a family therapy such as Short-term Mentalization and Relational Therapy (SMART) (Fearon et al., 2006), where parents and children work together to acquire a picture of each other's mental situation and learn some perspective on how much you can know about another person. If there has been no treatment as yet, from the point of view of stepped care, such a form is preferable. But if several care workers are already involved, we prefer to work with children and parents separately, because then we can focus in greater detail on building up the sense of self in both of them. Often, these are children and parents with a negative self-image, who need the exclusiveness of a relationship with a therapist in order to build up their sense of self by means of mentalizing interventions. By exclusiveness we do not mean intimacy. It has been our experience that empathy and proximity must be offered cautiously. The objective is certainly not to provide the affection that the child and the parent are lacking: this would show a complete misperception of the major damage caused by intensely emotionally charged interactions that require very specific repair work.

In carrying out the project, our goal was to develop a joint framework of concepts formulated on the basis of clinical empiricism. In the future we want to take this one step further. In writing this text, one of our objectives is to perform scientific research. The text describes techniques intended to promote specific aspects of a child's development. We hope very soon to be able to conduct scientific research to measure the effectiveness of this mentalization-based psychotherapy. On another front, the guidelines provided here aim to fill the need of practitioners to gain more insight into modified psychoanalytic treatment methods. In this light, the book can also be used as a textbook for training courses.

The structure of the volume is as follows. Chapter 2 describes the theories on which mentalization-based child therapy is based. The concepts involved and the theoretical framework are discussed at length. At the back of the book there is a glossary for easy reference, giving the meanings of the constructs described. Chapter 3 describes the group of children we work with and the diagnostic process. The description of the group is still largely based on theoretical considerations and diagnostic criteria that were formulated on this basis. These criteria can be operationalized with diagnostic instruments. Chapter 4 covers treatment strategy and guidelines in carrying out mentalization-based child therapy. This chapter sketches backgrounds and therapeutic frameworks to the treatment and concludes by formulating a few basic principles underlying this form of treatment. Chapter 5 describes the specific characteristics of guidance for parents with children in mentalization-based child therapy. Chapter 6 describes the procedure followed and the methods used to obtain the data that form the basis for this text. Chapters 7, 8, and 9 contain the empirically observed and identified mentalization-based child therapy techniques, classified into three groups: attention regulation, affect regulation, and mentalization (Bateman, 2002). These observation categories are useful when discussing the therapy during peer review meetings, for training purposes, and as a process measure in effect study. They offer a perspective on the practice of mentalization-based child therapy. These categories also form the basis for critical reflection and future adaptations. For ease of identification, the categories have been summarized and tabulated in Appendix A, and each has been provided with a short label. Chapter 10 summarizes issues that may come up in carrying out the treatment. The chapter discusses matters such as becoming acquainted, the therapeutic setting, and the various stages in the course of a treatment. Finally, in Chapter 11, research questions are formulated that point the way for future research and also show what aspects should be included in setting up research on the effectiveness of mentalization-based child therapy.

CHAPTER TWO

Theoretical concepts

Marcel G. J. Schmeets

This chapter takes a closer look at the concept of mentalization and the way in which this ability comes into being. The quality of the mother–child relationship seems to play a crucial role in this respect. In the process of learning to make representations, it is important that the child is given space by another person—for example, the mother—between the direct primary experience of the affect and being able to think about the affect. At this juncture, the capacity of the mother to make her own representations is decisive for the extent to which the child "learns" this ability from her. Intrapsychic processes in the mother are formative for the degree to which a child learns to mentalize. Traumatic experiences that are unmentalized in the mother will lead to blind (unmentalized) spots in the child. They are part of the information stored on a daily basis that helps to shape the structure of the brain, leading to personality traits and possibly also to psychopathology.

Introduction

Mentalization means the—often nonconscious—ability, when inter-
acting with others, to continually make the assumption that, like
yourself, others too have an internal world, with their own feelings,
thoughts, and desires (Fonagy, Gergely, et al., 2002). The ability to
mentalize is typically human. Mentalization presumes intentionality and second-order representation. The ability to mentalize might
be something that needs to be acquired in the course of the development. It resembles the concept of Theory of Mind because both
theorize about the possibility of reflecting on thoughts and feelings.
It differs in that the concept of mentalizing includes relationship
dynamics (e.g. Allen, 2006). Cognitive psychology assumes that a
Theory of Mind (Baron-Cohen, 1991; Leslie, 1987;) is an emergent
process—that is to say, it comes about by itself. The psychoanalytic
view of how the ability to mentalize develops starts from the assumption that not only is the basis laid during the child's early years,
but this ability is shaped in and by an affective relationship with the
caregiver. The quality of the intimate affective relationship between
parent and child is very decisive for developing the ability to mentalize, and being able to mentalize has, in turn, a great impact on a
child's ability to regulate himself. In order to develop a mentalizing
self-organization, exploration of the mental state of the sensitive
caregiver is of great importance. The child constructs a hypothetical representation of the caregiver's or mother's mind to explain
her behaviour towards him. In the mother's mind, the child finds a
picture of himself as motivated by thoughts, feelings, and intentions.
Mentalization includes not only this mind-reading ability, but also the
integrative role played by this capacity in the organization of the self
(Fonagy, Gergely, et al., 2002).

The capacity to mentalize can also be stimulated in a psychotherapeutic relationship. Mentalization-based child therapy used to
be called developmental therapy or psychoanalytic developmental
therapy. It initially emerged from classical child analysis (Schmeets,
2003). Child psychoanalysts soon spoke of adaptations to the classical technique to encourage the child's mental growth so that classical
psychoanalytic interventions could also do their therapeutic function
(Bion, 1962, 1967b; Winnicott, 1971). Recent developments in infant
research have lent support to the idea that mental functions, includ-

ing thinking and feeling, develop in an affective relationship, and that an affective relationship later in life can bring about changes in these mental functions. The essential human mental functions are nowadays summarized under the term "mentalization" (Fonagy, Gergely, et al., 2002). Deficiencies in the ability to mentalize are thought to be capable of change in a methodically manipulated, affectively charged relationship with a psychoanalyst or a psychotherapist (Bateman & Fonagy, 2006). In seriously disturbed children the mental processes necessary for this are blocked or underdeveloped (Hurry, 1998b). Setting the mental processes into motion is termed "mentalization-based psychotherapy". Mentalization-based child therapy consists of a number of techniques aimed at deficiencies and shortcomings in specific areas of psychological development. This chapter attempts to clarify the theoretical concepts and developmental phases that play a role in this form of treatment.

Developmental tasks of the infant

Fonagy, Gergely, and colleagues (2002)—building on the work of others—have formulated a theoretical model that states that in normal development an infant goes through five levels of "agency of self" of increasing complexity: physical, social, teleological, intentional, and representational. The experience of a child's own body—combining proprioceptive and sensory data—forms the basis for the self. The degree of predictability, or lack of contingency, in the infant's experiences contributes to the distinction between self and not-self. From birth, babies interact with the caregivers in their environment. The infant gradually gains an awareness that his physical actions have an effect on the behaviour and the emotions of the significant caregiver. This contributes to the development of the self as a "social agent".

Infant research has shown that in the first months of life a baby actively seeks interaction with his caregiver (Beebe & Lachmann, 1988). The facial expression of one of them is indicative for the facial expression the other will show within milliseconds (Beebe, Lachmann, & Jaffe, 1997). Just a few months after birth, an infant responds to the facial expression of its caregiver on the basis of stored information. An infant apparently already expects something of the other person.

These "expectations" are used to predict the other person's behaviour. The infant's ensuing behaviour can be regarded as rational in the sense that it is purposive. Reactions of the infant make it clear that it has an expectation about the behaviour of the physical objects around it. This is known as the teleological position (Fonagy, Gergely, et al., 2002; Fonagy & Target, 1997). For example, the infant can assume that, when it pushes away the spoon during feeding, the spoon will be presented once again, only to be pushed away again. In the teleological position, the infant's reaction is determined by all that is visible, audible, or tangible for him. In order to read the intention of another person, the infant focuses on the physical world. This is in contrast to the intentional position, in which the child's reaction is derived from the intention another person has with certain actions.

Gergely and Csibra (1997) presume that an infant is in the teleological position starting from the second half of the first year. An infant approaches both living and inanimate objects in the same way, because the only intentions he ascribes to living objects are those that are apparent from their physical appearance. It is only in human interaction that teleological models develop into intentional, mentalizing models. After all, intentions can only be ascribed to living creatures. The transition from teleological thinking to intentional thinking is shaped in the primary relationship of the infant with his caregiver. The quality of this primary relationship plays a decisive role here (Fonagy, Gergely, et al., 2002). The teleological position of thinking, a perfectly normal stage in an infant's development, can continue to dominate thinking later in life as well. Then it can be rather less functional, leading to problems. In a world dominated by teleological thinking, the intention of the other is deduced from the physical circumstances. For instance, when a person trips over another person's leg, his perception may be: "You stuck your leg out, so you tripped me up, which means you want to do me harm." Teleological thinking leaves no room for the assumption that the other person simply made an awkward move with his leg, without having the—conscious—intention to trip you up, or worse, that you might have caused yourself to trip. Only what is physical and visible is important: there is a leg and you trip over it, which means that someone tripped you up. This manner of thinking is presymbolic in the sense that thoughts and feelings are not deemed to be mentalized by the infant (Gergely & Csibra, 1997).

Around their second year, children develop the ability to understand that their actions are prompted by a mental state that preceded them. They also begin to be aware that their actions can bring about change not only in the physical body, but also in the mind. Pointing to an object in the assumption that this will cause another person to change his focus of attention is one expression of this. The preference of others is no longer thought to be the same as the infant's own preference. The intentional position makes its appearance. In the intentional position, it is not only the physical actions of another person that are decisive, but also the intention the other person has by carrying out these actions. By assuming that others have an intention, a child shows the first indication of being aware of a mental state in another person. It is the start of the ability to mentalize (Fonagy, Gergely, et al., 2002). Somewhat later, at around the age of 3 or 4, children begin to be aware of the possibility of mental causality, which allows them to understand epistemological constructs: moving away from the physical and towards the conceptual, the abstract. At this stage we may say that children can start to see *themselves* from a representational point of view: their internal intentional mental states are of a representational nature. Developing an understanding of the self, and the self as agent, presumes an increasing refinement of the awareness of mental states. To be able to think about mental states, we must have developed concepts that correspond with the actual internal experiences that cause them. The concept of fear is more than the actual experience of fear. It also refers to the physiological, the cognitive, and the behavioural aspects of fear. The actual internal experience is, then, the first-order or primary representation; the concept of fear is the second-order or secondary representation (Fonagy, Gergely, et al., 2002).

It is interesting to note that the same concepts and the term "representation" are also found in the neurosciences. In the neurosciences, the concept of representation refers to the general presumption that all mental activity has a representation in the brain. For example, when a person sees a chair, it is reflected in the activity of certain neurons in the visual cortex. The activity does not become the actual experience in this way, but apparently the experience has an effect on brain activity. We might speak of epiphenomena: the subjective experience goes together with the electrical activity in certain parts of the brain (Schore, 1994). Fonagy, Gergely, and colleagues (2002) adopt this way of thought when they see the primary representation as coinciding with the primary experience of the unrefined affect. This primary experience of the child is perceived and processed by the mother and then "given back". Secondary representation is then the representation of the primary affect as perceived by the other person (the mother) in the interaction. When the parent gives back a perceived and sufficiently marked experience, it leads to secondary representation in the infant. This brings about the mental space necessary to be able to have thoughts and feelings about the primary affect.

In sum, the transition from teleological to intentional and representational "manners of being" marks a very important distinction. It is presumed that psychopathology—and primarily personality psychopathology—can be understood as disorders in aspects of this capacity to make second-order representations, or disorders in the capacity to mentalize. We come back to this later in the chapter.

Gergely and Watson's social biofeedback theory of parental affect mirroring: the representation loop

If things go well, the parent approaches the child from the time of birth in the primarily nonconscious assumption that the child has an intention with his behaviour. It is assumed that this is a typically human point of view. The parent approaches the infant as if the infant has these internal mental states. The child's behaviour is not seen simply as a physical reaction to a physical world, but as an expression of intentionality (Fonagy, Gergely, et al., 2002). The verbalizations of the caregiver on the child's behaviour are punctuated with this type of assumption of intention. At the age of a few months, although not mentalized, cautiously formed representations of relationships between the self and others already start to vary in quality (Beebe, Lachmann, & Jaffe, 1997). Between the ages of 6 and 18 months, the infant is increasingly able to delineate his internal state from the mental state of the other person. The caregiver plays a crucial role in this process. She reflects, or mirrors, the infant's mental state. Mother and baby are continually in an affective exchange with one another, whereby the mother nonconsciously, almost reflexively, continually reacts to the supposed intentions and internal experiences of the child. She gives back to the baby—mirrors—what she sees and feels in the interaction with him. Winnicott (1971) calls it "giving the baby back its own self". We prefer to use the term representation loop. The primary experience of the baby is recognized and perceived in the mother's mind. She gives the baby's experience in daily interaction back to the baby. The baby in its turn starts to recognize itself in the mother (Gergely & Watson, 1996). It is a loop of representations that starts with the baby, as the primary affective state of the baby, and that the mother gives back to the baby, but now in the form of a secondary representation of the affective state. This organizes the baby's experiences, and the baby will begin to "know" what he feels: ultimately this leads to second-order affect representation. At the same time, it creates space between the baby's primary perception and the way in which the mother sees him. We might view this space as a further elaboration of Winnicott's (1971) concept of transitional space. It is this space that is of crucial importance for the development of the ability to mentalize.

The mother also ensures that there is regularity in their daily interaction, which makes it possible to start to recognize similar primary mental states experienced by the baby. For instance, the bedtime ritual may be composed of a succession of events, external as well as internal, which the baby starts to recognize. Subsequently the representations that are forming are ordered, arranged. Fonagy, Gergely, and colleagues (2002) call this representational mapping. Gradually a transition takes place from the teleological position to the mentalizing position. The caregiver metabolizes the baby's primary state, as it were, and gives it back to the baby in the form of a secondary representation. This is what the baby sees in the caregiver's mind. Along the same lines, the baby's different ways of crying lead to different verbal and nonverbal reactions in the parent. The baby uses the mother's representation as the basis for the development of his self and his self-organization. The research finding that in 75% (!) of the cases the attachment representation of the mother prior to the birth of the child leads to the same representation in the child at the age of 12 months is telling in this respect (Van IJzendoorn, 1995).

Initially, the baby takes the representation of the caregiver as the core of his own perception. After some time, as the child gets older and his primary perception has been given back often enough by his mother in the representation loop, he acquires the ability to represent his own primary perceptions as experience. Then the child is also able to compare the mental state represented by his mother with his own primary perception of the state. These two processes—recognition of his own perception and comparison of it to the secondary perception received from the mother—develop hand in hand (Fonagy, Gergely, et al., 2002). It will be evident that the mother's secondary representation should not be too different from the baby's primary representation, nor may it resemble this too closely. If it is too different, the secondary representation is not recognized as belonging to the primary representation. In extreme cases, when the child's feeling and the feeling given back by the mother are not the same, it leads to the formation of a false identification (false self, Winnicott, 1965). If the two are too similar, the primary representation coincides with the secondary representation and therefore cannot be distinguished from it (Fonagy, Gergely, et al., 2002). In that case, the representation given back by the mother cannot help define the child's own primary experience, and no contribution can be made to the capacity to symbolize and mentalize. Then the self and the other person become one: mental state and reality are equated. The symbolic potential of the exchanges between caregiver and child has been nullified. The difference between me and not-me is insufficiently delineated. Fonagy, Gergely, and colleagues (2002) speak of markedness here: the secondary representation must be sufficiently marked with respect to the primary representation. Only then can the internalized secondary representation lead to a mentalized representation.

It is of great importance to realize that the first mental states exchanged between the mother and the baby are strongly dominated by the affective state of that moment. This affective state must be regulated. On the one hand, regulation prevents the baby from being overwhelmed; on the other hand, it ensures that the baby is adequately curious. In the first year of life, the most important element of development is the emergence of a pattern of expectation in the baby that he will not be overwhelmed but can continue to show curiosity. The daily exchange between mother and child will lead to early frameworks that are presymbolic. Such frameworks are stored in the procedural memory. This part of the memory, in contrast to the declarative memory, cannot be accessed by conscious remembering, and it is not possible to reflect on its contents (Bleiberg, 2001). In the first year of life, the baby is already able to discover and represent relationships between events—a presymbolic form of representation. What is represented presymbolically is the dynamic interactive process, their playing together, as each partner influences the other from moment to moment. Stern (1998) speaks in this context of frameworks that are stored in the procedural memory (e.g. Pally, 2000). They will serve as the pattern on which to shape representations to be formed later, such as cognitions and beliefs.

Limitations in the capacity to mentalize

As stated above, the transition from the teleological to the intentional and representational manners of being is a very important moment in as child's development. Fonagy (1995) states that in order to mentalize, the child needs to have sufficient experience with three things: first of all, the child must have enough actual feelings and thoughts: organic brain damage causes a fundamental limitation to this first condition. Second, the child must have seen his own mental states reflected often enough in the mind of the other person. And third, these experiences must have been gained in the normal, everyday, reality-oriented perspective of the parent. The second aspect is very important: the child needs another person who takes part, so that the child sees his fantasy or idea represented in the mind of the other. Then the child can re-absorb this fantasy and use it as a representation of his own thinking. This is thought to be a purely human sequence of events, one that is unique to our species. It is a need that does not lessen or disappear as we mature, but one that stays with us all of our life. Infant researcher Tronick (1998) calls this the "dyadic expansion of consciousness". It is the interpersonal mechanism by which we communicate with one another and by which we can become attached to each other. It is an essential mechanism in interpersonal contact.

The representation by the parent of the child's mental contents can be used by the child as a crystallization point for his own symbolic thought, as a representation of his secondary representation. When his own thoughts are mirrored in the parent's representations, they can come to be seen as his own, as separate from reality, from actuality.

But what happens when the parent is unable to tolerate a certain mental content? The parent may not be able to recognize a thought, for example as a result of traumatization, because of the relationship of certain mental content of the child to the parent's inner reality. The parent will then not represent this mental content in the interaction with the child. The child will not see its own mental content in the parent, because that thought is too threatening for the parent. The parent will either not react, or will represent a content that is different from the content originally present in the child. In the first case, the actual primary perception will continue to determine behaviour; the second case will result in an as-if experience. It will be apparent that if this problem occurs with respect to a great deal of mental content, the child will not learn to perceive whole areas of his personality as intentional and representational. A familiar clinical example is the effect of the mother's depression on the child's development (Dawson et al., 1999). In her upbringing of the child, the mother is unable to go beyond her own limitations. This fundamental thought is in fact the elaboration at a human level of a non-genetic intergenerational system of transferring behaviour that has been accepted in biology for some time (Francis, Diorio, Liu, & Meaney, 1999; Meaney, 2001). The various limitations are discussed below.

Actual mode, pretend mode, and integrative mode

Are there clinical aspects that might cause one to suspect that a child has insufficient capacity to mentalize? Fonagy and Target (1996a, 1997, 2000; Target & Fonagy, 1996) present a psychoanalytic model of the development of thought. The ability to mentalize is directly linked to this. Their model provides a good basis for recognizing limitations in the ability to mentalize in clinical practice. Central to their model is the concept of "playing with reality". The model distinguishes three types of thinking. They are phases in normal development on the one hand, but on the other, they are different levels of thought that can occur simultaneously in patients.

Fonagy and Target termed the first manner of thinking the "actual mode". This means that a child in this mode equates reality and fantasy. Internal reality and external reality are not distinguished; fantasies are perceived as being reality. This mode is sometimes also called psychic equivalent mode or equation mode. What a thing seems to be and what it is are then equivalent. Thoughts are reality, reality is thoughts.

The second manner of thinking is the "pretend mode". This is the phase in which fantasy play comes to full development. The question of how play is related to reality is not asked. The boundary between reality and fantasy is upheld and closely guarded. When this boundary can no longer be maintained, the child stops playing. The child does not yet "know", is not yet "aware", that he is pretending. These two manners of thinking can co-exist, with the child availing himself of both of them. The child uses one mode, then the other, but they do not become integrated. Integration is characteristic of the second manner of thinking. In this phase, thinking can show substantial development, as long as the situation is sufficiently secure. Imagination and as-if play can be practised in the relationship with the caregiver. Thanks to the clear distinction between reality and fantasy, ideas can be experienced as not threatening, because they are no longer equated with reality, which is characteristic of thinking in the first phase. Playing is pretending, acting as-if, and the pretend mode of mental functioning is still a way of maintaining omnipotence and compensating for life's frustrations (Fonagy, 1995). When the parent and the child play, it creates a situation in which the child can gain an awareness of the internal world—both his own and the other person's. It is a defence mechanism against unacceptable ideas, shaped in the pretend world, in fantasy. Playing with reality is, then, a solution to the aspects of reality that are difficult to tolerate. But when playing with reality takes place in a secure environment, the mental processes of intentionality and representationality can come to full growth. The child learns to mentalize by playing. The relationship with the other person may facilitate this or may limit it, if the child experiences that certain thoughts or mental states cannot be shared with the parent.

The third manner of thinking is the integration of the two previous phases, called "integration mode". Essentially, this is when the child explores the relationship between pretend mode and reality. Not until he has reached this phase does the child fully understand that when he plays, he is pretending. Once he is fully aware of this, he is forced to give up the omnipotent fantasy. This is where guilt and shame about this fantasy enter the picture. The full-blown development of integration between the first two manners of thinking goes together with the ability to mentalize. In essence, the integrative manner of thinking is defined by Fonagy's (1995) statement: "treating ideas as ideas". This concisely puts into words what mentalization means: the capacity to actively regard ideas as representations of realities, both internal—psychic reality—and external—actual reality—in ourselves and in others, in the mind.

Manifestations of the inability to mentalize

The quality of the attachment relationship is described in terms of secure versus insecure. If a child is securely attached, it will be easier for him to learn to mentalize. This is the "normal" or non-pathological process as described at the beginning of this chapter. In children and adults who have developed insecure attachment representations, the capacity to mentalize has gone awry. This can be seen quite clearly in children or adults with a disorganized attachment representation, but to a lesser extent also in persons with avoidant or ambivalent attachment (Fonagy & Target, 1997). Their thinking does not take place in the integrated mode over long periods of time. It is often possible to recognize teleological ways of thinking. The actual mode or the pretend mode continues to predominate. The following three manifestations of the inability to mentalize have been mentioned by Fonagy, Gergely, and colleagues (2002; Bateman & Fonagy, 2004).

The teleological manner of thinking

All that matters is that which can be physically observed; there is no difference between what is physically observed and a person's intention. These children assess the intention behind a person's behaviour purely on the basis of what they can see. They do not accept any explanations or other possible interpretations that show an intention that is different from the one they saw in the physical behaviour. Bateman and Fonagy (2004) give a good example of an adult patient with a borderline personality disorder who argues about how the rules of the department are applied to another patient. Strictly speaking, she is right; but because she is unable to see that this is simply a nuance in the way the rules are applied, for her this burgeons into unreliability on the part of the departmental management. What the management has done is to take a humane decision, but this makes no difference to her: what she can see—in this case the physical circumstance that the department rules are not being applied to her fellow patient—is decisive, and for her this justifies her view that the management is unreliable. She cannot see that the actions of the management are determined by an interpretation of the rules and that they thus reflect an intention of the management.

The actual mode: the content of the primary representation is not represented

When an idea cannot be adequately represented in the pretend mode, the idea remains in psychic equivalence, where fantasy and reality are not distinguished from each other. This means that the idea remains reality, and as such it is threatening for the child. Development with regard to this specific thought content will then come to a standstill. If the parent's thinking has also not become sufficiently integrated, it is conceivable that the child experiences too much anxiety with respect to many thoughts to be able to experiment with them in pretend mode. These children cannot really play with their thoughts because they seem to be too genuine—too real. As they grow older, this problem will continue to occur, causing them excessive anxiety in relation to a great many thought contents. The second mode of thinking is not adequately developed, and patients often function in the actual mode. For them, because the second mode—the pretend mode—was blocked too early, a thought has reality value: they are in psychic equivalent mode. This leads to inaccurate interpretations of reality and, in extreme cases, to a distortion of reality. It results in great anxiety that often needs to be acted out.

The pretend mode: the content of the primary representation becomes an "as-if" experience

When a representation by the parent does take place, but this representation shows too little similarity with the primary representation, the pretend mode of thinking will dominate. Although the pretend mode has become active, the child is unable to link it to his own perception. These children show well-adjusted behaviour; they are able to put their experiences adequately into words, but their experiences in this mode are not linked to the actual primary experience at that moment. They do not feel their own emotions, or only very remotely. They view themselves as not very coherent; they have little sense of the self as agent (cf. Winnicott's concept of false self). The integrated manner of thinking has not been set in motion adequately. In practice, their functioning in pretend mode is often confused with a good ability to play. Whereas in younger children playing must be safeguarded so as to promote the development of thought, when older children use the pretend mode it can serve as a defence against intolerable affects. Child therapists will be familiar with children who go on playing for a long time, who show much fantasy in their play, but whose playing shows no change in the course of treatment, nor does the child's behaviour and symptoms change. Their stereotyped playing often only becomes apparent after some time. Then it also becomes apparent that their actual experiences in reality have little influence on them. If they feel hurt, for example, this is consistently kept at bay.

During their fantasy play, children whose development has taken place normally can step out of their fantasy when the pretend nature becomes threatening; they may say, for example, "I'm not really a princess!" Children who play out of a need for defence mechanisms will remain just out of reach of reality as something to go by. They make a great fuss of keeping reality outside. Such treatments often give the impression of being by-the-book therapies. Many therapists will recognize the observation that when a patient is able to make more use of humour, the treatment can be regarded as finished. Humour can only be understood, appreciated, and used when a thing can be perceived as real and as pretend at the same time. It is an outstanding example of integrated thinking.

In conclusion

The substrate of the mind, the brain, is receptive to structural change as long as an individual is intellectually active (Kandel, 2001). The brain's capacity for self-repair, termed neural plasticity, means more than functions being taken over by areas other than those damaged or injured. Neural plasticity can be useful in the everyday adaptation of the individual (Trojan & Pokorny, 1999). Environmental factors have a mediating influence on the genetic material, helping to produce a continually changing structure and function of the brain. Environmental factors, including the subjectively experienced inner world, can delay or obstruct development. Based on this knowledge, it is the task of the psychiatrist, psychologist, or psychotherapist to seek ways to manipulate that same environment so as to remove the obstacle or obstruction and so to decrease personal suffering. This is what mentalization-based child therapy is all about.

CHAPTER THREE

Assessment of mentalizing problems in children

Jolien Zevalkink

Having described in Chapter 2 the theory underlying our thinking about how problems with mentalization develop, the next step is to make these problems more easily recognizable by demarcating the group of children suitable for mentalization-based child therapy and by enlisting diagnostic instruments. Based on theory and clinical experience, Anne Hurry and Miriam Steele drew up a list of criteria to identify children for whom mentalization-based child therapy is appropriate. These criteria can be clinically observed during treatment sessions with the child. But it is also possible to make use of standardized instruments. Useful information can be obtained from instruments that yield data about attachment classifications, personality dynamics, cognitive functioning, anxiety, depression, and behavioural problems. By comparing and combining the results from clinical observation and instruments, it is possible to describe prototypes of children who may fall within the group suited to this form of treatment. Further research will have to show whether the criteria developed for this specific form of treatment were correct. This chapter gives a theoretical and psychiatric description of the target population, followed by the treatment indicator and the diagnostic instruments.

Target population

Theoretical and psychiatric description of the target population

The target population for mentalization-based child therapy comprises children who are inadequately able to mentalize in important developmental areas. In Chapter 2 we saw that there are children who function too much in the equivalent mode (or actual mode), children who only function in the pretend mode, but also children who operate in one or other of these modes alternately without integrating them. Alongside children who have had developmental problems from a very young age, there are also children who are unable to mentalize in a particular area (Bateman & Fonagy, 2006, p. 9). The latter seems to be more often the case in children who have gone through traumatic experiences. When these traumatic experiences involved the attachment system, more developmental areas seem to be disturbed (Allen, 2000). Concerning such cases, Bleiberg (1994) speaks of cumulative traumas. Rexwinkel (2003) writes in this respect: "Cumulative traumas have an effect on both affective and cognitive development and lead to defensive manoeuvres, in which affect is either minimized or maximized." Because fantasy, feeling, thinking, and wishing are impaired, these children develop mental process disorders (Fonagy, Moran, Edgcumbe, Kennedy, & Target, 1993). They are children who deal with their affect in a primitive manner and make frequent use of projective identification and splitting. In this chapter we try to translate this theoretical formulation into clinical practice. The objective is to arrive at a set of characteristics for this group of children, citing the well-known DSM–IV classifications wherever possible, while recognizing that there will always be some tension between diagnostics and in-depth assessment of a mental function, because they are different approaches to the same child.

In the first publication on mentalization-based psychotherapy, Bateman and Fonagy (2004) described the adult target population as patients with a borderline personality disorder. The DSM–IV or ICD–10 do not permit us to speak of a borderline personality disorder in children under the age of 18. Therefore, another route for assigning children to mentalization-based child therapy needs to be followed. In recent decades, various child analysts have written regularly about children who exhibited what was termed serious early pathology. The term "borderline child" was used to describe many of these children (e.g. Bleiberg, 2001; Frijling-Schreuder, 1969; Van Delsen & Meurs, 2004; Verhulst, 1981). The picture that emerges from these writings shows much overlap with a description of children who are suitable for mentalization-based child therapy. Bleiberg (2001, p. 149) summarizes vulnerabilities of children with a borderline personality disorder: unstable sense of self and others; subjective dyscontrol and hyperarousal; aloneness and vulnerability to separation; and rage. A psychiatric classification such as DSM–IV or ICD–10 does not permit an official classification of a borderline disorder in children (Cummings, Davies, & Campbell, 2000). However, both DSM–IV and ICD–10 allow disorders to be distinguished that are related to the problems of children who would be suitable for mentalization-based child therapy. These children clearly show a mixture of Axis I and Axis II problems (Fonagy & Target, 1996b; Meurs & Vliegen, 2004). In this respect, Bleiberg (2001, pp. 8–9) also focuses attention on children with narcissistic personality disorder, who will prototypically "organize their sense of self around an illusory conviction of perfection, power, or control". These children might also need to learn to mentalize about the states of mind of self and other. According to our own clinical experience, the following DSM–IV classifications can be added to the criteria we set for mentalization-based child therapy: pervasive development disorder (PDD–NOS); Asperger's syndrome; and disruptive disorders such as attention-deficit/hyperactivity disorder (ADHD), oppositional defiant disorder (ODD), and conduct disorder (CD) (Gerritzen, 2003).

Rothstein (2002) gives a psychoanalytic description of the mental functioning of children with ADHD. He writes that these children have difficulty with differentiations and shades of meaning, and that their impressions of their environment are disorganized and unpredictable. They are also less inclined to internalize and assimilate their impressions. It makes these children very sensitive to stimuli, causing them to come to conclusions rapidly—for example, about what another person has against them. These are often repetitive conclusions that are not really an answer to what actually takes place in their interaction with another person; they arise from a pattern of expectations stored in memory at an earlier point with respect to this type of contact. This very readily results in fixed, rigid, and simplistic ways of mentalization. Gilmore (2000, 2002) writes that ADHD involves a complex interaction of constitutional factors, intrapsychic dynamics, and disturbed basal ego functions. She cites a case showing how mentalization in children with ADHD has been obstructed. These children show structural deficits in the development of morality, superego, and the triadic level of functioning. The latter means that there is no room for reflection on what the child experiences in an interaction.

But classification on the basis of DSM–IV is not enough to assign a child to mentalization-based child therapy (e.g. Fonagy, Gergely, et al., 2002). The indicator criteria, which are discussed in the next section, cover a broader field. Relational dysfunctioning lies at the root of the problems (Bateman & Fonagy, 2006). When a child exhibits one of the aforementioned DSM disorders, it is important to investigate whether—often in the long term—the child will be able to enter into any form of contact. If a child suffers from mind blindness, as is the case with autism, then it is questionable whether an intervention aimed at mentalizing about oneself and other persons is useful (e.g. Baron-Cohen, Tager-Flusberg, & Cohen, 2000; Sharp, 2006). In children, precursors of personality disorders can be inferred from certain attachment patterns. Theoretically speaking, mentalization-based child therapy is closely related to attachment theory, and so it is useful to look more closely at the group of children with problems in the area of attachment. Three insecure attachment patterns can be distinguished: avoidant, ambivalent, and disorganized.

Bleiberg (2001) assumes—following Paulina Kernberg—that there is a relationship between disorganized attachment in young children and the development of a borderline personality disorder at a later stage. Bateman and Fonagy (2006, p. 14) also assume such a relationship. Children whose needs point to mentalization-based child therapy seem primarily to exhibit a disorganized attachment (Bleiberg, 2001; Brisch, 1999; Fonagy, 2001a; Solomon & George, 1999). Disorganized or disoriented attachment is the temporary collapse—or absence—of strategies in relation to attention and behaviour in dealing with attachment-related stress (Hesse & Main, 2000). Alongside great uncertainty about the emotional availability of others, the child finds it difficult to develop trust in his own capacity to observe. An important aspect in this process is defective mentalization, because it means that the child does not process the information leading to anxiety (Fonagy & Target, 1997). Disorganized attachment is found more often in children who have experienced neglect or abuse and in children of parents with mental problems than in children with other forms of insecure attachment (Cummings, Davies, & Campbell, 2000; Lyons-Ruth, Melnick, Bronfman, Sherry, & Llanas, 2004). Rather than speak of borderline children, as they are sometimes termed in the classical psychoanalytic literature, we prefer to speak of children with mental process disorders, to stress the fact that there is disorganization in primary relationships.

Children with ambivalent or avoidant attachment patterns also show insecure attachment. Main (2000) writes that these children are unable to focus their attention flexibly during attachment-related stress, but exhibit a rigid attention pattern by tenaciously concentrating on only one aspect of their surroundings. The strategy of the ambivalent child is to make sure he will not have to let go of the relationship, that of the avoidant child is one of not expecting very much of another person when it comes to fulfilling attachment needs. Precisely because the relationship—and with it the transference–countertransference constellation—occupies such an important role in this form of therapy, children with problems in their attachment pattern are preeminently suited for it. According to Bleiberg (2001), children who develop in a more narcissistic sense will often have had an avoidant attachment pattern as a child. This is their way of not becoming disorganized.

Within clinical practice, problems in the area of attachment are often referred to as attachment disorders, or disorders in the area of attachment development (De Lange, 1991; Gerritzen, 2000). This is not to say that an insecure attachment representation is always the same thing as an attachment disorder. According to the DSM, an attachment disorder is one that exhibits "clearly disturbed and developmentally inappropriate social ties in most situations starting before the fifth year" (APA, 1997). Zeanah (1996) distinguishes between a disorder and insecure attachment by judging the extent to which the emotions and behaviours shown by the child in his attachment relationship point to serious disturbances in his feelings of security. When children have an attachment disorder, we might ask ourselves whether mentalization-based child therapy is a suitable form of treatment, because usually these children have not learned to develop ties with others, and an ambulatory mentalization-based child therapy may well not be intensive enough (Brisch, 1999). In other words, a diagnosis of attachment disorder can only be made if there is serious pathology. Disturbed attachment relationships are always insecure attachment relationships, but insecure attachment relationships are probably only disturbed at the extreme end of each insecure type.

A form of therapy that shows similarities with mentalization-based child therapy was developed by Greenspan (1997); it is called "developmentally based psychotherapy". Greenspan focuses primarily on development or growth that has come to a standstill and the need for intensive psychotherapeutic treatment to get things moving again. According to him, the target population for this form of therapy should be persons "whose ability to construct day-to-day experiences is necessarily limited by the nature of their psychopathology. . . ." (Greenspan, 1997, p. 42). He distinguishes the following patients:

> for the individual whose neurotic structure pervades major and significant areas of his or her life, and where the capacity to construct growth-facilitating experiences with the consultation of the therapist is unlikely to occur, intensive therapeutic work may be indicated. Similarly, for the severe character pathologies, the borderline conditions, and severe disorders of affect, the most intensive approaches may be absolutely necessary, with, however, a focus on developmentally early issues and an understanding of the limited structural capacity of the individual. In this way, the therapeutic relationship would not overwhelm an already fragile person, but would initially create the support, regulatory, and interactive experiences for both stability and gradual change and growth. [Greenspan, 1997, p. 44]

The foregoing illustrates that there is a wide range of mental process disorders, depending on the area in which the child's development has stopped and what regulation profile the child uses (Greenspan, 1997). A person may have run into difficulties in a developmental field such as sense of reality or affect regulation, but it may also be due to excessive limitations in his experience or to not being open to new experiences. For example, it is possible for a child to show a sense of reality in carrying out a school assignment, but not when entering into relationships with peers. Greenspan (1997) advises drawing up a regulation profile for the child, and he suggests special attention to possible problems in sensorimotor regulation (Chapter 7). It is also important to draw a distinction between a child functioning in pretend mode or in equivalent mode, or alternating between them. Distinguishing and operationalizing diagnostic criteria can be a relevant starting point for treatment to discover in what areas a child has incurred developmental problems. The rest of this chapter is devoted to these criteria and its assessment in children with their own specific problems with respect to mentalization. Clustering, as it is done using the classification model of the DSM–IV, for example, is at cross-purposes to this.

Indicator criteria for mentalization-based child therapy

Anne Hurry is the editor of a book published in 1998 that describes developmental therapy, or mentalization-based child therapy. Although the book does not explicitly state indicator criteria, they are implicit in the various cases discussed. Working with these children and conducting diagnostic research with them ultimately led to the formulation of a list of indicator criteria for mentalization-based child therapy at the Anna Freud Centre. Miriam Steele presented this list at a workshop at the Netherlands Psychoanalytic Institute in November 2001. The Anna Freud Centre distinguished the following criteria (Steele, personal communication, 2001):

> defective mental representations of self and/or others;
> poor frustration tolerance;
> poor impulse control;
> low self-esteem;
> lack of coherence in inner world;
> inadequate self–object differentiation;
> inadequate structure, flexibility and functionality of defences;
> inadequate affect regulation;
> problems with social contacts;
> finds it difficult to perceive wishes and intentions of others;
> cognition: poor reality focus;
> cognition: weak attention span;
> cognition: poor memory function;

‣ cognition: problems with language comprehension in an emotional context.

Following these clinical guidelines, a child for whom mentalization-based child therapy is suitable will exhibit the majority of these criteria. It does not seem to be necessary for all criteria to be present at once. We do think that at least 6 of the 14 criteria should be present if a child is to fit within the target population, but further research is still needed. Some criteria seem to be closely interrelated but may also occur independently. For experienced clinicians, the child's functioning in the therapy room may be an indication of an impasse in the development of mental processes. Children who function in equivalent mode are a group for whom ideas can be threatening because they are experienced as reality. Precisely because fantasy can be so threatening, these children have great difficulty with play and imagination. There are also children who play and use their imagination very easily and who primarily function in pretend mode. In the playroom, it takes some time before the clinician notices that they often do nothing but play. Their play is often repetitive and one-sided. A therapist has a difficult time talking with these children about what happens in a play situation, what happens between therapist and child, or what happens outside therapy. In other words, the child does not allow the therapist to occupy a third position from which to look at, think, and speak as a therapist about what is taking place in that room. In contrast to more neurotic children, in whose play the therapist may see some development after giving an interpretation, if such a remark is made to these children, they are more likely to react with confusion, disintegration, acting out, or some other primitive defence (e.g. Bateman & Fonagy, 2006, p. 35). There are also children who function in reality and in fantasy alternately but are unable to integrate the two. If reality becomes too threatening, they flee into fantasy, and vice versa. They cannot find peace with either of these approaches. During clinical intake interviews with the child, the therapist can investigate the presence of one or more of the above criteria. There are several ways to set up the play situation (Frijling-Schreuder, Bakker, & Verhage, 1988; Rustin & Quagliata, 2000; Verhulst & Verheij, 2000).

In addition to the indicator criteria, which indicate the problem areas of children who are suitable for mentalization-based child therapy, there are certain prerequisites before the therapy can start. If these are not present, the therapy will not take place, in spite of the fact that the assessment for treatment was positive. First of all, the therapy must have the approval of the primary caregivers—probably the parents—and they must also make it possible in a practical sense by taking the child to and from therapy on time. As the target population does not always live in stable family circumstances, this prerequisite can sometimes present some difficulty. For example, the clinical material of the six children involved in the project showed that five of them lived in families without the biological father. Three of these five did see their biological father regularly on the basis of a visiting agreement. Second, parent guidance is an important aspect, and it is necessary that parents take part in it. Over time, not only practical but also more emotional matters will come up in parent guidance, such as whether the parents are able to permit the child to develop a special tie with the therapist (see Chapter 5).

A third prerequisite is that the child's problems may not be so serious as to preclude making and retaining any form of contact in the longer term, as is the case with serious cases of autism, psychotic children, attachment disorders according to DSM, or children with serious cognitive limitations. Miriam Steele (personal communication, 2002) states that there must be some sort of tie with at least one adult in order to start mentalization-based child therapy. But it is a grey area, and more research is needed to clarify the boundaries between the seriousness of the problems and the degree of treatability. These are nevertheless children with serious problems, as is apparent from the complaints of the six children in this project upon intake. It was clear that all six children had developed serious social and emotional problems. For half of them, the reason for registration was behavioural problems. Four of the six had difficulty in getting along with peers. Three children came into treatment with depressive complaints, and two with suicidal leanings. The clinical observation during the intake interviews showed insecure disorganized attachment representations in four of the six children, and in two an extreme form of insecure preoccupied attachment with serious separation–individuation themes.

In addition to gaining clinical information from intake interviews, it is also possible to use standardized research instruments to investigate whether the indicator criteria are in line with the child's problems. We turn our attention now to a discussion of this form of diagnostics.

Standardized diagnostics

Introduction

A variety of psychodiagnostic instruments can be enlisted in mental health care for children and adolescents (Verhulst & Verheij, 2000). After deliberation with academicians and psychoanalytic diagnosticians, the Netherlands Psychoanalytic Institute decided to work with the instruments described below. We chose instruments that can also be used as outcome measures for effectiveness research as well as for routine outcome monitoring (progress of individual patients). No instrument offers insight into all 14 indicator criteria. Table 3.1 shows which instrument will provide information about a specific indicator criterion. The list is not exhaustive, because if we work with a somewhat broader definition, additional information can also be obtained from other instruments. For example, the intelligence test can also say something about the degree of impulse control. The topics discussed are: measurement of attachment representation, personality dynamics, cognitive functioning, anxiety and depression, and behavioural problems as experienced by parents and/or teachers.

Insofar as possible, we illustrate the instruments based on the results obtained from the six children who took part in the project. Before the treatment, psychodiagnostic assessment of five of the six children was conducted at the Netherlands Psychoanalytic Institute. Psychodiagnostic assessment had already been done of the sixth child at a different mental health care agency. It is advisable to work with a tracking system, charting the beginning situation and the progress of clients using the same instruments, in a subsequent project.

Attachment representation

The classification of attachment representations can be divided into two main groups: secure and insecure (Ainsworth, Blehar, Waters, & Wall, 1978). In the main group with insecure attachment, three classifications are distinguished: two organized, non-pathological attachment patterns—avoidant and ambivalent—and one disorganized attachment classification (Hesse & Main, 2000; Main, 2000). For children aged between 5 and 10, an attachment instrument is available that allows the child to make known his attachment strategy

Table 3.1. Summary of diagnostic instruments in relation to indicators for mentalization-based child therapy

	Attachment	Rorschach (CS)	IQ	Anxiety and depression	Behavioural problems	DSM-IV
Defective mental representations of self and/or others	X					
Poor frustration tolerance		X			X	X
Poor impulse control	X	X			X	X
Low self-esteem		X		X	X	
Lack of coherence in inner world	X	X				
Inadequate self-object differentiation		X				
Inadequate structure, flexibility and functionality of defences		X				X
Inadequate affect regulation	X	X			X	
Problems with social contacts		X		X	X	
Finds it difficult to perceive wishes and intentions of others	X	X				X
Cognitions: poor reality focus	X	X				
Cognitions: weak attention span			X			
Cognitions: poor memory function			X		X	
Cognitions: problems with language comprehension in an emotional context	X					

using nonverbal and verbal reactions. The Attachment Story Completion Task (ASCT), also called the MacArthur Story-Stems Battery, was developed by Bretherton, Ridgeway, and Cassidy (1990). In the ASCT, a basic story and a standard scene, made up of figures and other items, is presented to the child. The conflicts or dilemmas in the stories involve dealing with situations that activate the attachment system, such as anxiety, pain, exclusion, and quarrelling. When playing, what the child reflects is not actually reality, but the way in which he reflects on reality. Via the detour of play (displacement), the child can show defence mechanisms (Hodges & Steele, 2000). At the Netherlands Psychoanalytic Institute we use a set of nine attachment-related stories and a coding system developed by Hodges, Hillmann, and Steele (Zevalkink, 2005; Zevalkink & Verheugt-Pleiter, 2005). This attachment instrument was administered to two children in the project group: Maartje (7 yrs) and Paul (9 yrs). To illustrate, here is a summary of Maartje's reaction to the story that starts with the child in the living room and father and mother cuddling on the sofa; the parents send the child away to her room because they want to be alone for a minute (Figure 3.1).

Maartje's reaction to "Exclusion" (abridged)

The child in the story says, "I know what you're doing, kissing!" in an injured tone. Then she says that she is going into the garden.

FIGURE 3.1.   "Exclusion" (ASCT)

She feels rather alone, and she cries. Then she says that it's their own fault and that she is leaving. The child says to the bed, "Come on, bed, I'm going to fly." She flies to a different father and mother. Then she goes back home.

Paul reacts as follows to the story in which the child is standing close to the cooker because he is so hungry; he knocks the dinner off the fire and burns his hand (Figure 3.2).

Paul's reaction to "Burnt hand" (abridged)

The mother is angry and tells the child to hold his hand under the tap and that now dinner is ruined. The child puts his hand under the tap. Then they see that the hand has fallen off, and the mother faints. The child gives the mother "cruel resuscitation" by stomping on her. The father calls out angrily, "Now look what you did, you stupid bastard! Your mother is dead." The child faints. And then the pan turns out to be able to work magic, and it makes both of them alive again. The child and his brother start making mischief, and together they eat everything. They wake up their parents, who know nothing about it.

The reactions to all stories were scored. These scores showed that Maartje's problems primarily lie in the area of defective mental rep-

FIGURE 3.2.   "Burnt hand" (ASCT)

resentations of herself and others. There is role confusion and substantial anxiety. Paul exhibits defective self–object differentiation and problems with impulse control. His stories evidence a great deal of aggression, which he later neutralizes. The stories show an inner world with little coherence. Both children have developed a disorganized attachment representation: Maartje shows more preoccupied and controlling reactions and Paul more aggressive ones. Both children exhibit much fear in their reactions to the attachment stories (for an interpretation, see Verheugt-Pleiter & Zevalkink, 2005).

Another way of looking at the quality of the attachment representations is by asking the child to draw its own family. Empirical research has shown that certain characteristics of family drawings correspond to the attachment history of the child. These characteristics were categorized under the attachment classifications of two methods, both of which distinguish four attachment patterns (Fury, Carlson, & Sroufe, 1997; Pianta, Longmaid, & Ferguson, 1999). The question the child is asked is: "Now I would like you to make me a drawing of your family." When the drawing is complete, the test administrator asks the child to identify the persons in it and to tell how they are related to the child. For example, "Whom have you drawn?" And then, "And who is this?" The child is at liberty to leave out members of the family if he so wishes. This counts as a relevant clinical observation.

Geert (8) made a drawing of his family. Geert has some problems with his motor system, and this becomes apparent as he draws. He is pleased that he does not need to draw the entire family, because there are eight children in his father's house. He draws his mother, father, himself, and his two-year-old brother; while drawing, he mentions a few characteristics of pre-schoolers and says that his brother is going through preschool puberty. With the exception of his mother's glasses and the younger brother's smaller appearance, the figures do not have any identifying characteristics. They all smile in the same way. No one has any hands or feet, and their bodies are drawn in the shape of balloons. Judging by these characteristics, Geert seems to have an avoidant attachment representation, possibly with some disorganized elements because of the missing extremities (Figure 3.3).

Figure 3.3.   Drawing of the family (Geert).

Personality dynamics

For more insight into the personality dynamics of a child, diagnosticians often make use of projective material (Slijper, 2000). A test that can also be used as an outcome measure is the Rorschach. The Rorschach is known as a projective test, but it can also function as a perceptual test. The Rorschach appraises a person's personality structure and personality dynamics (de Ruiter & Cohen, 1994; Weiner, 1998). It is a relatively unstructured personality test. The items ask for both perceptual–cognitive and highly imaginative reactions. For this reason, the test also serves as a measure for perception and association (Van der Ree, 2006). The most frequently used and best studied scoring system for the Rorschach is the Comprehensive System developed by John E. Exner, Jr (Weiner, 1998). It distinguishes seven clusters: information processing, cognitive mediation, thought, control, affect, self-perception and interpersonal perception. Various variables or indices fall within these clusters. Combinations of indices give information about the following special indices: perceptual thinking (PTI), depression (DEPI), coping deficit (CDI), hypervigilance (HVI), and obsessive style (OBS). Research has been done on the psychometric traits and the outcomes of the Rorschach used with adult clients and to a lesser extent with children. The Rorschach can be used from the age of 5 onward.

To illustrate the diagnostic use of the Rorschach, we describe the results of Paul and Maartje on the assessment prior to treatment. The Rorschach–CS is a comprehensive scoring system, providing information on a great many aspects of the child's functioning. These illustrations are primarily focused on the indicator criteria for mentalization-based child therapy.

Paul has a high score on the special index for coping problems. This points to defences that are inadequate as to structure, flexibility, and functionality. He may have poor frustration tolerance, because his ambition is great but the inner resources that should feed his ambition are barely available. Along with other possible causes, this leads to depressive feelings. Another perspective from which his moroseness can be viewed is that, in his social dealings with others, Paul often seems to stand empty-handed. There is much emptiness in his relationships with others and also much averted affect. At the same time, Paul is a child who is quite pleased to receive an emotional appeal. His low self-esteem is based on doubts about himself and the fear that he does not have himself under control. Paul gives an excessive number of anatomical responses to images, not all of which are clearly anatomical. This points to a very early self-esteem problem, where a caregiver who was experienced as intrusive caused confusion in relation to his physical autonomy and integrity. It will not come as a surprise that Paul experiences much oppositional, averted anger, which is partly an adequate answer to the intrusions he has experienced and partly makes for problems because it involves a loss of reality testing.

The Special Indices of the Rorschach administered to Maartje show that she has a high score on coping problems. Further study of the variables paints the following picture:

Maartje shows herself to be a child who plunges headlong into her environment with heart and soul, is alert to every detail, and very actively tries to discover a great many relationships. At the same time, she has difficulty observing feelings, fantasies, thoughts, and needs in herself and others. Thought and action seem to lie entirely on the same line, so that in social contacts she may be perceived as an impulsive, overactive girl who does not take kindly to prohibitions, postponements, and/or frustrations. Her frustration tolerance is poor in the sense that she has few inner resources available to her to fall back on in times of stress or in taking difficult decisions. Her affect regulation is somewhat unmodulated but is adequate for her age: after all, she is only 6. However, there are problems in this area: if an emotional appeal is made to Maartje, she is at a loss as to what to do with her feelings, to such an extent that her reality testing is adversely affected to a substantial extent. The quality of her thinking can be greatly influenced by her fantasies and her sometimes excessive associative ability. Maartje's self-esteem is extremely distressed. She hardly dares to have pleasant thoughts about others or herself. At the same time, she gives a very great many white space responses, pointing to oppositional behaviour and much averted anger.

The Rorschach gives extensive information about the personality dynamics of these two children (Table 3.1: 10 of the 14 criteria). Paul seems to function primarily in equivalent mode and Maartje to move between the two modes. The descriptions also show that the children have problems in specific developmental areas; Paul has developed more depressivity and Maartje more problems with impulse control. Both children feel lonely and have a distressed self-esteem.

Cognitive function

Intelligence tests such as the WISC–R are used to investigate a child's cognitive function. They provide information about the span of attention and memory function (see Table 3.1). From a psychoanalytic point of view, the results of intelligence tests are also indicative of regulation problems and problems with mentalization (e.g. Halberstadt-Freud, 1983).

The results on the WISC–R are known for four children in the mentalization-based child therapy group; it is striking that all four score at least 10 points lower on the performance part of the test than on the verbal part. In two of them the difference is significant, and they clearly exhibit a disharmonic profile, possibly suggesting a nonverbal learning disorder.

Questionnaires for anxiety and depression

The questionnaires for anxiety and depression also give insight into a number of mentalization-based child therapy indicator criteria (Table 3.1), of which self-esteem is an important aspect. The Netherlands Psychoanalytic Institute uses the following questionnaires in its tracking system. The Children's Depression Inventory (CDI) is a self-reporting questionnaire for children aged 8 to 17 that is intended to measure depression. The overall score gives an indication of the seriousness of self-reported depressive symptoms. The CDI is used as a screening instrument to identify children who are at risk of developing a depressive disorder, whether or not in the presence of other Axis I disorders. The instrument has shown itself to be sufficiently sensitive to investigate the effectiveness of therapeutic interventions (see, e.g., Kendall, 1994). The CDI consists of 27 questions and can be administered in less than 15 minutes.

The Multidimensional Anxiety Scale for Children (MASC), a questionnaire that measures anxiety dimensions in children and adolescents, was developed by March and colleagues (1997; Utens & Ferdinand, 2000). The MASC consists of 39 items and can be administered in around 10 minutes. It can be used as a general screening instrument to identify children and adolescents with anxiety-related problems. It can also be used as a diagnostic aid; interpretation of the results, together with clinical observations, gives a more comprehensive and systematic picture of a person than does the use of one single information source (March et al., 1997). The MASC–10 was developed to chart progress in treatment. Ten of the original MASC items are used in a short questionnaire for repeated measurements (March et al., 1997). The MASC has been shown to be reliable and valid for clinical populations and the factors correspond with DSM–IV diagnostic clusters of social phobia, separation anxiety, and generalized anxiety disorder—taking the average of the four factors (March, Parker, Sullivan, Stallings, & Conners, 1997; Utens, 2001). There are four basic scales: physical symptoms, damage avoidance, social anxiety, and separation anxiety.

Behavioural problems according to parents and teacher

The Child Behavior Checklist (CBCL/6–18) is a self-reporting questionnaire for parents with a child aged between 6 and 18. Versions are also available that are suitable for problems in younger children. The questionnaire measures the competence and behavioural problems of the child from the parents' perspective in a standardized manner (Verhulst, Van der Ende, & Koot, 1996). Based on the same pattern, a questionnaire has been developed for school heads or teachers—the Teacher Report Form (TRF) (Verhulst, Van der Ende, & Koot, 1997). It consists of two parts: a competence section and a section on behavioural problems. The competence section consists of 20 items. The behavioural section contains a total of 118 questions that can be scored on a three-point scale and two open-ended questions.

In conclusion

The target population for mentalization-based child therapy consists primarily of children who are at an impasse in the development of mental processes. They mentalize inadequately in a number of important developmental areas; their deficiency in social and emotional areas is striking. These children have difficulty in entering into relationships with others and in coping with emotions in a balanced, stable manner. This undermines their self-esteem and gives them a sense of loneliness that can lead to depression, but also to impulsive and attention-seeking behaviour. By seeking concrete indications for indicator criteria in clinical interviews and during standardized diagnostic study, the researcher can decide whether the problems of the child are such that mentalization-based child therapy is appropriate.

CHAPTER FOUR

Treatment strategy

Annelies J. E. Verheugt-Pleiter

In this chapter the most important strategic underpinnings of mentalization-based child therapy are discussed. First we briefly review a number of important authors who proffered innovative ideas with respect to this technique; then we go on to discuss the framework and principles of treatment. The framework of treatment includes the notion of involvement of and cooperation between therapists and other adults, the representational mismatch, the setting, the therapist as development object, and working "in" the transference. Treatment principles include working in the here and now, accepting the child's level of mental functioning and relating at the same level, giving reality value to inner experiences, playing with reality, and the importance of the process, which takes precedence over the technique. The chapter concludes with some remarks on ending the treatment.

Introduction

The most significant disorder in children who have difficulty with mental processes is one in the perception of the self as agent.[1] For these children, the most important objective in treatment is to foster the emergence of a coherent self, a sense of agency, and a capacity to defer, modulate, and regulate emotional responses (Tyson, 2005). This objective is different from that in traditional psychoanalytic treatment aimed at children with a mental representation disorder involving conflict in or between their mental representations. Gaining insight into and resolving unconscious conflicts cannot be the objective when a disorder in a mental process is involved. It might possibly come up in a later stage of treatment, when children can mentalize and may develop conflicts. But mentalization-based child therapy is first and foremost intended for children who have little or no ability to mentalize.

In real life there is no clear-cut difference between mental process and mental representation disorders. In periods of stress the ability to mentalize decreases for all children. More chronic stressful times in the family, such as severe illness or divorce, might affect the mentalizing capacity in children who were had previously had no such problems. Furthermore, children with a mental process disorder might have domains in which they are still able to mentalize. Therefore, the environmental context is always important to consider. Also, developmental changes might influence the ability to mentalize. Under the influence of biological puberty, for example, it might fluctuate and significantly reduce in certain circumstances. In sum, a mental process disorder can be temporary or more permanent and partial or not. For didactical reasons, we speak here of mental process and mental representation disorders as if they were easily distinctive entities.

A psychoanalytic frame of reference is indispensable in working with children with a mental process disorder because psychoanalysis traditionally gives priority to inner experiences and to putting them into words. Mentalization-based child therapy, in conjunction with attachment theory, focuses on the safe—and the unsafe—relationship, and primarily on the implicit, *nonconscious* factors. The impact of the transference brings the implicit procedures experienced by the child in an attachment relationship into the treatment. Classical psychoanalytic theory places greater emphasis on *unconscious* factors on account of its focus on conflict and repression. Making the child aware of inner conflicts is an important instrument in the treatment of a mental representation disorder. A mental process disorder involves the inability to develop mental representations. Although a therapist sometimes works for a longer period at a behavioural or "superficial" level, psychoanalytic concepts such as transference and countertransference set the course for mentalization-based child therapy and illustrate the distinction between it and cognitive behavioural therapy. A mentalization-based therapist tries to bring to development a transitional space, a playroom between fantasy and reality; this is a prerequisite for the promotion of mentalization and the development of a coherent self. In the end, if children can call up their own mental representations, they will increasingly become the authors of their own behaviour. They will also be able to tell a life story that is more or less their own.

In this chapter we first review the work of several authors with new and innovative ideas about the technique; we then sketch the main lines of the therapeutic strategy in mentalization-based child therapy in a discussion of the framework of treatment and the basic principles on which the treatment is based.

Backgrounds

Quite a number of strategies have been designed based on a psychoanalytic frame of reference to work therapeutically with children who—as we now put it—have mental process disorders. In practical situations, therapists have devised a variety of adjustments to psychoanalytic technique because such traditionally important techniques as the use of metaphor and complex interpretations proved not to be effective for children with these types of problems. In mentalization-based child therapy, form is more important than content: there is no conflict the child can be made aware of; in fact—strangely enough—the content sometimes seems not to matter so much. The use of conflict-oriented techniques assumes that children already have mental representations. The term "mental representations" implies that the child's experiences are recognized and acknowledged—are represented—by another person—parent, therapist—or by the child. In the development process, the parent first generates these representations; later, the child learns to internalize this function. If children can generate representations of their own internal perceptions, then they can cope with the difference between internal and external, between fantasy and reality. It is sometimes likened to the faithfully reproduced pipe in a painting by René Magritte, below which he wrote "*Ceci n'est pas une pipe*". What you see is not a pipe, but a painting of a pipe, a canvas covered in paint, in a frame: it represents a pipe in a certain context, but it is not a real pipe. It is a mental representation, and so it differs from reality. Some children develop hardly any mental representations because their experiences were too painful and their early attachment relationship was not safe enough.

When a mother assumes that her child's crying means that the child's nappy needs to be changed, in fact she is acknowledging the child's experiences and interpreting them as a need. The mother picks up the baby and accompanies her actions with words—for example, she says, "I think you would like a nice clean nappy"; she relates her contact with the child to the child's experience, and in this way she contributes to the affective representation of the child's primary experiences.

The experiences are affectively represented because the mother gives them reality. Later, when children can do this themselves, they can bring their affects to expression (can say: "I want a clean nappy"). Particularly when children are firmly in a teleological phase (see Chapter 2), they are unable to accept interpretations that reveal an intention that is different from that manifested in physical behaviour, such as needs and wishes. The parents of these children have not properly represented their children's perceptions, and so the children are unable to work with a mental picture instead of a physical one. And when a parent is seriously remiss, it means "that instead of an understanding internal object, the child has an wilfully misunderstanding object with which it is identified" (Mitrani, 2001, p. 1090). A child usually deals with this alien self by externalizing it. The need for projective identification then occurs over and over again, in every attachment relationship.

Maartje

Maartje's mother always brings her to therapy. One day, still in the initial stages of the therapy, her mother brings her early, so that Maartje has to sit alone in the waiting room until the therapist comes to get her when it is time for her appointment (five minutes later). She is furious and asks, "Where were you?" She is absolutely convinced that T [the therapist] did not want her today; she puts this across nonverbally and will not allow her mind to be changed. From a cognitive point of view, she understands perfectly well that some things—such as a therapy—start and end at a certain time, but this is different. T says she understands that Maartje is angry because things took so long. She says that today things are different from usual, because Maartje's mother usually comes inside with her for a minute, and they are not usually early. But it doesn't help. When T says she should have realized straight away that Maartje was sitting all alone and bored in the waiting room, there is a hint of confirmation. But Maartje remains on her guard throughout the session. She interprets the physical situation of sitting in the waiting room without her mother and without the therapist literally as being left in the lurch and not wanted. She is not yet able to put into words the enormous anxiety this has aroused in her. She is anxious, but she does not feel it as anxiety. Her response to a verbalization of the anxiety would be one of great humiliation. She would feel that she was not understood. A verbalization does not correspond to her point of view, and so it is false.

Already in 1986, Cluckers pointed out the importance of mentalization when he observed that therapy would help children with weak egos to gradually shape a mental space in which they could contain themselves: "Based on the relationship with the therapist as his container, little by little the child will grow able to experience, to control and to understand himself" (Cluckers, 1986, p. 26). He cited as the main objective of treatment "making contact with the child's experiences, making them communicable and manageable" (p. 35). Cluckers named a number of important methods that a therapist can use. They have much in common with mentalization-based child therapy, particularly his warning not to interpret background conflicts and feelings. What is missing, however, is a theory on the actual process of mentalization, and so he assumes that a child has feelings—whether they underlie his actions or not—and can express them in words. The theory on mentalization stresses the distinction between *being* sad and its mental representation, *feeling* sad. If a child has a mental process disorder and does not have any mental representations in a certain aspect of mental life, then if an affect in that area is verbalized incorrectly, it can seriously interfere with the relationship. The child will not recognize what the verbalization refers to, which will contribute to his sense of not being recognized or acknowledged. Only long and patient work, often in a preverbal sense as well, can lead to some form of representation and make affect verbalizations possible.[2]

At the Tavistock Clinic in London, Alvarez (1992) worked for a long time with extremely difficult, atypical, and often autistic children. Starting from a psychoanalytic frame of reference, she added many technical innovations to her therapeutic practice with these children. Analysts are used to emphasizing underlying depressive positions, and certainly the Kleinians among them consider these positions to be of great therapeutic importance. Alvarez counters by saying that one can also focus on hope and light-heartedness, sometimes on fantasies of omnipotence, to experiment with new identities. In some cases, Alvarez even sees "forgetting" (of sexual abuse) as a form of adaptation that may be favourable, because it allows children to shift their attention and to move on to further development (Hamilton, 2001). Although our group of children is less extreme than that of Alvarez, she does offer a number of suggestions that we can put to good use for children with less serious mental process disorders. According to Fonagy (2001b), Alvarez has led us to make two changes in our understanding of therapeutic effectiveness. Instead of talking about removing repression, we now speak of expanding the borders of the self so as to regain (by means of containment on the part of the analyst) the parts that have been split off. And a meta-theory has been developed that is less mechanistic and more relational, one that is better able to comprise renewal and the mentalness of mind.

Anne Hurry's *Psychoanalysis and Developmental Therapy* (Hurry, 1998b) was an important step towards recognizing the importance of techniques to promote mentalization. At the time of publication, the theoretical chapters were innovative in that they introduced the concept of mentalization. The cases described reveal the early stages of a theory on the technique. The technique is formulated as follows: "certain more supportive techniques may shift from the status of parameter to mutative components, at least in the early stages of what is likely to be a prolonged analysis" (Hurry, 1998b, p. 29). The analyst must create an environment in which it is safe, perhaps for the first time, to think about feelings and ideas. This gives children an opportunity to view themselves as thinking and feeling persons in the mind of their analyst. The analyst must yield to the huge pressure to accept the child's externalizations, because a refusal will mean a return of the alien object and put the child at risk of destruction of the self. It is the task of the analyst to stay in touch with the child's perspective despite the sometimes disruptive enactments. Some of the techniques cited challenge the child's mental abilities by verbalizing internal states, differentiating feelings, breaking down unmanageable experiences that evoke anxiety into simpler, more manageable units, helping the child to develop a pretend mode in which ideas can be seen as ideas and distinguished from external realities. The book advocates moving from an attitude of stimulating development to an attitude of interpreting, depending on what the child needs and can cope with. The abused child who challenges the analyst to enter into a sexualized interaction will not initially profit from an interpretation of his need to repeat, but will profit from an explication of his need to be sure that the analyst will not let it happen again. The child may perhaps be able to profit from interpretations later in the treatment, when more transitional space has been created.

Bleiberg (2001) wrote a treatment programme for children and adolescents with personality disorders. He too focuses on promoting mentalization in his emphasis on strengthening the reflective function. He advocates cross-fertilization between psychoanalytically oriented psychotherapy and other more empirical supporting treatments such as cognitive behavioural therapy and interpersonal psychotherapy. An advantage of Bleiberg's approach is the clarity with which he describes goals in each phase of the therapy process. Because of this, his approach sounds perhaps more cognitive than it really is. In any case the bridge to cognitive treatments is very clear.

Bateman and Fonagy (2004) introduced the term "mentalization-based treatment" and elaborated it into a treatment policy for borderline personality disorder. Although this book is about adult clients in an institutionalized setting, in an adapted form it still has much to offer by way of insights for the ambulatory treatment of children with mental process disorders. The authors name various techniques—for instance, increasing a person's capacity for mentalization and bridging the gap between affects and their representations. But the treatment situation with a child in the playroom has very different requirements and possibilities compared to the case of an adult. An adult's motivation and suffering are usually quite different from those of children brought in by their parents for treatment. The big discrepancy in cognitive development is another important factor with respect to synthesis and integration. Naturally, cognitive development refers not to intelligence, but to the differences in the ability to think in the abstract that are related to emotional development.

Framework of the treatment

Working with the adults in the child's life

As is further explained in Chapter 5, mentalization-based child therapy can succeed only if important adults can be involved. This refers in the first place to the therapist and the advisor for parent guidance, but other practitioners or the school may come into play. For children with a mental process disorder, it is extremely important to work with a consistent policy on all fronts. The child's manner of mental functioning must be the starting point for all agreements about a supportive, clear, consistent child-rearing climate that responds to the child.

In particular, the child therapist and the parent counsellor need to share a perspective of this child and this family. It is important that their relationship includes a sort of intermediate space in which the often primitive parallel processes can be put into words and given meaning. Because in this type of treatment both therapist and parent counsellor can readily find themselves in a situation in which their own integrative capacity is put under pressure, peer review meetings in a safe climate are indispensable.

Considering the objective of treatment, it must be assumed that this will be an intensive, long-term process. Both long and intensive child therapy and long-term parent guidance are needed because safe attachment relationships are not formed in a short period of time, and a safe attachment relationship is essential for the development of mentalization.

The representational mismatch

Bleiberg (2001) uses the term "representational mismatch" for what may occur when parents and caregivers start acting like competent and consistent child rearers.[3] Bleiberg's vision of the crucial role of parent guidance (Bleiberg, 2001) is discussed in Chapter 5. Here we will only remark that he ascribes high priority to improving effective parenting, if only because it leads to a representational mismatch for the child. The child's expectations no longer tally. The omnipotence invoked by narcissistic and narcissistic–antisocial children and their view of others as weak and incompetent are in jeopardy. Borderline children will experience a mismatch if their parents start to offer protection against maladjusted behaviour—for example, if they have temper tantrums or are impulsive. Their expectation that parents are indifferent or rejecting is no longer confirmed. Bleiberg thinks this mismatch is necessary to help parents to move more purposefully towards a safe base, but more particularly, to challenge children's coping mechanisms. Although their symptomatology will initially let them hold on to their illusion of control, treatment starts and is aimed at altering their unproductive compulsive and unmentalized exchanges into an initial awareness of reciprocity. For Bleiberg, the first objective of treatment is to move from an initial contractual co-operation—such as agreements as to times, payment—to therapeutic cooperation. This is more complicated with children than with adults with the same problems. Adults are more aware of their suffering, and they opt for treatment themselves, whereas children are registered for treatment by their caregivers.

Setting of child therapy

In consultation with the parents and parent counsellors, agreements are made as to frequency, dates and times, holidays, and so on. For how this works in practice, see Chapter 10. It is essential that every-thing about the setting is reliable. The first ingredient for building up trust in another person is their continual availability; this is a prereq-uisite with a view to building up a safe relationship.

Disorders in the ability to mentalize may be masked, for exam-ple, by parentification: in such a case, children are quite well able to read the thoughts and feelings of adults, but not their own. If they are bright children, it may sometimes seem that they do understand the complexity of alternative perspectives. But they prove not to be able to carry over thoughts and desires from one session to the next. There is no consistency in their experiences with others, so that they may idealize the therapist at one moment and be disparaging of him or her at the next. It is the task of the therapist to accept the child's perspective. Instead of telling a child that at the last session he had a completely different opinion about something, the therapist can try to understand the differences in perspective together with the child.

The therapist's typical attachment representation and regulatory capacity play a role from the beginning. Particularly in the early phases of treatment, when there is a representational mismatch and the child's vehemence and urge to control increase, it is necessary for the therapist to retain some inner space in which to think. With such often greatly over-stimulated children, the therapist needs this space in order to find the right tone and physical expression that can get the child to relax a little. Initially, the therapeutic process takes place via the therapist, who tries to contain all the child's vehemence by focus-ing attention on internal priorities. She tries to digest the vehemence of the affects and then give them back to the child in detoxified form by adding an incompatible affect such as comfort or reassurance, while retaining her own calm and quiet.

The therapist as development object

Cluckers (1986) is one of the authors who point out that the therapist is also an identification figure for the child. The therapist offers her-self as an identification model and, by means of holding and contain-ment, creates a safe framework so that the relationship stays good, thus offsetting the child's chaos. The structure of the self is reinforced because the therapist supports the child's narcissism: the child experiences that his person—what he says and thinks—are important for someone else. The experience of continuity and coherence that the therapist attempts to create also serves this purpose. The child's experience that the therapist is there and is helpful forms the basis on which to develop a safe object relationship.

At the same time the therapist must remain in the role of therapist and not become caught up in a real relationship. As a new object, of course, the therapist offers a real new relationship, but not in the form of a parent substitute. These children can be extremely demanding, asking for care and expecting to be treated as exceptions. Some children are looking for a warm and special relationship with the therapist. In reaction to this, the therapist may become distant and reticent, which can lead to destructive interaction. Then it is crucial to restore the representational mismatch—for example, by showing that the therapist understands what it is like if no one takes care of you. These can be crucial moments for the success of the treatment. If the therapist finds a way—without loss of face for the child but with great empathy for the child's needs—to maintain the contractual framework (time of the appointment, no visits to school performances, etc.), a great deal will have been gained. As Mannoni so clearly describes it, such an attitude makes it impossible for a child to "parasitize" or freeload (Pleiter, 1983). The child sees that, if he does not have the chance to insist that his often destructive demands are met, then—paradoxically enough—he is taken more seriously as a person in his own right. If the child cannot use the other to go his own way, he becomes more focused on his own inner self, on the question of "what do I really want".

It is also important to set limits for destructive behaviour, such as the child hurting himself or the therapist or breaking things. If there are clear boundaries, the child knows what he can expect, and this contributes to the sense of safety. It helps the child to build up an inner structure (Tyson, 2005). A complicated aspect is the fact that the therapist must not go along with the child's acting out, whereas it is inevitable that she will find herself in enactments with the child, and this is a good thing. Bateman and Fonagy (2004) speak of a benign split in which the therapist must steer a middle course: she takes the roles ascribed to her upon herself, including

the more implicit, sometimes nonverbal attributions that the therapist is usually only aware of in retrospect. At the same time she
must be able to continue mentalizing as the therapist, which can be
extremely difficult at times.

It is difficult to manoeuvre between remaining in the role of the
therapist and taking part without reinforcing the child's concretely
demanding attitude. It will sometimes be necessary to say something
about the "real" relationship. For example, when a child whose therapist was absent had become convinced that it meant the end of his
treatment, the therapist responded by writing the time and date for
the next appointment on a card to restore the child's faith that she
would be there. Vivian Green describes a therapy of a 5-year-old boy
whose mother had died a year earlier. Because breaks in the therapy
were really desertions for him, she asked him if he wanted a message
from her, and she sent him a card (Hurry, 1998b, p. 149).

Working "in" the transference

Transference is used here to refer to latent or implicit habits, expectations, and views that become clear, organized around and evoked by
the intensity of the therapeutic relationship. Nothing is constructed!
Transference is the aspect of the interaction in which the child's mental functioning can be played out in the treatment; it is a new emotional experience that, although it is influenced by the past, is not a
repetition of it. Working in the transference is a therapeutic means by
which the therapist and the child together try to understand what is
going on. Transference interpretations are out of the question as long
as a child functions in the equivalent mode. An interpretation of the
transference might cause the child to feel that what goes on in the
therapy is not real. For example, if the therapist were to suggest that
the child tends to make her more powerful than is actually the case,
intimating that the child's perception is distorted, the child could
find himself in a pretend world—one dissociated from his mental
functioning. Or the child might withdraw because he has not felt
understood. The therapist must always be prepared for differences
between the child's perspective and her own. If the therapist feels
she is being blamed for something, the child may see it completely

differently. It is important that they both start from a position of "*not knowing*", but "*trying to understand*". It is important to remember that many children with personality problems become very anxious in intimate relationships because of the paradox in their disorganized attachment system: the person you most want to be with is at the same time the one who scares you. Because of this, too much emphasis on the relationship can lead to panic. This can be regulated by working in the transference. Basically, if the therapist always sees the different positions and places the child's perspective first and foremost, safety will increase. Sometimes it is better not to focus on the therapeutic relation because this triggers too much anxiety. It can be more useful to talk about other relations—for example, between the figures in a play. This is a form of "displacement" (e.g. Verheugt-Pleiter & Zevalkink, 2005).

In the treatment, the way the therapist acts with the child is parallel to the process through which the parent's intentional attitude provides feedback on the child's emotional state and thus promotes the child's development. It is important, as we have seen, that the therapist clearly distinguishes between her own feelings and those of the child. This is not always easy when countertransference reactions provoke the therapist to act rather than to think. In these treatments, the therapist must accept the fact that in order to train her focus on the child's mental functioning, she will sometimes see herself do things that do not suit her. She must also become what the child wants her to be while at the same time continuing to think about what takes place.

In fact, the therapist only needs to be "good enough" at recognizing the child's state of mind. A mismatch can also lead to a fruitful exchange. It is important that the therapist feels free to absorb whatever comes up in the relationship.

Maartje

In the middle phase of therapy Maartje is almost chronically angry with the therapist. As the positive transference increases, the unsafe attachment, of the preoccupied type, becomes more palpable in the relationship. For instance, she has an increasingly difficult time with the end of the session. At a certain point she wants to play a game of marbles. She cheats a lot and is basically out to get the nicest marbles, not to play by the rules—which is usual in young children. She enjoys the game. When the time is up, she grabs a handful of marbles, flings them into the room, and leaves with the remark, "You stay here!" She does not say goodbye. T is left behind, angry and dismayed. She has to pick up the marbles and get them out of the way before the next client comes. At the next session she tries to talk about this with Maartje when she takes out the marbles to play the game. Maartje doesn't want to talk, but to play: "Shut up." At the end of the session she again reaches into the jar of marbles and flings the marbles into the room. Again she doesn't say goodbye but gives T a chilling look. T feels quite wretched. She tries to pick up the marbles, but feels completely lost. Looking and not finding. T realizes that Maartje wants to change their positive relationship, because she thinks that the relationship has been spoiled. Better to make a mess of it and see anxiety in the other person than to be small and dependent on an adult, on someone she cannot and dare not trust. T decides that she will put the marbles away for the next session and let Maartje know how dreadful it is to have lost everything, how very lost you can feel. Maartje says nothing to this, but she is much calmer. T has tried to bring to development the feeling of being lost and not "found".

Countertransference is an important instrument in sensing what it is at stake. And not just the countertransference as discussed above, where the therapist takes on the roles ascribed to her. The more implicit, sometimes nonverbal reactions of the therapist to the child are important as well. Sometimes the therapist finds herself stalemated by her own unresolved conflicts. In such a case, peer review or supervision is needed, or perhaps even treatment.

Bleiberg (2001) shows that the countertransference can be used productively because the therapist can give a real-life demonstration of how a vicious circle of not understanding and not being understood can be broken by verbalizing a sequence of her own internal activities. Clarifying what the child has said ("let me see if I heard what you said correctly. . . .") also helps in verbalizing internal states; he recommends adopting a playful attitude as a way of offsetting the feeling of being overwhelmed by experiences.

*Principles behind the technique
of mentalization-based child therapy*

Working in the here and now of the relationship

Various authors have looked for alternative strategies for the treatment of children with difficulties in the area of mental processes, for
instance, because they have observed that classical interpretations
do not work with this group of children, who are more seriously
disturbed than neurotic children. Cluckers (1986) concluded that,
for many children with weak egos, who have relatively little inner
strength and ability to cope, reconstructive psychotherapy does not
offer a solution. He described expansions and adaptations of reconstructive therapy, calling it ego-supportive or ego-strengthening
therapy. The objective of this therapy is to create the conditions that
can optimize ego development.

Chethik (1989) is another author who modified psychoanalytic
psychotherapy and psychoanalysis for borderline children, children
with narcissistic problems, and children with character pathology.
Adjustments are primarily needed for impulsive children. These children have great difficulty bearing reconstructions of their life story,
possibly because of the enormous anxiety it evokes. He therefore
restricts himself to analysing defences. He tries to make behaviour
and character traits explicit and less ego-syntonic. In this way, he aims
to make the child aware of the underlying motivations and so make
them more acceptable.

With borderline children, therapy that provides insight is not possible, according to Chethik (1989); like Cluckers, he looks to support
and strengthening of the ego. Basically, his strategy is to slowly join
the child's fantasy world and from that position to help the child integrate aspects of the frightening real world. On account of the child's
poor defences and lack of reflection, the objective is to tie down the
material and bring it under control. He structures on the one hand
and dramatizes on the other, rather like the mother who points to
the heater and says to the young child "HOT HOT", so that it is extremely clear. With children with narcissistic disorders, on the other
hand, he uses more techniques that provide insight, such as interpretation and reconstruction. According to him, the chief problem here

is the same as that with borderline children: integrating the primitive aggression. The difference with the treatment of neurosis lies in the specific content, because much more early material and mechanisms such as splitting are under scrutiny. All in all, Chethik's treatment remains within the conflict model.

Bleiberg (2001) goes one step further. He does not want to link the child's mental functioning with dissociated, repressed experiences or experiences from the past. He focuses instead on the circumstances leading up to an aggressive act—for example, in a situation in which the child did not feel understood. The therapist helps him to gain control of his automatic reactions.

Greenspan (1997) also distances himself from classical interpretation and focuses primarily on ego structure alongside the dynamic contents always considered so important. In his opinion, the various types of psychotherapy have had much too limited a focus on symbolic verbal interaction, and it has even been considered possible to treat preverbal interaction patterns using verbal reflective therapeutic techniques. Greenspan offers a comprehensive vision of socio-emotional development in the child, on the basis of which he develops a therapy model that is suitable for children—and adults—with mental process disorders.[4] An important transition in Greenspan's development model is the transition from the behavioural level (toddler phase) to the representational phase, and he puts forward an impressive series of intervention techniques to facilitate this transition in therapy.

Fonagy, Gergely, and colleagues (2002) conclude that psychoanalytic metaphors for stagnations in development that are traditionally used in the explanation of pathology and treatment strategy can be hollow and circular because they cannot define the consequences of psychological problems at a young age. On the basis of cases such as that of Rebecca (Fonagy, Gergely, et al., 2002, pp. 278ff.), they show what can go wrong when moving from a non-representational to a representational mental reality. Rebecca could not make a representation of the pain and the shame of being fatherless, leaving a psychotic island in her subjective perception, an island where subjective experience was equated with reality, thus becoming a source of acute anxiety. This girl benefited from the relationship with a therapist who could tone down her ideas so that she could re-form them herself and create a mental reality that was no longer either fantasy or external reality. In playing and talking with the therapist, her ideas could be altered and transformed because, thanks to the therapist's containment of her, she saw a reflection of *her own* mental state and not the preoccupations or defences of the adult. Because the therapist *acknowledges* the coercive reality of the child's experiences and enters into the pretend world of the child, there is room for change. Gradually the therapist can show that these are representations that you can share, that you can play with, and that you can change. This means promoting mentalization in the child.

Bion (1967a) advises the therapist to work "without memory or desire". Memory, for example in relation to a patient's past history, is misleading because it is always distorted by unconscious processes and desires. For instance, the desire to give the patient something interferes with the therapist's capacity to observe, which is so essential in order to form an opinion. It is not about what happened or what will happen, but what is happening. Mitrani writes: "what we hope to achieve is a state of being with the patient in the present so that he/she can eventually bear to be him or herself, with him/herself" (Mitrani, 2001, p. 1099). Working in the here and now in a new relationship with a therapist who, thanks to his containment of the child, gives a marked reflection of the child's inner world, offers the best chance of setting in motion mentalization in the child.

Recognizing the child's level of mental functioning and meeting at the same level

To restart development processes in the child, in the first place it is important to attune to the child's natural tendencies and interests (Greenspan, 1997). We have seen that therapists often address the child too abstractly because they assume that affects are available and that a child will have the ability to talk about them. These children can be highly inconsistent in what they say. They are not lying: it is just impossible for them to understand the various representations. They are all true and the therapist will simply have to work with them.

The first instrument with which the therapist responds to the child's level of mental functioning is what Winnicott (1960) referred to as "holding". In the first place, Winnicott refers to holding as the mother physically holding her child. There are mothers who are un-able to do this. The holding function of the analyst often takes on a verbal form in the sense that the analyst knows and understands the client's deepest fears (Winnicott, 1963). The very earliest form of holding by the child's mother involves transforming the otherness of time for the child and creating the illusion of a world that is attuned to the physical and psychological rhythm of the child. With an older child, the function of physical holding changes into holding the more object-related manners of being alive, such as providing a psycho-logical space in which the child can bring himself together. Winnicott also uses this concept to investigate the changing intrapsychic and interpersonal ways in which a sense of continuity of being in time can be retained (1960). Mentalization-based child therapy is intended to bring about an internalization of these functions of holding in the child, both in the basic sense and in the more developed sense, so that the child can develop a mind of his own. In children in whom the self is as yet so little developed—and who have little capacity to mentalize—it is important that the therapist uses holding to stimulate development. For this purpose he must meet the child's level accu-rately: if the child is in the equivalent mode of mental functioning, this is the perspective to which the therapist must relate.

Greenspan (1997) in particular is a strong advocate of relating to what he terms pre-representational levels in development. These levels focus more on the structure of the self—Greenspan speaks of ego—than on the content of the material. He names four pre-rep-resentational levels along with appropriate strategic suggestions if there are problems in these areas:

1. helping the child achieve a state of calm and focused regulation;
2. working on the child's ability to make contacts;
3. working on limits and the basis for intentional behaviour;
4. stimulating preverbal interactions that make possible self and other attributions.

These levels are further elaborated in the discussion of attention regulation in Chapter 7.

Giving reality value to inner experiences

The therapist works with what manifests itself as affects in the here and now. Not much is to be gained by focusing on the past. Even if the child himself continually brings up the past, it is advisable to get him back on the track of the present—the events that take place during the session.

Once the child can accurately identify an affect within the relationship, exploration can be set in motion: not by the therapist putting into words how the child feels, because this can cause confusion about whose feelings are being discussed; but the therapist can help by exploring whatever is expressed in the child's actual behaviour.

> If the child says that the therapist is acting very stupid today, it is important to ask questions about when the child thinks so and in relation to what. Perhaps it will turn out that the child has new shoes and is very disappointed that the therapist—who usually notices things like this—has not seen them today. The therapist gives reality value to the child's feeling of disappointment by saying that she understands perfectly that the child thinks this is stupid of her. She says, "You are right about that. I should have noticed. It is certainly no fun—in fact, it is quite stupid—for you to have something new and then no one notices it. In fact it means that no one is paying any attention to you!"

In the therapy, it is therefore important to explicitly state the experience aspect from the child's perspective, thus giving it reality value. Stating them helps build up an inner structure so that the child can bring affects to expression himself at a certain point: the secondary affect representations. In the long run the child will develop the ability to reflect about feelings and to correct misconnections.

Seeking out with the child the emotional antecedents of his enactments can help achieve this. If attacked, the therapist must remain calm and show that words and thoughts can express more than behaviour can. Summarizing behavioural patterns—for example, going back and recounting how something quite unpleasant happened—can serve to create a shared experience in the here and now. If the therapist recognizes the experience, it takes on reality value and the existence of the child's self is confirmed.

Often the child will start by giving a very broad indication of affects: "I feel bad." The most highly developed representation and expression of affect is when we talk about affects that have a combined affective and cognitive significance. There, feelings and their symbolic elaborations are combined, which means that the child can represent his own affects. In normal development, this level is achieved around the age of 3 to 5. Then children know that certain behaviour of theirs or of another person may be related to an emotional state. *Thinking* about the affect representations is an even higher level; at this level, a child begins to realize that another person can feel quite differently about the same event. When a child can start to think from several perspectives, we speak of mentalization. This is discussed further in Chapter 9.

The most important question is how the therapist can help the child to make the transition to a truly representational level. The most frequent error—and quite an understandable one when speaking from the experience of a person who does mentalize—is to routinely ask a child who functions at a behavioural level what something reminds him of (Bateman & Fonagy, 2004). If the child gives some explanation, the therapist can empathically summarize the material in terms of the feelings that he thinks are implied. But if the child has spoken about behaviour and not about feelings, he will not understand the concepts presented. Perhaps he will even feel attacked or otherwise overwhelmed by the therapist. In such a case it is much more effective to jointly focus on the child's behavioural pattern and to see his perspective in this. This can give a sense of a *shared* experience in the present, one at the child's current level.

If the child can name an affect within the relationship, the therapist and the child can then follow this up together. In practice, a great deal of work will go into carefully following and exploring what the child exhibits in his current behaviour or mood. The shared experience can lead to recognition and acknowledgement, thus forming the basis for the child to start thinking about his own behaviour or mood. The interaction promotes mentalization, and the child will develop mental representations as a result.

It is easy for a child to show aggression. When children feel they have suffered a humiliation or some other threat to their sense of self, a temper tantrum often follows. This happens when the intention of the other person is poorly understood, or when the child feels threatened by something inside him. For example, if a child feels continually and intensely critical of himself and is unable to regulate his self-criticism, the result is strong anxiety. Without self-regulation, a feeling of anxiety can easily be converted into destructive behaviour because it facilitates the externalization of an unbearable feeling. The child wants to be rid of his alien self! Writing about the model of mentalization-based treatment, Verheugt-Pleiter and Deben-Mager (2006) state:

> Rather than of aggression, the model generally speaks of disintegrating tendencies, that can express themselves in extreme panic or in hostility. In this model, aggression is seen as the final stronghold against the unbearable fear of the barren, empty inner landscape and the awareness that your parent, your attachment figure, does not really "see" you, and may even hate you. [p. 308]

If the anxiety is verbalized too quickly, it often has the opposite effect, because the child may well regard the verbalization as an attack. Bateman and Fonagy (2004) describe how a patient can terrorize the therapist just to see him show anxiety. It calms the patient, and the externalized alien self remains firmly anchored in the relationship. In that case it is necessary to supervise or to shift the tension very patiently and with much compassion, and at a certain point to start understanding it. Luckily, much can be worked out in play in child therapies. The various techniques used in affect regulation are discussed in greater detail in Chapter 8.

Playing with reality

There are children who cannot play at all: they cannot or dare not think in pretend terms.[5] Theoretically, this can be understood as a consequence of the parent having been too realistic and not having markedly mirrored the child's affects (see Chapter 2). If a child experiences a negative state of mind and the parent reacts in kind, the child does not learn to regulate his own inner experiences. The lack of containment leads to projective forms of identification because the inner world has become unbearable and much too real. These children stay extremely focused on the physical reality outside themselves instead of on mental reality, and they are overly sensitive to the emotional reactions of others. They are caught in the equivalent mode of mental functioning, which means that thoughts and feelings are taken literally. Because they cannot perceive themselves as entities from the inside out, they are forced to perceive themselves from the outside by means of enactments (Bateman & Fonagy, 2004). They project onto the other that which is elicited in them by the alien self, the unknown. It is important to remember that the therapist does *not* know it either, but does try *to understand it together with the child.*

There are also children in whom the emphasis of their experiences is on the pretend manner of mental functioning; they only perceive things from the inside out. Theoretically this can be understood as a situation in which the parents did not give the young child congruent feedback on his primary experiences (see Chapter 2). The child has not given any grip for inner perceptions. In a dissociative disorder, nothing is related or linked: fantasy and reality are completely separate. This can later lead to a compulsive search for meaning to dispel the sense of emptiness brought on by the pretend mode (Bateman & Fonagy, 2004). Characteristic of the borderline personality organization in adults is the oscillation between these two manners of being. It can be seen in children as well.

When children play, both the pretend mode and the equivalent mode may be present, and sometimes they may alternate. It is always important to be aware of the child's perspective and to meet that same level. In child development, playing "pretend" is one step beyond the equivalent mode, because the need for immediate action has been replaced and a mental representation has been made of it. Pretend play can be a way of generating fantasies and images, but its link to reality is an important point. In normal development, playing with reality at the parent's initiative and in a safe environment is what leads to an integration of the two modes. Only then does the child really understand what it means to pretend (see Chapter 2). Many children are not yet able to do so. In that case, it is important—for example—to dramatize play so that the child is encouraged to move more into pretend mode: the therapist is an active commentator, reacting to the child's play and trying to invite the child to enlarge on important moments. Separations are often important moments. Loss and mourning are higher-level affects that are not yet felt as such. Greenspan (1997) therefore points out the importance, for example, of visualization or making a person who is not there present using other sensory channels. This is a form of playing with reality. A discussion of defences such as, during a treatment of neurosis, not wanting to talk about a loved one who is absent is not appropriate here. Making the presence of that person imaginable through visualization or some other sense (smell, hearing, etc.) can help the child to retain a picture and to develop an initial mental representation of loss and sadness.

An interruption to the therapy is another very important topic that will be approached in a different way than it is in the treatment of neurosis. It is assumed (Stoker, 2005) that an interruption calls up great anxiety, because then there is no longer anyone to give words to the child's experiences, assuming that the child cannot yet do this himself. Interpreting the child's anger at the interruption is completely wide of the mark. Stoker says that anxiety about an interruption in the therapy must always be discussed explicitly *in advance*. At the same time it is important to keep in mind the child's great need to exist for the other person, to be understood. For the retention of his thoughts, the child is literally dependent on the therapist. When there is a separation, the development object is gone, and the child feels overcome by the perception of diffuse nothingness, which is very frightening. Separation is so difficult because it is a threat to the self. In these treatments, it is basically the enormously vulnerable sense of self that cries out for recognition.

Psychoanalysts have traditionally placed great emphasis on separation and absence. Alvarez (1992), on the other hand, follows Bowlby in her emphasis on experiences of reunion and nearness. For instance, she explains children's pleasure at playing hide-and-seek as pleasure in having a person want to find them. For these children, the focus on reunion and finding one another is often a more important experience than coping with separation (for an example, see Verheugt-Pleiter, 2003). The pleasure in finding is the result of the discovery that when a person goes away, it does not mean that he or she is literally gone. It is an initial awareness that things are not always what they seem—an understanding of the pretend mode in mental functioning. The huge pleasure children take in playing hide-and-seek is because it allows them to play with reality, thus bringing an integration of the two modes one step closer.

Playing with reality: with some children, the therapist will look for greater differentiation in their playing to increase their sensitivity.

With other children he will name the larger whole, if it can make a repetitive form of play more colourful, for example.

The process is more important than the technique

In describing the treatment, it is tempting to assume a hierarchy in the techniques. As is the case in normal development, the child must first be capable of calm sensorimotor regulation, so that he is no longer simply overwhelmed by vehement affect states, before he can start to recognize and regulate affects; and so this would seem to be the right order in therapy as well. But reality is not so clear-cut. In the first place, a child in the latency period cannot be likened to a baby. In certain fields development has continued, while in specific areas it has stagnated. Development processes seldom proceed at an equal pace on all fronts. It is known that some adult borderline patients can maintain themselves well in work and social life while their personal relationships are disasters; children with mental process disorders also exhibit great difficulties with their social contacts with both children and adults. Still, one child will feel a terrific sense of disintegration if his wish to withdraw is under pressure, while another child panics when her possibilities to gain control of a situation disintegrate. The therapist must retain space so that he can be surprised by what comes up in the relationship, primarily in its unconscious aspects. He will sometimes find himself caught in an enactment or have to find a way to understand what unregulated areas in himself are being called upon in the relationship.

Sometimes constructive work is done in a therapy for a time, and then suddenly a regression occurs because something comes up in the child's playing that cannot be understood immediately. Inevitably, the therapist works by trial and error. But, just as in normal development, for the perception of the self as agent, it is crucial that the relationship is restored and, if possible, that the therapist and the child see how the interruption occurred. Being a person who experiences this gives a sturdier basis to the child's sense of self. This may be just a moment, one that Daniel Stern (2004) calls a "now moment" or a "moment of meeting". Such a moment is usually not verbalized, but it is a time when both parties implicitly know that something essential has changed in their relationship. And to this one might add: and in the perception of the self as agent.

In a workshop in 2004, Bateman and Fonagy gave excellent examples of a therapeutic mismatch:

> A patient with self-undermining behaviour brings the therapist to make an empathic and perhaps too intrusive comment. The patient defends himself by attacking the therapist (attributes an unacceptable quality of his to the therapist). The therapist has difficulty with this, gets the feeling that he is failing and tries to compensate (activates his attachment system) by offering an extra session. This causes the patient to withdraw further, thinking that there is no point in it anyway.

Acting to promote mentalization means, therefore:

1. Remaining in the here and now: how does it feel for you to sit there and say I am worthless?

2. Going through the entire sequence one more time, to understand together what happened in the patient when the therapist said or did something.

3. Taking responsibility for the mismatch upon yourself as therapist by acknowledging the mismatch: "I do think that my reaction was not very sensitive." Recognize how difficult it is for the patient to be approached like this, and then describe the emotional state, adding an incompatible affect (containment)—for example: "I understand that it makes you feel anxious if I say something with so much force. That is a highly unpleasant feeling. But you know, we can talk about it."

A more traditional treatment would probably look at an actualization of internal objects in the patient; mentalization-based child therapy is about the interaction in the here and now. The various techniques as elaborated in Chapters 7, 8, and 9 are important tools. But they are only tools that serve the process, which largely takes place in the nonconscious, in the implicit relationship. The term "process" "implies dynamics, an event, a certain course" (Berkouwer, 2004, p. 28). In the past century, the psychoanalytic treatment process has been conceptualized in very different ways. In general it may be stated—

according to Berkouwer—that we have more and more come to view and describe the psychoanalytic process as a process that takes place between partners, as an intersubjective event. Mentalization-based child therapy is one example of this. Promoting mentalization is the objective, and the various techniques discussed in Chapters 7, 8, and 9 can be used to achieve this objective.

Ending the treatment

At the beginning of this chapter the most important objective of the treatment was formulated: promoting the emergence of a coherent self, a sense of agency, and a capacity to defer, modulate, and regulate emotional reactions (Tyson, 2005). We have indicated how important it is to meet the child's development level and to his equivalent or pretend mode of functioning. We do this in order to give reality value to the child's experiences. This means the child begins to exist in the eyes of another person and so in his own eyes as well. This is the basis on which to build up a sense of self in a safe relationship. The child will only have a coherent self, a sense of agency, and a capacity to defer, modulate, and regulate emotional reactions if he has also made the step from primary affect representations to secondary representations and has gradually developed a competence for interpretative self-regulation. The therapist starts by recognizing the coercive reality of the child's experiences and, by making contact with the child's mental world, gradually starts to show the child that it contains a number of representations that can be shared, that you can play with, and that can be changed (Fonagy, Gergely, et al., 2002)—mental representations of self and of the therapist as beings that think and feel, together with and independent of one another. Here the core of a sense of self is formed, with a capacity to represent ideas and opinions, and the basis is laid for a relationship that will ultimately offer new possibilities of separation and intimacy (Fonagy, Gergely, et al., 2002).

We might well ask whether the objective can be set so high in every treatment. Sometimes there is an obvious limit to what can be achieved at a certain point, in a certain developmental phase, with this particular child, and in this family. The changes discussed in this chapter are so fundamental that sometimes we must be satisfied with a developmental step by which the child moves in the direction of safe attachment and can mentalize in some areas but not in all, one where the parents are better able to have thoughts and ideas about this child, so that the child has acquired more right to exist in a psychological sense. Then in a later phase—for example, during adolescence—when cognitive development is rapid, perhaps further work can be done in a therapeutic relationship. Perhaps it is better to let the family first benefit from the improvements on their own for a while. It has been our experience so far that these children often stop treatment when their development in important fields such as school or relationships with peers has started to go forward again. These children may need a multiple-entry ticket so they can come back in a later phase and go through another course of treatment, perhaps accompanied by parent guidance, perhaps on their own.

The objective of the treatment is to facilitate the emergence of a coherent self. With children, this objective is best served if we are able to get their development moving again, even if a child has not yet really reached the stage of a mentalizing self. The principles of treatment discussed in this chapter are elaborated for the various intervention techniques in Chapters 7, 8, and 9.

Notes

1. The self as agent refers to a concept of self and others as intentional mental organizers (Fonagy, Gergely, et al., 2002, p. 204). Fonagy distinguishes the following stages in development: (1) the self as physical agent, (2) the self as social agent, (3) the self as teleological agent, (4) the self as intentional mental agent, and (5) the self as representational agent and the autobiographical self, at around the age of 4 or 5.

2. There is much confusion in the literature about the terms "affect", "feeling", and "emotion". Damasio (2004) reserves the term "emotions" for "actions or movements that are often public, visible to others in the way they are shown by a person's face, voice, or specific behaviour". In contrast, "feelings" are always hidden, as are all other mental images: "they are observed exclusively by their lawful owner and they are the most personal possession of the organism in whose brains they occur" (Damasio, 2004, p. 32). He uses the term "affect" to refer to both emotions and feelings.

3. These are often—but not always—children of parents who also have a mental process disorder (see Chapter 5). There are also children who have

sensitive parents but have developed a mental process disorder on account of a trauma at an earlier age.

4. Greenspan speaks of the absence of representations and reflection.

5. It was Winnicott (1971) who turned attention to the special connection between playing and reality. Play is not an inner reality; it is outside the individual, but is not the outside world. In playing, external phenomena are invested with a dream quality. In his article entitled "Playing with Reality: The Development of Psychic Reality and Its Malfunction in Borderline Personalities", Fonagy (1995) discusses how an analyst playing with a young child can help the child to get to know his inner world and to have the opportunity to make him more integrated and reflective.

CHAPTER FIVE

Helping parents to promote mentalization

Marja J. Rexwinkel and Annelies J. E. Verheugt-Pleiter

T his chapter focuses on guidance for parents, which takes place parallel with the child's therapy, as discussed in Chapter 4. A number of specific characteristics of parent guidance are examined, and the following techniques are discussed: giving reality value to the inner experiences of parents with their child, learning to observe and read the child's inner world, working in the here and now, and repairing misattunement. The specific difficulties of parent guidance in composite families are also considered. In conclusion, we touch on the importance of working together with other disciplines and the idea of representational mismatch.

Introduction

A child's specific psychopathology is an important reason to request therapy for a child, but every time a child is registered, it can also be seen as an expression of problems experienced in parenting. It is often the parents who experience problems in their relationship with the child. When parents register a child, it should thus also be viewed as way of expressing their uncertainty about themselves as parents. From this point of view, it is the parent who asks for help as a parent. In response to this request, a therapeutic relationship is offered which has come to be called parent guidance. When children are in psychoanalysis or psychotherapy, the parents are always offered parent guidance.

Parents of children with a mental process disorder often have their own difficulties with mentalization, though this is not always the case: it sometimes happens that a child grows up with emotionally available, mentalizing parents, but that, because of a predisposition or traumatic factors such as loss or illness, the child is unable to draw any benefit from this. A parent with a mental process disorder may have a defective picture of the child as a separate person with his own intentional existence. In that case, the child's behaviour is taken too literally, and if the child exhibits negative behaviour, the parent can literally feel made a fool of by the child. The parent cannot form an inner representation of the various intentions the child may have with his negative behaviour. For example, when children have been out with their parents all day and are exhausted in the afternoon from all the walking and all the impressions, they may have a temper tantrum if they are taken to the supermarket. A parent who is unable to put himself in the child's place can see the latter's behaviour as a personal attack: "You're terribly ungrateful. You've been the centre of attention all day, why are you pestering me now?" This only causes the situation to escalate.

In a parent–child relationship, it is essential that the parent is able to recognize that a child has his own feelings, thoughts, and wishes: he is "sad", she is "angry", he "likes" to sing songs, she "wants" to go outside, he "can tell" that he will soon have a meal. The capacity of parents to link this awareness of a child's inner experiences to behaviour or to their own inner experiences is the essential characteristic of mentalization (Slade, 2002). To put it in the terms of the foregoing example with the supermarket:

> "He had a temper tantrum in the supermarket [behaviour] *because* he was so *tired* and *hungry* [physical state] and I had been walking around with him all day and he had had *enough* of it [child's mental state]."

or

"Sometimes he gets so *frustrated and angry* [child's mental state] that I am not *entirely certain that I understand him properly* [link to mother's mental state]."

It will be clear that if a parent mentalizes, the meaning of behaviour can be discussed, while if a parent has a mental process disorder, the behaviour is perceived quite concretely and equated with the emotional inner world. With parents it is—just as we saw when talking about the disorders of children—also no clear demarcation line between problems with mental processes or representations. The ability to mentalize will depend on the level of stress and type of circumstances and can be partial or total. In this chapter we will first dwell on a number of general aspects of parent guidance and then elaborate them as they are used in helping parents to promote mentalization. When working with parents with a mental process disorder, different techniques are needed, so as to create conditions in which parents are better able to see and experience what goes on in their own inner world and that of their child. In the project we have described in this book, we focused on collecting information about child therapies intended to encourage mentalization. We did not also systematically collect material about parent guidance. Because parent guidance is so extremely important, in this chapter we will try to describe our first experiences, and we definitely view this as a work in progress. We made much use of the theory of Anthony Bateman and Peter Fonagy (2004) about borderline personality disorder and mentalization-based therapy.

General aspects of guidance for parents

It is important to bear in mind that every time parents request therapy for their child, it can also be regarded as an expression of problems of the parents with their parenting, as a request for help. parent guidance is a *sine qua non* for child therapy. It is an important link in the treatment process of the child (Slijper, 1998). The content of parent guidance can vary from an "exchange of information to a more process-oriented and therapeutic relationship with parents focusing on their position and their role as parents" (van der Maas & Tates, 1990).

According to the Association for Child and Adolescent Psychotherapy (VKJP, 1994), three basic objectives of parent guidance can be distinguished:

1. developing a working relationship with parents intended to support the growth of their child, whether the child is in therapy or not;
2. making it possible to exchange the necessary information about the child;
3. bringing about changes in the child's home environment and surroundings to open the way to further development.

These starting points all have a strong focus on the child. As parent guidance has developed as a discipline in its own right, the focus of the counsellor has shifted to the parent as a parent. While the child's diagnosis and treatment are often worked out in detail, relatively little attention has been paid to a further elaboration of parent guidance (Marcelis-Eerdmans, 2000). Parenting can be likened to child development in that it has its own developmental phases and developmental tasks. When we take parenting and its furtherance as the focus of parent guidance, the primary objectives can be expanded with:

4. the position to be adopted by the counsellor, meaning that the therapist must start by identifying with the parent instead of the "inviting" option of identifying with the child;
5. the therapist stands alongside the parent and tries to come into contact with the parent's inner world, with the intention of coming to understand the meaning the child has for the parent.

The position of the counsellor or therapist as described by van der Pas (1994, 1996) is based on three tenets that will help the therapist to work effectively. The therapist must be continually aware that:

▸ parenting implies an awareness of "being responsible" for the child;

> this feeling of "being responsible" makes parents vulnerable;

> the parent is the one who asks for help, and so the parent bears final responsibility.

If a therapist can see the parent as the one asking for help for his or her child, it makes it easier to identify with the parent, allowing the therapist to stand shoulder to shoulder with him or her.

parent guidance in the form of a process-oriented therapeutic relationship is most often used in combination with psychoanalytic therapies of children. A therapeutic relationship will look at the inner world of the parents, with their own conflicts in relation to the child brought in for therapy (Chethik, 2000; Marcelis-Eerdmans, 1994, 1999, 2000; van der Pas, 1994, 1996). Just as is the case with children with a mental process disorder, so when parents have a mental process disorder, guidance will not focus on conflicts in or between mental representations. Interventions aimed at gaining insight, giving meaning and resolving unconscious conflicts are too much for these parents. It has been our experience that, in working with these parents, the techniques used in parent guidance need to be adjusted. In the emotional and cognitive development of the young child, it is the parent who first generates representations, after which the child can gradually internalize them. If the parent finds it difficult to make a representation of the child, he will have a hard time dealing with the difference between within and without, between fantasy and reality, between self and the other, between the child and himself.

A predisposition such as temperament, intelligence, or vulnerability for psychopathology influence both parent and child in their behavioural, affective, and cognitive functioning. The biological makeup of the parent and the child mutually influence each other: they supplement, compensate, or strengthen one another (Fonagy, Gergely, et al., 2002). It is also important to see the relationship between parent and child in a broader context. A wide variety of environmental factors make their influence felt, such as living conditions, socio-economic status, culture, a new school, the family's phase of life, life events, and sibling order. It is beyond the scope of this chapter to discuss these aspects. But they do influence parent–child interaction, and they will need to be considered in the treatment.

Helping parents to promote mentalization

In addition to these general aspects of parent guidance, when parent guidance is intended to promote mentalization, it needs a specific focus as well. The emotional and psychological development of a child is greatly influenced by the internal attachment representations of the parents (Fonagy, Steele, Moran, & Higgitt, 1993; Van IJzendoorn, 1995). This means that influencing these internal representations can have a positive effect on the emotional and psychological development of both parent and child. The work of Fonagy, Steele, and colleagues (1993) has shown that the most crucial factor mediating the influence of parents on their children is the parents' capacity to mentalize. A child's secure attachment is predicted by the parents' capacity to represent the affective experiences of their child. The most important aspect of preventing psychopathology in early childhood lies therefore in increasing the capacity of the parents to mentalize (Fonagy, Steele, Moran, Steele, & Higgitt, 1991). We know that losses and traumatic experiences that are not worked through can be part of the intergenerational transfer of conflicts, also termed the "ghosts in the nursery" (Fraiberg, Adelson, & Shapiro, 1980). Parents who suffered early losses or traumatic experiences do not automatically transfer them to the next generation (Steele, Steele, & Fonagy, 1996). The key to breaking through such a vicious circle lies in the capacity to mentalize these experiences—in other words, to create a coherent story in which the affective impact and meanings of experiences are recognized (Fonagy, Steele, et al., 1995).

Parent guidance intended to promote mentalization is aimed at mindful parenting: to stimulate the parents' capacity to mentalize and, in this way, that of their children as well. Teaching parents competencies and communication skills, used quite successfully in many parenting courses, often does not work for parents with a mental process disorder. They often follow child-rearing advice much too literally because, although their need for advice is great, the framework for applying it as it was meant to be applied is not there. For parent guidance as it is discussed here, being able to put child-rearing advice to sensible use is more an end point than a starting point for treatment.

Family members need to have a fundamental basis of trust and attachment before they can learn communication skills and problem-solving skills. A child's trust grows as he repeatedly experiences reliable and responsive caregivers who are able to regulate their children's behaviour, to comfort them, and to watch over their safety. Concretely, this means that parents and children feel they have a bond, that parents can support their children both by giving them adequate holding and containment and by limiting their destructive or otherwise maladjusted behaviour (Bleiberg, 2001).

When children have a mental process disorder, parent guidance is aimed at learning and stimulating skills within a therapeutic relationship that will increase the parents' capacity to mentalize in the parent–child relationship. This is not to say that it is enough for these children if their parents can gain a mentalized representation of their child. As stated in chapter 4, it is often necessary for the child to undergo a new experience within a therapeutic relationship with a mentalizing adult—in this case the therapist. In the case of children under the age of 4, often a single therapist works with both parent and child (this parent–infant therapy is not discussed further in this chapter).

The parent guidance framework

It only makes sense to increase a child's capacity to mentalize in therapy if this is accompanied by changes in the child's interpersonal context. Factors in the parent–child relationship, in the school context, and in the broader social context influence the parent–child relationship, and they require specific attention in treatment. Working with other specialists, such as speech therapists, social workers, or psychomotor therapists, is often of great importance if development patterns that have run aground are to be set in motion once again. There is a great deal of research to confirm that structured programmes in which parents are helped to be more effective can break through maladaptive behavioural patterns of children (Beckwith, 2000).

In their book on the treatment of people with a borderline personality structure, Bateman and Fonagy (2004) also stress the importance of a clearly structured framework, within which interventions to encourage mentalization can take place. We think that this same framework is important as a basis in child therapy and parent guidance intended to promote mentalization. Objectives and boundaries of both child therapy and parent guidance must be formulated clearly and in understandable terms. Discussing the structure of the treatment with the parents makes the process more transparent for them, ensures that treatment is consistent, and emphasizes the relationship as being the heart of the treatment (Bleiberg, 2001). It is important that treatment be consistent, because inconsistency undermines the capacity to mentalize.

It is possible that parents do not recognize themselves or their child in the picture sketched by the researchers or therapists. Parents need to have the scope to agree as well as to disagree with the way the problems of their child and the treatment objectives are formulated (Bleiberg, 2001). It is the responsibility of the parent counsellor to ensure that they all share a picture of the child, so that everyone knows what the treatment is aimed at and can give it their support. The child brought to therapy by the parents and the child as the therapist sees him must be "the same child". It is essential to take plenty of time to create this "same child" before the child therapy starts. Often this picture consists of a number of concrete forms of behaviour at first, and parents do not have an internal picture of their child. It may be helpful, for example, to discuss with the parents one of the attachment stories completed by the child (see Chapter 3)—but of course only if the child gives permission for it. If, upon hearing such an attachment story, the parents can begin to see that their child often does certain things or has temper tantrums out of fear, because he expects only to be punished and not to be helped, then something truly has been gained.

Many parents of children with serious personality disorders experience the world—and so also the therapists—as hostile and frightening. If in an initial advisory meeting the parent counsellor confronts the parents with their role in maintaining the problems, this merely confirms the parents' assumption that treatment will expose them to abuse, shame, and pain. The first objective in parent guidance is therefore to arrive at a working relationship with the parents in which they feel they are understood and taken seriously in their questions and their issues with parenting.

When children have serious behavioural problems, there is often a great deal of suffering, and parents can feel they are being helped if the therapist starts by discussing the concrete forms of behaviour and tries, together with the parents, to develop more possibilities for regulation. This can be done by investigating with the parents how they can be more effective and consistent in setting limits, in watching over boundaries in general, and how parents can invest more effort in making the roles played by their children in relations within the family a subject of discussion. Boundaries contribute to a sense of safety and help build up inner structure. Instead of finding themselves at the mercy of emotional and behavioural outbursts, both their child's and their own, parents can start to feel more competent in their parenting role and gain new experiences, thus also reinforcing their working relationship with the therapist. Here it is important that the therapist does not offer too much concrete advice: if the therapist proffers a solution at a behavioural level too quickly, it is a missed opportunity to explore the parent's thoughts about what the child experiences, and why the child breaks a rule, for example. A non-directive attitude offers the best chance of helping the parents to strengthen their ability to mentalize (cf. Greenspan, 1997). Exploring behavioural patterns together with the parents can help reinforce their ability to make representations. By seeing the positions of the various family members and then placing the parents' perspective first and foremost, safety is increased.

If a parent still functions in equivalent mode, this is the perspective to which the therapist must attune, and other meanings cannot yet be explored. Asking parents who function at a behavioural level what they are reminded of, what they feel when talking about the child, is a mismatch. The parent talks about concrete behaviour and not about feelings, will not understand the concepts put forward, and may feel attacked or overwhelmed. It is then much more effective to focus on the child's behavioural pattern and to see the parent's point of view on it. This can give the feeling of a shared experience. Also, verbalizing feelings of fear or anger too quickly can be counterproductive because the parent may view the verbalization as an attack, in the sense that the therapist causes the parent to feel anxious or angry. The subjective perception is equated with reality and becomes a source of anxiety and aggression.

Such a lack of containment on the part of the therapist can lead to projective identification because the parent's inner world has become unbearable and too realistic. These intolerable feelings are expelled by the parent and often focused on the child. By placing the perspective of the parent first and foremost, safety is increased. The countertransference feelings of the therapist can be used, for example, to put into words the sequences of not understanding and not being understood. If the therapist verbalizes these sequences of internal activities—for example, in reaction to an angry and frustrated parent who is cross with the therapist, who does not understand him or her—this can set into motion a shift from the behavioural to the representational level.

When parents can come to see the treatment as a cooperative relationship between parents and therapists, there is a basis for developing mentalization. Starting from the relationship with the therapist as the container of intolerable feelings, parents can come to experience, understand, and regulate themselves.

An example from the parent guidance of Maartje's mother

Ms A is ambivalent about her daughter Maartje's therapy. She sees that it is necessary and that Maartje benefits by it, but she finds it difficult to accept the dependence of a therapeutic relationship and of parent guidance. From a childhood of neglect she has retained the maxim that you should never make yourself dependent on anyone; this is not a feeling but a concrete reality. This aspect of her is therefore unmentalized. She does not regulate the vehement affects evoked by the therapy of her daughter and her own parent guidance by talking about them, but in a very concrete manner: by controlling the frequency of the appointments and thus the pace. She determines how long it will be until the next appointment. The parent counsellor allows this. Ms A asks for support and exploration, but at the same time she does not want it, because she wants to find things out herself. By being allowed to regulate distance and closeness in the appointments very concretely, she gradually comes to feel safer, which makes it possible to link her concrete regulation of appointments to feelings and to put into words her conflicting needs, so they can ultimately be linked to the conflicts in Maartje's behaviour.

Mentalizing techniques

Entering into a parent guidance relationship with parents implies recognition of their request for help. This implies vulnerability and activates the parents' attachment system. Asking for help is extremely complex, particularly if the parents do not have secure attachment representations of their own. For a person who feels unsafe or whose attachment is disorganized (see Chapter 2), asking for help can be a dangerous undertaking. If, as a child, a parent asked for help from a parent who was frightening or abusive, asking for help has by definition become an inconsistent state. Making this inconsistent state explicit can be very important for the working relationship.

In this chapter the following techniques are discussed:

1. giving reality value to the inner experience of the parents with their child;
2. learning to observe and read the child's inner world;
3. working in the here and now;
4. repairing misattunement

Giving reality value to the inner experience of the parents with their child

Parents who have a mental process disorder know very little about their own inner world and that of their children. They are often powerless; their lives are ruled by a succession of concrete events on which they have no grip. To come into contact with their inner world, it is important to remain very close to the primary affective experiences. In this way, reality value is given to the parents' experiences. If parents know that they are understood, it creates room to explore their inner world and that of their child. Responding to the primary affective experiences is highly complex because the therapist must often be willing to—consciously or unconsciously—go along with a projected picture with which she does not agree. For example: the parent counsellor may not only have to accept that a child, the other parent, or the child's therapist is maligned, but also have to go along empathically with such a perception. Sometimes the parent counsellor can only come into contact with a client if a divorced parent is allowed to talk at length at every session about how bad the other parent is as a parent. At this stage of treatment, it is essential to simply leave these projections as they are and to give the accompanying perceptions reality value: "I understand that it makes you furious that he doesn't watch your children properly and lets them go to bed far too late; I understand that it is extremely inconvenient that he is the father of your children!" Often no one else has ever validated these feelings in this way before; it brings the parents' perceptions to "life" and makes them "real". These parents often had non-mentalizing parents of their own. When parents' experiences are validated, it leads to an initial awareness of being a person with a perception world of your own. Sometimes there are doubts as to whether parents will be able to accept asking for help for their child and for themselves. Then it is sometimes suggested to start out with parent guidance, so that this can be explored further.

An example from the parent guidance of Paul's mother

Ms B is not yet able to accept the advice to start the parent guidance and to postpone the child therapy. She is not good at mentalizing and is used to taking immediate action. If there must be child therapy, then let it be right away. The therapists agree to this, because they think that otherwise the child will be lost completely. During the first two months, the mother continually cancels appointments. The appointments go more smoothly when Ms B has her appointments at the same time as her son has therapy. While she sits in the waiting room, she has no idea what to do: she often falls asleep there. The way she puts it is that she disappears if she does not know what to do. She feels she has been heard properly when the counsellor shows understanding and adjusts her own schedule so that she can see Ms B at the time her son has therapy. Her vulnerable sense of self apparently requires a lot of action and aggression towards others in order to keep it up. Ms B regularly flies into a rage about the father of her children, calling him a loser, an overgrown child. On the other hand, she lets the children visit their father frequently if it is convenient for her. Clearly, Ms B needs to be able to moan about the father, and the counsellor responds by showing her understanding of how difficult things must be for her with such a childish husband. It looks as if she has projected part of herself into him and that she manages to stay on her feet because she can accommodate this bad aspect with another person. She does the same thing with the teachers at the school, referring to them as bitches and fishwives. And she contrasts them with a previous teacher, whom she praises to the skies. She is unable to accept very much from the counsellor. Nor does she want any advice; she is the only one who knows how to handle Paul: cuddle him to death, make lots of jokes and wisecracks. The counsellor tries to link this to her need for control and competence but also adds, in passing, that she is all on her own and always has to be on her toes, always thinking what to do with such a troublesome child.

Learning to observe and read the child's inner world

The objective of treatment is to give parents, in addition to child-rearing tools, a mental toolkit as well, so that parents start to develop ideas about how their child experiences life, and come to have representations and hypotheses about this. If parents come to feel that their own powerlessness and desperation is understood, gradually the various aspects of their relationship with their child can be explored. There is sometimes little communication between parent and child about the child's needs or wishes. Matters are resolved by means of a power struggle, with a simple "yes" or "no", without exploring the child's experiences. It is important that the counsellor does not allow himself to be tempted to give interpretations ("When you were small, you often felt that way yourself, so now. . . .") or explanations about the child ("The child is angry or anxious because. . . ."). Rather, parents need to be encouraged to think about behavioural patterns, about their own reactions and to learn to communicate about this with their child. Once they have gained such experiences during parent guidance, they can share them with their child, and this opens the door to the representation of an affect. An important aspect here is to unravel which affective state belongs to whom, because often parent and child are not well demarcated and the parent's inner world and that of the child are intermingled. The following excerpt from a session with a divorced mother (Ms C) illustrates this.

An example from the treatment of a divorced mother

Ms C: "Sophie's father gave her such a tacky-looking coat. She wanted to wear it to school." [*She cries.*] "So awful, she looked so awful! It was simply a fright. I was so embarrassed. I told her I wouldn't allow it, but then I feel so bad. Sophie thought it was a gorgeous coat, and she got cross."

T: "Tacky-looking?"

C: "Yes, something that looked nice and smart on my sister looked common and tatty on me. Sophie has the same thing: unkempt, frumpish. Shabby and cheap. What kind of mother has this child?"

T: "I think it makes you feel quite horrid, that common, tacky, tatty, cheap look . . . I think you're afraid that everyone, me included, will think you are a bad mother, to let your child go around in a coat like that."

C: "Yes, then I'm a bad mother."

T: "You really want to protect her, and that's why you won't allow it, but then Sophie gets cross and then you also feel like a bad mother. When she is so cross with you, it is just as if you truly *are* bad!"

C: [*cries*] "And I am!"

T: "You know, it's so hard for you because you're trapped: if you let her wear that coat, you think that I and everyone else will think you are a bad mother, but if you don't allow it, Sophie gets cross and then her anger tells you that you are a bad mother."

Now this can gradually be sifted through: what is the difference between concrete reality and reality as it is perceived, what is the difference between the child's affect and that of the mother. In this vignette no interpretation was given about the link between her relationship with her daughter and that with her sister. For a non-mentalizing parent, this might be the concrete confirmation that nothing has changed compared to the past.

Working in the here and now

The interpersonal context in the here and now is the most important focus of attention and offers the best chance that the here-and-now situation will set something in motion that will be a new experience for the parent.

An example from the parent guidance of Paul's mother

Ms B comes in, and the counsellor notices that something is different about her facial expression. She looks radiant. She complains very little about her ex-husband, and she sees her son's problems much more positively. When the counsellor lets slip that it almost seems as if her client is in love, she is so delighted with everything today, this turns out to be the case. She tells all about it, and says that she indeed feels much better. Ms B seems to feel that she is understood because the counsellor has "read" her inner world; now that she has been "seen", she is able to talk about all the times when she felt so terrible and was unable to cope with being a mother. When the love affair is over, she is able to share her grief in the parent guidance sessions. The working relationship showed great improvement after these interactions.

In parents and children with mental process disorders, techniques such as metaphors, pointing out a similarity with the parent's own past, focusing on conflicts, or even simply focusing on content often does not work. These techniques are based on the assumption that people are able to retain different mental representations over time, but this is precisely one of the problems when people are unable to mentalize (Bateman & Fonagy, 2004). In the parent guidance sessions, the gap between a concrete emotional experience and the representation of this experience must be bridged anew each time.

An important objective of parent guidance is to strengthen the secondary representational system. Feelings of transference and countertransference are used by the counsellor to demonstrate alternative perspectives in the here and now, not as a means of reconstructing the past. The past is present in the current perception of both parent and counsellor. Feelings of transference represent the early internal object representations of the parents; now they are played out in the here-and-now situation, in the current relationship with their child and with the counsellor. They are not interpreted, but used to clarify what is at stake and what is going on in the relationship between counsellor and parent, between parent and child.

Repairing misattunement

Deben-Mager and Verheugt-Pleiter (2004) described the different therapeutic attitude in the treatment of children and adults with a mental process disorder:

> Whereas in classical psychoanalytic technique a therapist can interpret something about the patient while remaining more or less absent—which, in theory, can increase the distance to the client—in the approach described here it is of great importance to place the interaction and oneself central in the here and now. In other words, the perspective is therapist-centred instead of client-centered. [p. 29]

Too abstinent an approach creates specific problems in the therapy: the therapist may be perceived as remote, authoritarian, with a lack of empathy, unsympathetic. If the therapist adopts a wait-and-see attitude, it can be taken literally in the sense of "you don't hear what I'm saying", "I am not important", and this is likely to interfere with the relationship. This can stimulate paranoid fantasies and lead to angry reactions and growing anxiety. But showing too much empathy with the affect state of the parent can also cause problems. For example, the therapist may too quickly respond empathically to behaviour with which a parent in fact defeats himself or herself. If the therapist responds to such a devaluation with too much empathy, she may inadvertently be perceived as intrusive. Anxiety can mount. If such a misattunement occurs between counsellor and parent, the parent may angrily withdraw from the relationship. By externalizing and becoming angry at the counsellor, who "doesn't understand a thing about it", the parent restores control.

An example from the parent guidance of Ivo's mother

At one point in the parent guidance it comes out that Ms D still drives her 12-year-old son to school. Because Ivo has many problems in his relationships with other children, the counsellor realizes how much this would put him at a distance from his classmates, who do go to school on their own. When first asked about this, Ms D says that her son really doesn't like to go by himself. The counsellor notes how anxious the mother has become after this conversation, which is in fact about separation. She commiserates. From that point on, Ms D avoids this subject, and their relationship becomes awkward. When the client talks about her own mother, whom she sees or speaks to every day, her fear of independence becomes very clear to the therapist. Now she understands better why the client has withdrawn from their relationship, and now she can clearly say how horrid it must be for her when a person just starts talking about things that you simply can't talk about, they make you so anxious. Only when the therapist has explicitly said that she had not properly understood can they really talk about the child and differentiate between his fears and hers. Once she has been able to contain the unnameable fear, there is scope to get a clear focus on how frightening it is to let her own child go to school alone.

The more stress a person experiences, the more difficult it becomes to mentalize. The attitude of the therapist in dealing with children and adults with mental process disorders is more open, more transparent, more aimed at collaboration, and more active than the classical psychoanalytic attitude. It is important that the counsellor explore her own countertransference without immediately presenting it to the parents, but she must first consider whether the feelings aroused in her as the parent counsellor are pertinent to the parent or the child, and whether verbalizing them can help in offering a different perspective. Parents with mental process disorders can evoke vehement feelings in the counsellor, implicating a feeling of a lack of safety, to which the parent counsellor may react by overactivating her own attachment system. For instance, she may become even more active in the relationship, or withdraw from it, depending on her style of attachment. Countertransference here explicitly includes nonconscious, implicit factors.

Adjusting to the parent's level of mental functioning is the most useful direction for the counsellor to set to work. Sometimes this will be more at a behavioural level so as to bring experiences of the parent into focus and thus to strengthen the parental role. At another level, verbal representations can be used. Naturally, the development level can change when a new theme comes up. There are families whose mentalization is active until matters such as jealousy or aggression are involved. Then the parent may suddenly be completely unable to mentalize and show little affect representation. In that case, the counsellor will need to adjust her strategy and attitude.

In parent guidance, just as in any other form of treatment, misattunement may occur (see Chapter 4). If this is the case, it is important that the therapist take the blame for it. For instance, she might say: "I think I didn't react very sensitively. I don't know why, but that's just how it went today; let's go back and see if we can understand it." This can make it possible for the parent and the counsellor to go over the entire sequence of events and feelings so that the parent becomes aware of what feelings are aroused if the counsellor is too empathic or too remote.

Parent guidance: one, two, or more parents

Parent guidance takes place sometimes with one parent, usually with two, and with parents in composite families, sometimes with several parents as well as stepparents. Here, too, the same mentalizing techniques are used: giving reality value to the inner experiences of the parents with their child; learning to observe and read the child's inner world; working in the here and now; repairing misattunement. Working with two or more parents is complex; there may be conflicting interests and feelings and, in situations of divorce, experiences that have not been worked through and power struggles. Specific processes characteristic of new composite families may play a role: for example, aggression may be focused on the stepparent, so that the child can stay on good terms with his own parent. In such cases the therapeutic framework and the therapeutic attitude are of great importance. The counsellor must be able to work with what is termed multiple partiality: the ability to identify, work with, and contain the perspectives of both parents and child (Böszörményi-Nagy, 1987). Often, feelings that are intolerable for the parent are projected onto the other parent, or one parent identifies more with the child or with one aspect of a feeling and the other parent with the other aspect. A common example is feelings of powerlessness in one parent and firm control in the other, or feelings of love in one and hate in the other. Each parent represents one aspect of a mental state, but because they are not yet able to tolerate much ambivalence, difficult feelings are often projected onto the other and then attacked. In this case, interpretations will only serve to foster a further split, because they give back the threatening feeling that the parent is unable to tolerate. Here too it is important to be able to show different perspectives and to allow several perspectives to exist alongside each other. Experimenting with alternatives can gradually make it easier to accept intolerable feelings. This improves the integration of the parent's inner world. Gradually the parents can come to feel that they are both concerned, but that they each emphasize different sides of the same coin. This helps parents to become more sensitive to their child's level of mental functioning and to learn to read their child's signals. In the parent guidance sessions, the gap between a concrete emotional experience and the representation of this experience must be bridged anew each time. What makes working with two or more parents so complex is that the transference may be spread out, with various aspects of a concrete experience residing in each parent. It is important to make sure that the concrete experience is shared before setting to work on the representations of this experience in the parents. When there are heated conflicts between parents, the mentalizing capacity of the psychotherapist is at risk.

An example from parent guidance

Mr E and Ms F have been living together for a short time. Both have children from a previous marriage, and there is much controversy about the way they are brought up. Mr E's eldest daughter E is in psychotherapy, and both parents have parent interviews. Mr E starts out by complimenting Ms F about the way she has dealt with his son, but in the same sentence he includes a remark to the effect that the way she sets limits for his eldest daughter is out of all proportion. Ms F is visibly confused by this double message; she feels attacked, and she says in a heated tone of voice that Mr E never set any boundaries for his children, that he thinks she is not a good mother, but that she has raised her own children well. It is not without reason, she adds, that his daughter is in therapy. This results in a fierce argument between the two parents. Mr E says that the parent guidance has not helped so far either. The counsellor is confused by Mr E's double message and by the vehemence of the argument between the parents. It takes a while before she is again able to think and then she goes over the sequence again with the parents: what exactly has taken place since they came into the room; together, they set down the various perspectives.

Growing up in more than one family may mean that children have to deal with parental systems that differ in their capacity to mentalize. In such a case, it is often very difficult for parents to find a shared perspective, and here lies an important task for the counsellor.

Collaboration with other therapists

There must be a balanced parent–child–parent counsellor triangle, in accordance with the rules for triads. When parent guidance is intended to promote mentalization, it is crucial that the counsellor and the child therapist share the same perspective. Without this shared perspective, treatment cannot start. Each participant in the treatment must respect the others and be willing to work within a framework of mentalization. This means that in these treatments the match between counsellor and child therapist is more delicate than in a more classical combination of parent guidance and child psychotherapy or psychoanalysis. Does it click between the counsellor and the child therapist? Space will have to be created within the framework of treatment to talk about this. If too much energy starts to go into righting the relationship between parent counsellor and child psychotherapist, neither of them will be able to mentalize properly. This will have repercussions on the treatment.

It has been our experience that parallel processes regularly take place in parent guidance and child therapy. Such parallel processes are always found in working with children, but here they are of a different order than in psychotherapy with children who do not have a mental process disorder. In working with children and parents with a mental process disorder, counsellor and child therapist will often react in equivalent mode: feelings and differences of opinion are more vehement, and they can no longer be seen as different perspectives, but as the "truth". It is in the relationship between counsellor and child therapist where a rudimentary sort of intermediate space can emerge in which these primitive parallel processes can be recognized. Then it is possible to feel the difference between a concrete reality and a subjective reality, a mental state. Often this will require teamwork and peer review.

As mentioned in the introductory chapter to this book, the core techniques of child therapy and parent guidance to promote mentalization are not incompatible with other therapy models, such as cognitive behavioural therapy, systemic therapy, training in social skills, speech therapy, physiotherapy, or remedial teaching. Since these children often have special needs and deficiencies in development, two or more therapists, working from different frameworks and disciplines, may be involved with the child. At the heart of their collaboration is coming together and thinking together about the child and the parents within a mentalizing framework and integrating other treatment goals in a way that can be understood by all those involved. It is crucial to have a shared perspective before the treatment can start. Bleiberg (2001) said that the most essential and also most difficult aspect of a combined or multidisciplinary treatment is not the integration of therapies, but the integration of therapists. Each participant in the treatment must respect the others and be willing to work within a framework of mentalization. A teacher may benefit from the knowledge that a child can react only with concrete behaviour in certain areas, such as in contacts with other children. This knowledge can be helpful in not locking into battle with the child. It may be very helpful to the therapist to hear from the teacher how the child functions in a classroom and in social contacts. Physiotherapy, speech therapy, or sensorimotor therapy increase the child's capacity to utilize the therapy; conversely, child therapy increases a child's capacity to profit from other treatments.

In conclusion

Bleiberg (2001) sees a representational mismatch when external reality is on a tense footing with internal expectations. In the case of children with a mental process disorder, a representational mismatch is created for the child if parents and therapists show effectiveness and consistency in the way they deal with the child. This is a new situation for the child, thanks to which he may be better able to profit from the therapy. The counsellor tries to stand alongside the parents, based on the conviction that they are essential to the success of the treatment. Bear in mind that it is well worth taking plenty of time to ensure that the therapist and the parents see eye to eye before starting the child's treatment. If parents are the ones asking for help, working out a shared picture of their child will need to start from their own psychological capacities. The awareness of "being responsible" for their child may have a different meaning for parents with a mental process disorder than it would for parents who are able to make themselves well-balanced mental representations of their child, no matter how neurotic and guilt-laden they may be. The objective of guidance for parents with a mental process disorder is to help them to generate representations about themselves as parents, about their parenthood, and about their child. Once parents start to feel that they have scope to think about parenting and about their child, they can start to think about themselves and their child as people who want, think, or feel something without having to translate this into immediate action. This brings greater understanding of the child and of themselves as parents, who sometimes turn to destructive action because they feel powerless and frustrated. Then there is greater solidarity between parents and child, and the sense of self is strengthened in both.

CHAPTER SIX

Observation method

Jolien Zevalkink

Observing children systematically during treatment has greatly expanded our knowledge and understanding of mentalization and significantly contributed to the development of the treatment model explained in the next chapters. Therapists turned out to be invaluable in this process. From behind a one-way screen therapists observed interventions of other therapists and systematically described interventions they considered beneficial to the child's ability to mentalize. These observations have opened the door to empirical research into mentalization-based child therapy and—perhaps more importantly—given other therapists an opportunity to learn to work with the method. This chapter describes a brief history of the process of this project. Furthermore, it describes the selection of suitable cases for treatment, agreements prior to data collection, reactions of children to the observer and to the video recorder, the systematic collection of observations, and discussion of the interventions in peer review meetings. As the observation method was refined, it gradually became an observation system that can be used to study the types of interventions used in therapy sessions. The categories used in the observation system are described in the following chapters.

Identifying intervention techniques: a brief history

Three phases preceded the actual development of our method for observation: studying the literature, contacting experts, and drawing up a plan of action. We started in the years between 1998 to 2001 by studying the literature and holding monthly discussions of publications on psychoanalytic developmental therapy. The book on psychoanalysis and developmental therapy edited by Anne Hurry (1998b) was of particular importance. After reading this book and the Child Therapy Manual of the Anna Freud Centre (AFC & UCL, 1999), an idea began to take shape: why not investigate whether it was possible to observe, describe, and name the developmental therapy interventions. On the basis of these initial efforts, 14 different types of intervention techniques used in mentalization-based child therapy were distinguished and classified into four main groups: working on affect; mirroring and/or containment; brief specific interpretations; and recognizing projective identification (chapters 7, 8, and 9 describe the interventions as they ultimately came to be categorized). The participants felt a need to link clinical practice to this theoretical knowledge.

After this, experts were contacted, and in November 2001 a workshop was organized to which Miriam Steele of the Anna Freud Centre was invited as an expert. The workshop was intended to help therapists recognize children who were suitable for mentalization-based child therapy (based on indicator criteria), to identify suitable research instruments that are useful both clinically and in scientific research, to become acquainted with mentalization-based child therapy techniques, to discuss case material, and to use mentalization-based child therapy techniques for different age groups. This led to lively discussions and was good preparation for a seminar on mentalization-based child therapy held by the Netherlands Psychoanalytic Institute in January 2002.

Lastly, a project group was set up to deal with mentalization-based child therapies. Based on previous experiences, the project group drew up a plan the objective of which was to systematically list, describe, and further develop therapeutic techniques (Verheugt-Pleiter, 2002). Then the project group investigated whether children who were on a waiting list for therapy or were already in therapy might be suitable for mentalization-based child therapy. Six therapists were involved in the project; one treatment of each of them would be observed. The therapies of six children were followed between September 2002 and July 2003. The rest of this chapter is devoted to the implementation of the action plan.

Working method for the observation of interventions in mentalization-based child therapy

Introduction

To systematically describe interventions, consensus about the method of observation is a necessity in order to be able to draw some conclusions. Some parameters need to be set, because observations are always dependent on subjective perception. Subjectivity can be decreased by systematizing the method of observation and by making clear-cut agreements of exactly what to observe. Then if the same observer starts to see the same thing in the repeated occurrence of the same phenomenon, the observation is reliable, and if others see the same thing, we may speak of interrater reliability (Galtung, 1973). The first agreement that needs to be made concerns the unit of observation. In this project we decided to work with event sampling, thus taking a complete interaction sequence as the unit of observation (Reuling, 1987). This is in contrast to time sampling, in which behaviour is observed during an agreed unit of time. Other systematic agreements were set down in the first mentalization-based child therapy plan of action (Verheugt-Pleiter, 2002). The plan of action comprises a number of aspects, including references to the selection of suitable cases for treatment, agreements about data collection, some reactions of children to the observer and to the video recorder, the systematic collection of the observations, and the need to discuss the interventions in peer review meetings.

Selection of suitable cases

The selected cases came from a pool of ongoing treatments. Initially we wanted the group to satisfy the following criteria:

▷ treatment indicators for mentalization-based child therapy (see Chapter 3);

▷ the frequency of sessions was not fixed, but would ideally be at least two sessions a week, one of which would be recorded on video;

▷ the treatments were to be distributed as evenly as possible over early, middle, and final stages;

▷ the children selected should show a representative distribution as to age, sex, and, if possible, DSM classification.

Permission of the parents was required for observation and to make use of the material from their child's sessions in developing the manual.

How did selection of the six cases take place in practice? Several meetings had to be devoted to a discussion of the first requirement: the indicator criteria. But it was also not always easy to adhere to the other, more practical, criteria. As to the number of sessions, it was difficult to include a higher frequency than twice a week. Four of the children had two sessions weekly and two of them only one. The Anna Freud Centre (Steele, personal communication, 2002) was also unable to work with a higher frequency—despite the fact that the treatment advice was more intensive treatment—on account of practical objections, plus the added burden of a high frequency on the agenda of the entire family. They generally also opted for two sessions a week.

The distribution over the three stages of treatment was quite skewed. Five of the treatments were in the initial stages, and one treatment was midway. This was primarily because it was difficult to pinpoint the indicator criteria for mentalization-based child therapy if treatment had already started. It proved to be easier to assess children's needs for mentalization-based child therapy immediately after registration for treatment. The observation of treatments in the initial stages probably gives a distorted picture of the identification of interventions. It will mean that interventions that can be made at a more advanced stage of treatment will be less readily apparent. However, because the treatments were followed for 12 weeks, some shifts in technique were observed.

We had intended to achieve a representative distribution over three child-specific characteristics: age, sex, and DSM classification. The group we studied consisted of five boys and one girl, ranging in age from 7 to 12 years, with an average age of 9 years 7 months at the start of treatment. Distribution as to age was reasonably successful, but with regard to gender we might have done better with a second girl. In this age group, the Netherlands Psychoanalytic Institute registers around three times as many boys as girls (NPI, 2002). The six children were proportionately distributed over DSM classifications. All children had serious problems: several Axis I disorders were diagnosed and in two cases Axis II disorders as well. All in all, the trial group for mentalization-based child therapy is a rather good reflection of the group for whom the treatment is intended on these three characteristics.

In some cases, obtaining the informed consent of the parents turned out to be rather problematic. One child who had been selected was withdrawn by the parents at a late stage, and a newly selected child was only able to take part in the final weeks of the project. The parents of these children also had a wide variety of problems of their own (see Chapter 5). What may have played a role here is that we chose to describe the project orally and not provide them with an additional written project description. In future projects it would be useful to work with written information as well—something parents can take home with them to read before they decide whether or not to participate. But, in the end parents of six children signed the informed consent. With children of this age, the parents are the legal representatives, but we went to some lengths to get the children's informal consent as well. In the end, all the children whose parents had given permission took part in the project. For several reasons—in addition to the legal obligation—it was useful to ask for an official statement of consent. In a practical sense, it was necessary to ensure that the data collected could be used in developing the manual and for training purposes. From a methodological point of view, giving explicit consent for a treatment to be observed may lower the degree of reactivity. The act of observing and the presence of an observer are intrusive, and they increase the chance of changes in the behaviour to be observed. Methodologists call this undesired change "reactivity". One way of decreasing this effect is to explain clearly to the children and their parents the purpose of the observations, which is to watch the therapist in order to improve the treatment in the future (Jones, 1996). During meetings of the project group, therapists discussed reactions of parents, children, and themselves to being observed: one purpose of these discussions was to avoid socially desirable behaviour and to encourage natural behaviour on their part.

Agreements prior to data collection

The data collection had two purposes. First of all, it yielded material on which to base development of the observation system, and this material would be discussed in the context of the techniques used and possible alternatives. The second objective was important for the further development of the treatment method, and it was discussed at length in the project group meetings. In the light of these two objectives, the following agreements were made:

▷ Once a week, a colleague in the project group would observe a session through the one-way screen or from the recording room and also ensure that the session was recorded on video.

▷ The observed session would be discussed by the therapist and the observer immediately after it was over, and during this discussion they would select three mentalization-enhancing interventions from the material on the session observed.

▷ The observer would watch the video recording and write down the three interventions, using a maximum of one sheet of A4 paper per vignette, transcribing verbatim the statements of the therapist and the child.

▷ The observer would be responsible for formulating the final transcript of the interventions. In the event of a difference of opinion, the therapist would be able to add a note.

▷ The observer would as soon as possible pass on the three written interventions to the project leader, who would work them up into a classification proposal for the next project meeting.

In the course of the project, both peer review and project group meetings about the mentalization-based child therapies were held on a monthly basis. This means that there was a meeting every other week, first for a clinical, then for a research purpose. After the project group meeting, the project leader revised and clarified the formulations in the intervention scenario and added new vignettes.

Reactions of children to the observer and the video recorder

Three pairs of therapists performed the data collection, with one of them acting as therapist while the other was given the role of observer; they switched roles in the other therapy. The observer sat behind the one-way screen and/or the video recorder to observe the session and to ensure that the sessions were recorded on video tape (Figure 6.1). Once the parents and the child had given their consent at the first session to be recorded, the therapist further explained the procedure to the child. The child was introduced to the observer and allowed to look around the recording room. The therapist paid particular attention to helping the child get used to the idea that he would be observed in order to safeguard the therapeutic process and

Figure 6.1.   The view of the playroom from the video recording room.

to lessen the chance of reactivity (Jones, 1996). The observer did not sit in the therapy room so as not to function as a third person in the relationship between the child and the therapist.

Reactions of children to the observer and to the video recorder were rather diverse. What follows are illustrations: a child who acted as if the camera was non-existent, a child who involved the camera in the therapy as a third person in several ways, and a child who reversed the roles so as to counteract the humiliation of being observed.

Ivo

The video recording was just fine with Ivo (12), and he was glad to come. His mother assumed that she would be able to take a seat behind the screen and observe her son. Based on the way she controlled Ivo's life, this was a logical train of thought for her. She was therefore surprised and rather angry that we did not allow this. Ivo had no objection whatsoever to a recording being made, or to his mother's wish to sit behind the one-way screen. This showed just how interwoven he was with his mother, how he lacked individuation, but also how powerless he was towards this intrusive tendency of his mother. During the sessions Ivo did not once refer to the researcher behind the screen; for him, she did not exist; he just thought her away. This was part of his pathology: a fear of freely entering into contact with others, which he fended off by ignoring them. In his treatment it became evident again and again that others were not important to him. So his not wanting or being able to make a distinction between the therapist and the observer ran parallel to his not being able to distinguish between other adults and his mother. Sometimes he was aware of—and had difficulty with—the video recorder, as shown by a description in Chapter 7. After the project the treatment continued at the therapist's home. About nine months later—in the process of winding up the treatment—Ivo was asked for a final session before the screen. At that moment he no longer felt any need to come, and he declined. Other adults—which included the observer and the therapist—had become part of his life, and at the moment they became important; this made him feel observed, and he therefore rejected it.

A different reaction to the video recorder was shown by a 9-year-old boy.

Xander

Xander's parents only gave their consent for sessions to be recorded on video after some hesitation. Xander also had a bit of a fright when he heard that some sessions would be recorded: he fantasized that he would be on television. When he was first registered, one of his complaints was that he thought other children could spy on him. The first time he absolutely refused to be introduced to the observer. Nor did he want to see the video room. He acted—at least outwardly—as if the video was not there. But in the meantime, the fact that the camera was playing a major role—a third person in the room, as it were—soon became apparent. Often, when he was standing with his back to the therapist, Xander gave it a hasty look. Also striking was that, precisely on the days when sessions were recorded, he took something along from home to show in detail. However, he did not react when the therapist made a remark about this. This changed as he felt more and more at ease. When, in Session 9, a bit after the therapist had once again remarked that he really kept a good watch on that camera, Xander started shooting paper arrows at it in a playful, teasing manner. In the next session he continued on this same course, now trying to tape over the lens of the camera—hesitantly at first, keeping his eye on the therapist's reaction, but later enjoying it to the full. He was curious whether he had managed to prevent the recordings. Now he very readily accepted an invitation to check this out. Being introduced to the observer was apparently no longer a problem. For the rest of the session he ran excitedly back and forth between the therapy room and the observation room, carrying out all kinds of experiments to boycott the recording. Things grew calmer in subsequent sessions. The video now more openly played a role in the background, in a more relaxed manner. Xander gave demonstrations of acrobatic feats, he whispered a sex joke to the camera the therapist was not allowed to hear. On the final day of recording he was sorry that the project was over. Later on, Xander again asked about the video; he had forgotten that recordings were no longer being made.

The fact that the reaction to the recording can be even more vehement, with the child trying to capitalize on this situation or turn it to her advantage, is illustrated by Maartje

Maartje

During this session, Maartje (6) goes to the toilet and sneaks a look in the observation room. It seems that, as the sessions go on, Maartje finds it more and more difficult to be observed. This is what she thinks up. After going to the toilet, Maartje storms into the observation room. She wants to talk with the therapist from the observation room. She shouts and later uses the microphone to try to get in touch with T. She directs T so that she can see her on the monitor and then thunders: "You have to stand like that the whole time." Maartje gets very worked up about this game, and she starts to shriek even louder. Even so, her actions continue to be coherent. From the therapy room, T says in various wordings, "I am the one who is responsible for the fact that you are always watched here. You thought that was very stupid of me. And so I deserve to be punished and you want us to change places! I deserve to be punished." The observer, who has been waiting in the hallway, finally goes over to Maartje as she is about to turn off the monitors, gently guiding her back to the therapy room. When she comes in, T says that she has certainly turned things topsy-turvy. Then they start to play school. Blissfully, Maartje drops into a chair and says, "Oh, so lovely." Role reversal often comes up in Maartje's therapy. Maartje cannot stand not being able to do something, or not as well as the therapist. T often goes along with the reversal so that she can explicitly point out the various aspects.

After this session, Maartje paid less attention to the camera. Sometimes it was clear that she was still aware that a session was being recorded, because sometimes she whispered to the therapist with one eye on the camera. She was cheerful, and whispering seemed to give her a sense of intimacy with the therapist. This was in contrast to Xander, who in a later session shared a whispered sex joke with the camera.

All in all, from the experiences with the camera we can conclude that the problems a child had sometimes seemed to be intensified by the presence of the video camera, but that the same problems came to the fore in the therapy room without the camera.

Systematic collection of the observations

According to the project plan, one session per week of each therapy would be observed and recorded on video for a period of 12 weeks. In each session, three interventions would be identified by the observer as developmental interventions and then described. A total of 62 sessions were recorded and 186 interventions described. Ten sessions had to be left out because of problems with the video equipment, illness of a child, a missed appointment, and the late intake of the last child.

In the data collection, use was made of the theory of mentalization as learned from the literature and of the broadly outlined techniques (see history). Initially, in choosing interventions, emphasis was placed on interventions that illustrated these techniques. Later the observers selected different interventions they had not yet observed in previous sessions. The method was one of non-randomized selection during the observation of a treatment session on the basis of clinical, theoretical, and empirical interest in a therapeutic intervention. An important advantage of this method is that relevant realistic observations are collected in a particular context. These observations served to develop an observation system and were also used as corrective feedback in arriving at agreement as to suitable interventions in mentalization-based child therapy. The disadvantage of direct observations is that they can introduce an unknown degree of selectivity to the data collection (Bickman & Rog, 1998). Another practical drawback is that it is a very time-consuming method of data collection. To decrease selectivity, the observation system was used again later to encode the entire video recording, including unselected interventions. A total of three steps can be distinguished in data collection for the observation system: selection during the treatment session, watching video recordings in retrospect to add unselected interventions, and then coding the video recording in full.

At first, observers primarily selected interventions that—starting from the theory—could illustrate the working method in

mentalization-based child therapy and were on the list of 14 intervention techniques (see history). During treatment sessions, the observers made notes and marked at what time on the recording they saw a
mentalization-based child therapy intervention. These interventions
were discussed with the therapist afterwards. An example is an intervention from Maartje's treatment, from which it is clear that the
therapist is working on affect. The intervention was written up as
shown in Exhibit 6.1.

The observer described the selected interventions in a standardized manner. In addition to the identification data[1] such as date of
registration and the child's initials, four classes of information were
distinguished:

> intervention (coded if possible);
> description of the situation;
> description of countertransference;
> argument in relation to this choice.

During its monthly meetings, the project group discussed the classification proposed by the project leader for the collected mentalization-based child therapy interventions. Every week at least 3 and
at most 18 new descriptions were added. For each intervention, the
project leader checked whether it could be added as an example
under an observation category already identified or whether a new
category would need to be created for it. The most important rule in
constructing a category was to "keep it simple" (Jones, 1996). When
observing behaviour, it is important to identify relatively simple
forms of conduct that are easy to see, so that others can observe
them as well. The idea is that it must also be possible to observe the
behaviour category or intervention while the therapy is taking place,
so that other therapists can watch and later discuss the techniques
used without having to resort to complicated observation methods.
Each category or group of interventions collected was noted under
a shared characteristic or description. Each description was defined
to determine the boundaries of the interventions classified under
that heading, and each intervention was defined to clearly delineate
it. Each intervention was given an abbreviation or a code. The joint
group discussion of the interventions was useful in identifying and

Exhibit 6.1. Intervention from Maartje's treatment

Intervention
Working on affect, but step by step. First naming the child's feeling through the fantasy figure, after that the child's feeling through an abstract person.

Description of the situation
In the corridor, Maartje is telling about a talk she will give at school. Maartje goes straight to the box of animals and screens them: how dull, how stupid do they look. She laughs at the stupid animals and flings them around the room. She says, "This one is stupid, this one isn't." T says, "What do you mean?" Maartje says that they look like complete dopes. Maartje asks T, "Do you think this one looks silly?" Maartje decides: no, a dolt! T says, "*Do you suppose he feels stupid?*" Maartje says, "No." T: "Only how you look, not how you feel?" Maartje goes on making her selection, finds a small animal and is touched. She makes groups of families and animals that are alone.

Description of countertransference
T has heard from the parent supervisor that Maartje will be repeating the school year; she is not a good student. T did not know this; she thought that Maartje was doing well at school. Because of this, T starts to see their playing school in previous sessions in a different light.

Arguments in relation to this choice
Working step by step towards naming a feeling is an intervention we have not yet had. Via the fantasy figure, T moves to the person of Maartje, but by formulating it impersonally, she remains at some distance.

demarcating the mentalization-based child therapy techniques, but also for an observer of subsequent therapy sessions looking for examples of types of interventions other than those already collected. Many new categories were identified during this period, including categories that could later be merged. An example of a new category that was later incorporated into an existing category from Xander's therapy is shown in Exhibit 6.2.

The second step was watching the video recordings at a later stage in a research group. This had two purposes: first, to investigate whether the interventions identified could be found and scored in unselected portions from the session, and, second, to find interventions that had been missed but that had to be included when coding an entire session. The research group watched parts of randomly selected treatment sessions of each child. The observation system

Exhibit 6.2.   Intervention from Xander's therapy

Intervention

Putting into words thoughts with aggressive undertones

Description of the situation

Xander has asked T what her favourite animal is. They are talking about this and Xander says that he would rather have a mouse than the rabbit he has now, but that he has to wait until the rabbit is dead. T says, *"Do you sometimes secretly think, if only the rabbit was dead?"* Xander laughs in confirmation of this. He tells how long he will have to wait, probably for ten years.

Description of countertransference

T had some difficulty with his lack of loyalty to animals. Later it became more understandable. His disappointment is primarily prompted by the fact that neither the dog nor the rabbit will allow itself to be cuddled. Getting ahead of events, as he does, he is now hoping for a mouse, but then the rabbit first has to die.

Arguments in relation to this choice

Secret thoughts with overtones of aggression is an important topic in Xander's treatment.

---

was further expanded, chiefly by adding interventions focused on attention regulation. Many of the interactions in the first sessions between therapist and child proved to be aimed at establishing contact and jointly focusing their attention on their surroundings. A brief outline of the codes to be used was drawn up at this time as well. Ultimately, no more new categories were discovered, and some categories needed to be merged, because the behaviour occurred too infrequently or because it was difficult to mark the boundaries between two categories.

The final step in completing the observation system consisted of independently assigning codes to a video recording. Separately, two project group members watched the same 15 minutes of a random session of the treatment of a child in which the person who originally did the coding had not been involved either as therapist or observer. Observers worked with an observation form. The observation form had a time line on which the interventions could be recorded using brief markings or abbreviations. The person assigning codes wrote the behaviour of the therapist above the line. If the behaviour was circled, it meant that it was a direct reaction to the child's behaviour. Below the line the reactions of the child were briefly described.

For the project, we chose not to categorize the child's behaviour because attention was focused on the interventions of the therapist (e.g. Argyle, 1975). Nor was the child's behaviour involved in naming the categories; it was only described to illustrate a technique. Lines drawn between the behaviour of the therapist and that of the child show that it is an interaction chain. An interaction chain was taken as the unit of observation, and the behaviour of the therapist in that interaction was coded. This means, for example, that several attempts to establish contact during an interaction chain are scored only once. The agreements for the observation method are referred to collectively as the behaviour code; it contains a detailed description of certain conducts and events observed, along with the exact rules about making observations (Jones, 1996). The behaviour code is necessary in order to conduct research (see Chapter 11).

Discussing interventions in peer review meetings

In addition to the project group meetings, where the technical aspects and classification of the interventions were discussed, peer review meetings were also held. In these meetings therapists worked on aspects such as developing a shared conceptual framework, learning to look at interventions in the same way, and formulating possible alternative mentalization-based child therapy interventions. Observing the recordings and re-reading the interventions were important resources during peer review. The therapists scrutinized moments in a treatment when progress flagged. Because the group jointly thought about and discussed possible interventions, it could help the therapist in question to overcome an impasse, basically because she again found room to think about it. At the same time this honed the theoretical principles to daily practice. Putting a theoretical frame of reference into practice in a uniform manner demands much consultation. As they exchanged observations and ideas, colleagues began to mentalize among themselves about the treatment. Alongside the inspiration derived from working like this, the joint observation also had a corrective aspect. An example of the corrective feedback comes after the following intervention, which falls into the observation category "Focus on the child's qualities" under the heading of improving attention regulation:

Intervention

"You are a good hunter. You have food for the whole village. . . . It's so very reassuring."

During the entire session in which this intervention occurred, Xander has been very much occupied with talking about how very good he is, that he is a good shot, and that he has a very handsome bow and arrow. The therapist responds to this with generous confirmation, as appears from the foregoing intervention. In any case, it allows Xander to enjoy the game and to go on playing one game for a long time. Following the peer review meeting, the therapist decides to see whether she can take more active part in Xander's playing. She describes this as follows:

> "The active posture was made very easy for me in this session. Xander is still full of school camp and its theme of cave dwellers: he has brought along a beautiful bow and arrow, made for him by his grandfather for this purpose; he sets up camp and goes out hunting. I join in as 'mother at the fireside', who keeps the camp clean, tends the fire, and is full of praise about all the game that my hunter brings home with him."

Without the comments of the other therapists, the therapist in question would have remained on the sidelines longer, paying compliments, and would not have joined in so quickly. Joining in is one of the mentalization-based child therapy techniques, and it helps the child in his pretend play.

A mentalization-based child therapy intervention demands much inventiveness from a therapist. Because colleagues are watching behind the one-way screen or on the video recorder, they can point out to a therapist the possibility of alternative interventions. It gives the therapist fresh ideas about how to approach a child.

Another advantage of peer review was the shared thinking about the child. Sometimes a therapist could no longer keep a child in focus and was in danger of losing her picture of the child, while others were preoccupied with this. By observing and discussing the child with colleagues, it was easier to identify these transference processes. Intensive collaboration with the parent counsellors also proved to be important (see Chapters 5 and 10). Unfortunately, the parent guidance sessions were not recorded on video, which might have made it possible to observe processes parallel to those in the treatment of their children.

The peer review meetings thus proved to be highly necessary with this group of children, and the same can be said of mentalization-based therapy for adults (Bateman & Fonagy, 2006). It also brought collaboration between colleagues to a new and different level, because therapists could only put themselves in the vulnerable position of allowing their own way of treatment to be observed by trusting one another and creating a secure atmosphere. With all the pressure of ordinary therapy work, there is not always time for this. As one of the participants put it, thanks to the peer review, the group came to be a haven of "unexpected safety".

In conclusion

Translating the knowledge gained during our literature study into clinical practice was very instructive. As we observed, we were able to give more thought to the theory. It was concluded that a therapist also needs to work in practice in order to think, and that the theory is helpful to working in practice, so that therapists learn to specify what it is they do during a treatment. The techniques observed proved to be very useful for this.

Note

1. Identification data refers to: date of registration, child's initials, initials of observer and therapist, number of session observed (starting from the beginning of treatment), intervention found on the VHS tape in number of minutes after the start of the session, and a composite code added, consisting of initials of child, date of registration, and number of intervention (A, B, or C).

CHAPTER SEVEN

Intervention techniques: attention regulation

Annelies J. E. Verheugt-Pleiter

The objective of Chapters 7, 8, and 9 is to give a picture of mentalization-based child therapy intervention techniques so that therapists in a clinical setting can learn to recognize what strategy they can best adopt in their relationship with the child in order to set the mentalization process in motion. As we began to list interventions, it soon became clear that they could be classified roughly into three groups as distinguished by Anthony Bateman (symposium, December 2002) in discussing the treatment of adult borderline patients: attention regulation, affect regulation, and mentalization. This chapter discusses intervention techniques that have to do with attention regulation. For each type, examples of interventions illustrate the intervention technique.

Introduction

The general basic principles of mentalization-based child therapy as discussed at length in Chapter 4 are worked out in a practical sense in Chapter 7 (attention regulation), Chapter 8 (affect regulation), and

Chapter 9 (mentalization) by relating them to concrete categories observed during treatment sessions. The principles are:

▷ working in the here and now of the relationship;
▷ attuning to the child's mental functioning at the same level;
▷ giving reality value to inner experiences;
▷ playing with reality;
▷ the process is more important than the technique.

This chapter focuses on attention regulation. Why is it important? The theoretical framework set forth in this book assumes that *thinking*, just like *self*, does not exist at birth but is developed in an attachment relationship with the primary caregivers. A baby may have innate expectations about perfect synchronization with its parent—Bion speaks of "pre-conceptions"—for example, of being fed. But only when these expectations are fulfilled, which implies the attachment figure, do conceptions arise, does thinking have content (Bion, 1962). If the perfect synchronization is not achieved—and this is inevitable in every parent–baby pair because there is no such thing as perfection—it leads to frustration. The ability to tolerate frustration is identical to the acquisition of thinking, which makes it possible to fantasize about imminent or future satisfaction and to postpone satisfaction. Without this mental system, the baby's primitive disintegration anxiety is unbearable. In its initial form, this mental system arises from learning to tolerate frustration—something a baby can learn only in the interaction of an attachment relationship. Control of primary affects, so that actions are not determined by impulse, is the first step towards a focus on internal perceptions, on one's own affects and ideas, by which the initial sense of self can be reinforced. Controlling impulsiveness, developing or learning primary mental content, and the framework of a reciprocal relationship are the three basic elements of the earliest regulation processes. When discussing the interventions in this chapter, we always refer to these three aspects, which are, in fact, three facets of the same process.

What is attention regulation?

This chapter is about the group of interventions that can be summed up under the heading of "attention regulation". If a child has hardly any ability to mentalize in a certain field, the therapist will start by working with the child on finding or creating attention to his inner self. Children need help so that they are not overwhelmed by severe anxiety and so that they can create a state of calm and alert regulation. The term "attention" is used here in a broad sense. Normally it is used to refer to attentiveness, perceptivity, interest, suggesting a primarily cognitive function. Here it goes further and also refers to the ability to control impulsiveness—something that can be learned in a safe relationship. A great deal of research shows that self-control and the ability to focus attention are related (Bateman & Fonagy, 2004, p. 18). The early attachment relationship in which the mother diverts the child's attention from an impulse that presents itself with great urgency in the child ultimately makes it possible for the child to internalize this capacity (its mother's). The ability to gain control of impulses that arise from within is an essential condition for the capacity to mentalize: it requires being able to give priority to a mental state over a physical reality. And the reverse is also true: without stable internal representations, it is not possible to have firm control of affect. The creation of a safe space is essential to this process and to this ability. Within the confines of a firmly fixed and safe framework, the therapist ensures that his relationship with the child stays "good": he protects the child against too much frustration, anxiety, chaos, and excitation (Cluckers, 1986, p. 23). In Chapter 4 we used the word "holding", or tuning in to the child's physical and psychological rhythm.

The techniques are interventions that encourage the development of attention skills: learning to control, focus, and manage attention. Of prime importance is learning to control an overwhelming response in favour of a subdominant response. This covers all verbal and nonverbal interventions that are attempts to rearrange the child's attention to impulses in the here and now (for example, immediate satisfaction of needs from a teleological viewpoint), such as when the mother comforts, distracts, or adds another affect to regulate the child's attention. This means all interventions intended by the therapist to turn the child's attention inward—for example, in first instance, by aiming it at the therapist's regulation model. It is the intention of the therapist to make the child less dependent on the sensory input from the external world, so that he can follow a more internally dictated set of priorities. All interventions within this main group concern the regulation of arousal—impulsive actions involving an often strong emotional arousal. Greenspan (1997) calls them pre-representational interventions, by which he means that they are based on the assumption that a child does not yet have detailed mental representations of affects. This group of interventions appeals to the therapist's capacity to adjust his reactions to the child's mental functioning level and to create an atmosphere of acceptance, one in which the child will feel room to explore some aspect of his tense and often impulsive inner world.

Within this group we distinguish:

1. Accepting the child's regulation profile and attuning to the same level;

2. working on the child's ability to make contacts;

3. working on the basis for intentional behaviour;

4. giving reality value to preverbal interactions by taking the child's own style seriously.

Accepting the child's regulation profile and attuning to the same level

The first phase of development is about gaining confidence in the ability to lead life in a calm, regulated, and interested manner, and to feel safe with the workings of one's body, specifically the perceptual and motor systems. Problems in this phase express themselves in a feeling of being overwhelmed, of disintegration, in attempts to achieve omnipotent over-control. Some children with a mental process disorder have difficulty with this. Mood, panic, or anxiety are too overwhelming for them to be able to do anything. This becomes apparent in the very first phase of therapy. The therapist will then seek ways to ensure that the child feels calm: regulated and interested in the world around him. The abnormal regulation processes influence development in numerous ways, and it will be clear that the child can best become calm if his specific pattern is understood. The therapist can adapt his responses to the child's specific regulation profile and attempt to find a pattern that will best help this child to focus his attention and to utilize his energy. The first step named by Greenspan (1997) is for the therapist to watch the child at play or in conversation and to adjust his responses to the child's interaction pattern. This may mean that the therapist adjusts the pitch of his voice, his use of facial expression, and so on.

Greenspan (1997) distinguishes a number of regulation patterns that have to do with constitution or maturity, which must be given attention if the therapy is to move to a higher level. They are:

▷ over- or undersensitivity to sounds, light and new images;
▷ tactile defensiveness or underreacting to touch or pain;
▷ over- or undersensitivity to movement in the room, scents, temperature;
▷ poor locomotor tension;
▷ less-than-age-adequate motor planning skills, abilities to modulate motor activity and/or fine motor skills;
▷ less-than-age-adequate visual–spatial processing capacities and/or ability to focus and retain without being excessively distracted.

A child who cannot listen or play because, for example, he is completely focused on a fly in the room needs an adult who makes contact at this level. Once the two have developed a sense of mutual engagement, they can explore the problems encountered by the child with this type of thing. The therapist can then help the child to anticipate difficult situations. The therapist will listen closely to descriptions of behaviour and pick out moments when something resembling a feeling is named. Exploring this—for example, how it feels to be so overwhelmed—can make the child more flexible. If the child, together with the therapist, can gain some empathy for his problems, they can work out together some of the child's basic assumptions: for example, the idea that you immediately get up, leave the room, and slam the door if you feel uncomfortable with something. Step by step, the therapist can help the child to gain more alternatives. These interventions are appropriate to the child's behavioural level and perspective and not to his presumed feelings, because the child does not yet have these at the ready: he will freeze up or become worked up if too quickly asked about emotions.

Based on the material collected (see Chapter 6), within this sub-group of interventions we discuss:

a. attention to the content of the child's play or activity/introducing structure in play or story;

b. naming/describing physical states;

c. naming/describing behaviour aimed at the naming of mental content (cognitions and feelings);

d. naming/describing anxiety or feeling threatened; and

e. naming/describing a state of animosity.

Attention to the content of the child's play or activity/introducing structure in play or story

In the first place, this refers to remarks and behaviour about the content of the child's activities. The therapist moves along with the child's rhythm. This is more about creating patterns of being together than about what is actually said. Doing the same thing together rhythmically, often repetitively, is reminiscent of a children's song. The process agenda is ultimately at the service of the content agenda (Stern, 2004): in other words, in this phase the fact that you share such a rhythm may well be more important than what precisely is being exchanged. The introduction of structure during a game or story that is in danger of becoming unstructured is meant to refocus the child's attention. As long as the therapist joins in the child's game, when a child is in danger of becoming worked up, the therapist can try to weave in some sort of line, thus offering the child some sort of grip.

Remarkably, the activities of the therapist that were classified under this heading were only identified in a second round, during which we observed much more precisely what the therapists actually did. We became convinced that many activities seem to be so very automatic that a therapist is scarcely aware of what happens. Nevertheless, it is important to name or describe these things that tend to be taken for granted in order to get some idea of how they work.

Paul

Paul is a boy who readily becomes wound up and has difficulty in playing. Whenever Paul manages to do anything resembling play, T tries to respond at the same level and to take it very seriously, resulting in a sort of shared cadence. Paul is doing something with water and a surfboard. T pays much attention to what he is doing, in the hope that this will give it more content for him as well. For instance, she asks, *"Do you think the surfboard will float on this?"*

Naming/describing physical states

Focusing attention on aspects of behaviour that can express a physical sensation is highly concrete and mainly intended to name sensory information. In this category, a physical sensation is not regarded as a metaphor for something mental. The fact that the body is something you can give some thought to, something another person might be interested in, can be seen as a building block for the development of self as agent (see Chapter 4). If your body is something you can think about and can share thoughts about, you are working towards the regulation of physical processes.

Paul

While playing Monopoly, Paul becomes increasingly restless physically. He shows this by extending his arms, opening and closing his hands in a particular way, pulling faces, and fidgeting on his chair. This physical unrest starts on a small scale but becomes more and more obvious. During the previous session, Paul showed himself insensitive to a description of what made the game so "exciting". Now that Paul is so restless, it seems to be sufficiently observable and so close to the surface that a remark might be made about it, and T decides to ask, *"Um, how do you like this chair?"* (Paul is sitting on a different chair this time.)

Geert

Geert says that he won a lollipop because he stood still in the class with a book on his head for 20 minutes. He tells this in passing, as if it is perfectly ordinary. T is confused by what Geert says. He relates something he is good at and which was apparently confirmed by his teacher as something special that he can do. But it is also an odd sort of trick with which to earn the admiration of teacher and pupils. It is an example of the great control Geert has of himself. T tries to link a physical perception to this by asking, *"I'm trying to imagine it, standing for 20 minutes with a book on your head, how do you manage that?"*

Here the therapist uses her own mental state to try to get Geert to dwell on a physical experience (as a precursor to an emotional experience).

Naming/describing behaviour aimed at the naming of mental content (cognitions and feelings)

Focusing attention on aspects of behaviour and ascribing a *possible* expression of emotion or cognition to them is a first step towards highlighting an inner experience.

Maartje

Maartje and T are sitting at the table, cutting and pasting. Both of them are making a collage, but T has to hand hers over to Maartje if it turns out better. It is as if T has to feed Maartje her work, which looks nicer. Maartje also wants T's admiration for what she produces. If T were to name all these aspects at this point, the fact that they are working together would be undone. By saying *"Aren't we working hard!"* she names the sensorimotor pleasure and the fact that they are working *together*. Maartje cannot tolerate the idea that she is unable to do something. Now and then T admits that she thinks something is difficult, thus implicitly giving the child permission to admit this as well.

With her intervention, the therapist indicates that the fact that they are doing this together helps you to tolerate and regulate such disquieting feelings (can I do this? am I doing it right?).

Naming/describing anxiety and feeling threatened

This involves directing attention to unsafe situations in which a person can feel threatened and anxious, and how to deal with them.

Maartje

Maartje wants to have a sword fight. She pretends to fall down, and T has to follow suit. She waves her sword so dangerously in front of T's nose that T says, "*I want to defend myself*" and takes a shield. But Maartje won't let her. She says, "I'll stab you straight through your head." T is afraid that the sword fight will get out of hand, because Maartje can be rather impulsive. She plays along but responds very slowly, and puts into words that she feels unsafe and wants protection. Finally, she says it is a dangerous game. Maartje then stops playing, saying that it is more a game for boys.

The therapist expresses her own sense of feeling unsafe to make it clear to Maartje that she is allowed to feel anxious in such a situation, while also giving her a coping mechanism: you can defend yourself (with a shield).

Maartje

Maartje has a game full of excitement: a great deal goes on during the game, and she shrieks a lot. Maartje is playing with the castle, and a kitten is climbing in it. Maartje allows T to ascribe feelings to the kitten: "*Is there a safe way too?*" "*Will the kitty be all right?*" and responds well to T's interventions. This makes T feel she can go one step further in naming the kitten's feelings: they stand for the feelings of Maartje, who does dangerous things in reality (at home), such as threatening to jump off the balcony. Once or twice T tries to link the game to reality, but Maartje does not accept this, so T abandons her attempts. (Figure 7.1)

FIGURE 7.1. Will the kitty be all right?

Naming/describing a state of animosity

This involves showing the child in a playful manner that anger may be present but does not necessarily have a direct effect on behaviour. This category may also include naming the fact that the same object can evoke opposing feelings.

Ivo

> At a certain point, Ivo turns towards the one-way screen and feints with his sword towards the mirror. T says: *"It looks like a shadow fight against the unknown person behind the mirror."* And she asks him, *"Is it still so bad?"* It's not so bad, he says, "And now it's your turn." So he sidesteps it. Ivo sometimes loses control and hurts T, rapping her fingers. (Figure 7.2)

The remark about the shadow fight in the mirror symbolizes Ivo's anger about the screen and how you can deal with it by pretending. It is not a real fight, but a shadow fight, a pretend fight. The

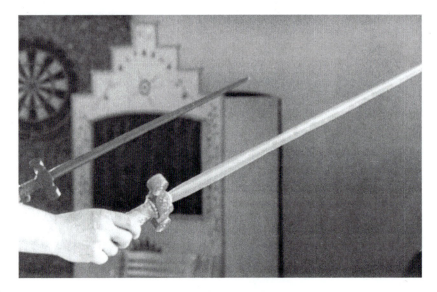

Figure 7.2.   It looks like a shadow fight against the unknown person behind the mirror.

intervention helps him to allow his feelings of anger and appeals to his cognitive skills.

Paul

While they are playing Monopoly, T decides that this time she really will buy the Boardwalk. Paul obviously does not like this. On his next turn he winds up on the Boardwalk and has to pay a huge fine. He grabs half the money from the bank instead of from his own pile, then corrects himself. Looks in the mirror. A little later, when he again lands on one of T's streets, he tries to distract her by calling, "Quick, quick, a monster is coming!" T laughs. *"Are you trying to distract me?"* Reluctantly, Paul pays. T, breezily: *"I can tell by looking at you, you're out for revenge."*

By adopting a playful attitude, the therapist offsets Paul's whining, pestering, and cheating without touching his narcissism—moreover, while drawing his attention to the fact that he is doing this. This engenders a sense of the two of them together instead of "you're cheating, I caught you, and I'll get you back, you can count on it". It is more along the lines of "let's pretend we're cheating" instead of "we're cheating".

Ivo

Ivo likes to play darts, but he seems to get a little anxious about the cracks that he says it makes in the dartboard; he also often shoots his darts into the wall or the woodwork, very close to the window. When he does this, he recounts his fantasy that a dart will hit a passer-by in his head and frighten him. After having made another crack (a very small one), he says, "I'm getting stronger, I think." T asks, "How does that make you feel?" Ivo: "Bad." T: "Getting stronger feels bad?" In response, Ivo again shoots the dart pistol, confirming as it were both the anxiety and the aggression. A while later he says that he almost wrecked the doll house, giggling very hard all the while. T goes along in the half-laughing, half-serious situation by saying, "*It is not easy to divide your strength, is it?*"

With this intervention the therapist shares the child's emotional and physical rhythm. There is little point in asking him for the reason behind the damage he causes. The aggression is therefore not discussed as such: the attention to the anger is used to interest him in interaction.

Working on the ability to make contact

A safe attachment relationship must be developed in order to learn to control impulsive behaviour and to turn attention inward. Although this aspect plays a role in all interventions, in some cases it stands in the foreground, so that these interventions are discussed separately. We are talking here about the first steps towards developing a capacity to make commitments and to take part in and maintain an intimate relationship. Many children have serious limitations when it comes to feeling a link to another person: this aspect, too, soon comes forward in therapy. Many children cannot say in words that they feel empty or without any ties. In such a case, the therapist watches for signs of connectedness such as a smile, a quick glance. As came up indirectly in the previous series of interventions, working on the capacity to make contact, especially in withdrawn children, means first and foremost incorporating yourself into the child's play. In this way you show the child that it is possible to stay connected and even start to feel better about an unpleasant mood or undifferentiated affect. The subtle message is that it is better to experience strong, overwhelming affects within a relationship than to feel withdrawn from all contact. At these moments it is not yet possible to experience the painful affect states at a representational level.

The following topics are discussed:

a. maintaining contact and introducing continuity in contact;

b. creating a safe environment; and

c. naming/describing interactions.

Maintaining contact and introducing continuity in contact

Sometimes maintaining contact will require verbalizations without naming or describing behaviour or feelings. Many children experience little continuity in their contact with others. References to matters that came up in a previous session or that may play a role in several different sessions will have to be made cautiously. If the child has a hard time retaining images from previous sessions, a reference to them by the therapist may be experienced as criticism, and it means that the therapist is not relating to the child's perspective. It is still possible for the therapist to show that she is thinking about what the child says and does. In the long run, this can provide a form of continuity for the child.

Paul

When the session comes to an end, Paul does not want to stop. He is very wound up, and it is difficult to understand what he is talking about. Finally it becomes clear that he is talking about a game on MTV. T: ". . . so it's a game in which people hurt themselves?" Paul: "Yes and they do things like. . . ." He shows some examples and with a flying leap, lets himself fall hard to the ground. T: *"We'll have to talk about that next week."* This calms Paul; together, they leave the room.

The therapist has observed that with Paul, it is possible and helpful to come back to a vehement affect at a later time by "the two of us thinking about it once more" or "I've been thinking about that". What probably makes this effective is the fact that she more or less takes the responsibility. Although she does not respond to the content, she lets him know that she can keep it in her thoughts.

Creating a safe environment

Within the context of a permanent and safe framework, the therapist ensures that the relationship stays "good": she protects the child against too much frustration, chaos, and excitation. The therapist ensures that the affect does not become overwhelming and the child does not hurt himself or get himself into difficulty in some other way. In the first example the therapist is simply offering care. In the second example something more is needed, because the child does not tolerate dependence very well.

Maartje

Maartje is painting. While she mixes the colours and starts painting, T is busy cleaning up the spilled paint. A few times, she asks Maartje if she wants her to push up her sleeves. T offers help when the painting seems to be in danger of turning out badly. "It's all wrong", says Maartje; T: "put some black over it and then you won't see it." Maartje accepts all these caring interventions on the part of T. T also praises the results when Maartje asks her to. Maartje says, for example, "A masterpiece" and gazes with satisfaction at the result. T confirms this. Because Maartje is not very neat about painting and because there is a carpet on the floor and Maartje is in danger of making herself dirty, T has a lot of work cleaning up the mess. Maartje patiently accepts this.

Here the therapist is acting like a mother who lets a 3-year-old paint, supports her and backs her up, protects her from too much disappointment and failure. The therapist uses her nonverbal inter-ventions—cleaning up, avoiding messes and spills—to create an at-mosphere of care for Maartje in which Maartje can produce work she is pleased with and which the therapist can admire. The atmosphere is pleasant and safe, so that Maartje enjoys painting, messing about, and producing a nice result.

Paul

Paul and T are playing football in the room. Although he is acting tough, he also shows some vulnerability. He expresses this physi-cally: if he lets the ball through, he finds his failure very hurtful and expresses it as physical pain. Paul has already had several drinks of water; he gets so very thirsty from playing football. This time he even starts putting water on his hair. T says: "You got all hot and sweaty, did you?" and picks up the box of tissues and offers them: "Else it'll run down into your sweater." Paul: "But that feels good." T: "It cools you off." Paul says he holds the water in his mouth but does not drink it. T: "So you just let it run out again . . . (half stating a fact, half asking). . . . Is that a nice feeling?" Paul asks if there is also hot water; they check this out together. T asks: "Are you cooler now?" And adds, *"You can tell what a hard match it was, can't you."*

The therapist was unsure whether her picking up the box of tis-sues might not detract from the "tough" image Paul wants so badly, whether it might not tend to confirm him in his idea of being "only a small boy who doesn't amount to much". At the same time, drinking the water and putting his head under the tap were not at all tough, but rather more of an appeal: "are you [T] concerned about how I feel physically?" The addition of "You can tell . . ." is a reference to the tough aspect of the game.

Naming/describing explicit interactions

Naming or describing what can take place between people is an im-portant way of preparing for being able to put yourself in another's place. Children with a mental process disorder often have a very difficult time imagining the world as others perceive it. The therapist can encourage the child to imagine or picture this, provided she manages to reach the child's mental functioning level.

Xander

Xander is sitting at the table with T and playing with the castle and a knight on horseback in front of it. Xander: "This knight wants to conquer the castle. They don't have any more weapons in the castle." T: "So he doesn't need to be afraid?" Silence. *"Why didn't he like the people in the castle?"* asks T. Xander: "They were naughty all the time." T: "What did they do?" Xander: "They were calling us names all the time." (Figure 7.3)

Pursuit and feeling pursued is a theme in Xander's therapy and in his life. The intervention elicits from Xander the response of putting into words through his play something that occupies him very much: being called names and being left out. This question allows him to make a very spontaneous remark about what he feels within without

FIGURE 7.3.   Why didn't he like the people in the castle?

having to let go of the tough exterior that is so important to him. It is a first step on the way towards understanding interactions.

Ivo

> T and Ivo are each assembling an army. Ivo says that it is really a pretty unfair fight. T confirms that she has much more equipment and asks whether he wants to have some of hers. Ivo doesn't want any because he has mainly soldiers. And soldiers are more important, he says; they are well trained. At which point T says, *"You're right, people are more important."*

Ivo still thinks about relationships in fairly instrumental terms. It is an area in which Ivo still has a lot to learn. He has always lived very much in his own world and has very little idea of what people can mean for each other outside strict instrumentality.

Working on the basis for intentional behaviour

A third group of interventions is concerned with simple intentional gestures—the exchange of nods, frowns, and other social signals that also define boundaries between people. Take, for example, the very young child who uses sign language to show that she wants to be picked up: if the parent responds to this "intention", an initial feeling of self will acquire validity and credibility. Although there are no verbal representations yet, there are circles of communication: these are opened and closed. The child reaches, opening the circle. The parent picks her up in response. If the child then smiles, the circle is closed again. It will be obvious that it can have a disorganizing effect if the circle cannot be closed again (Greenspan, 1997).

In the therapy situation it is important that the therapist's style does not hamper the child. A therapist who is too still or withdrawn can further disorganize a child or make him intensely angry. The therapist can emanate continuous regulation and acceptance via his gestures and make interaction possible by opening and closing communication circles in this nonverbal area. If the child is withdrawn, he can easily draw the therapist into a game of wait-and-see. If the child has a real problem in this area, it is up to the therapist to respond with properly distributed warmth and attention. The therapist's facial expression may become a bit livelier, the way a parent will intuitively do with a child who is too overwhelmed to be able to answer verbally. But the child's disorganization can also be passed on to the adult, and so the adult will have to regulate himself and can use this in his contact with the child.

The following topic is discussed:

a.   joining into the child's activities visually and/or in gestures.

Joining in with the child's activities visually and/or in gestures

Nonverbally, the therapist will note all communicative or potentially communicative gestures and respond with regulation and acceptance. It is important to pay particular visual attention to the child and his activities—such as very intently following the child's actions visually or physically, for example, in gestures—engenders a nonverbal involvement, and the child gets a clearer idea of what he wants (see the example from Eduard' therapy). By exaggerating his attitude, facial expressions, or intonation, the therapist can present or express difficult feelings, thus promoting their acceptance (see the example from Maartje' therapy). It is not necessary to use moderation. The therapist's facial expressions do not need to be repressed—on the contrary (see the example from Geert' therapy). The child may be able to use these reactions to gain a better understanding of what he wants.

Eduard

Eduard says, "... maybe play a game again?" Since the last session, he has apparently decided that he enjoys this. He chooses a new game, The Game of Life. Neither Eduard nor T knows how it goes. Eduard takes the initiative, reads the instructions, is active in a relaxed way, really puts some work into it; he clearly seems to take pleasure in it. T just sits and watches with amusement, nonverbally recognizing him in his new role.

The fact that the therapist did not know the game gave Eduard the chance to take the initiative. The nonverbal recognition of this by the therapist, the way she observed his intention to take the lead, gave Eduard room to grow in his role, and this made it clear that the "role reversal" really seemed to do him good. This is an entirely different Eduard from the Eduard who has such a hard time complying with the therapy requirements!

Maartje

Maartje sits at the table with T and is making a drawing for Christmas. As so often, Maartje wants T to do exactly the same thing she does—and when T does so, it is usually not good enough for Maartje. If T's drawing is better, Maartje immediately exchanges them, which T allows. In their interaction, Maartje is the strict and irritated teacher who criticizes the child. For instance, she angrily commands T: "It has to be perfectly straight! And then you take this, and you do like this." But she is also the teacher who helps and gives instructions: "And now we will take the . . . orange." T constantly repeats that she has a hard time making the drawing. For instance, she says, "I'm not so sure I'm very good at it, I don't really understand, it would be nice if I had a better idea of what you wanted, I think it's awfully hard." Despite the criticism that is heaped on her and despite the fact that her work is not good enough, T simply goes on with her drawing.

The therapist responds to Maartje's intentions by going along in the role Maartje has given her, which is that of a child with shortcomings. But she adds something to it: she also plays the role of the child who is not afraid to express her uncertainty about what she can do, who does not let the criticism upset or distract her, and who nonverbally shows that she stays calm despite her failings and the teacher's curt words, simply getting on with her work. The fact that she allows the drawings to be exchanged is a nonverbal sign that the therapist can accept being used like this. In a classroom situation with another child, an adult would have drawn a line here: there, of course, it is not all right for drawings to be exchanged. It would only serve to feed the child's anxiety, because she would be overstepping someone's else boundaries. But in this phase of the therapy, something different is at stake. The therapist is now genuinely an object that the child can use for her development. The therapist gives a light-hearted indication that the child is not crossing her boundaries; the therapist plays the game too and shows by her actions how to deal with frustration.

Geert

Once again, T and Geert are playing Monopoly. Geert is wound up: he is physically restless and shows it in his movements. Only incidentally does he make eye contact with T, and then it is fleeting. When Geert does make eye contact, T mirrors it by returning Geert's slightly wound-up expression.

Geert is wound up and restless from the Monopoly game. The mirroring of the facial expression by the therapist seems to serve as a form of regulation, but also as a way to draw Geert into the contact. The therapist exaggerates her facial expression, but also delays it, mirroring enthusiasm, joy, and disappointment. It is, as it were, an invitation to Geert to view himself as a person who is enthusiastic or disappointed.

Giving reality value to preverbal interactions
by taking the child's own style seriously

Rather like the way a toddler uses a complex behavioural repertoire to express in a preverbal fashion psychological feelings such as dependence and independence, pride and admiration, envy and competition, love and care for others, here a pre-symbolic complex sense of self and other is established within an attachment relationship. When the gesture system does not work, it leads to fixated views and attitudes. Greenspan (1997) describes how many enactments take place in this field, and how a therapist can confirm the dependent attitude of an adult patient simply by his intonation and attitude. A change of tactics in this nonverbal area (for example, the therapist does not wait for the patient to lower his eyes, but lowers his own first) can increase the patient's independence.

Becoming aware of subtle forms of communication may imply that the therapist shows admiration for the child without being patronizing. It is a tactical error to start discussing feelings when they are not yet recognized by the child at a behavioural level. Sometimes there is only a vague somatic reference (tense muscles, stomach ache). Then the therapist will patiently ask after the source of the child's discomfort and invite the child to talk about his physical sensations. If there is interaction with respect to the behavioural level, the corresponding affects can come up as well. For instance, a therapist may simply comment on the intensity: "That is an intense look." Or point out to the child at the end of the session that he seems to be stuck to his chair. Children with a mental process disorder understand this type of thing better than talking about anxiety, desire, or missing.

If the parents have not really seen the child as a person in his own right, if they have given too little social biofeedback, the child has had too little opportunity to link its own inner sensations to an affective state, or to a representation that is not perceived to be "true" or "real". The child must first experience affective states at the level of behaviour and gestures before he can make mental representations of them. They must first be given reality value, and the therapist can help in this respect. This aspect often involves naming intensities, pointing out behavioural sequences that are important to the child and communicating admiration of the child and his behaviour as the very first form of help in starting to see his own qualities.

To be discussed here:

a.   directing attention at describing behaviour;
b.   focusing on the child's qualities.

Directing attention at describing behaviour

This category includes giving descriptions of behaviour and/or asking questions at a behavioural level. It is important that a child comes to see that he is viewed as an independent person, as the pilot of his own behaviour. By describing a behavioural sequence once again but then from his own perspective, it can become clear to him—for example—that it is very understandable that he has responded in a certain way, even if it was a tantrum or panic. His behaviour and his manner of reacting take on reality value if the therapist discusses with him very seriously exactly how something has taken place (see the example from Xander's therapy). And discussing how something will take place can give the child the feeling that he can influence the course of the events (see the example from Eduard's therapy).

Xander

When he arrives, Xander has with him materials and attributes that he uses in his games with his friends in the hut, where they fight each other with poison. In the therapy, Xander has spent much time playing with poison in several variants. It is unclear why he thinks this is so important, although the therapist makes a great many indirect remarks about it. Now T asks, "What gives you all these ideas about poison?" There is a sudden silence, and then Xander says, "Well, the war in Iraq."

This question, asked with a strongly interrogative intonation, resulted in a genuine reply from Xander instead of a silly or evasive remark. Earlier on the therapist had felt the temptation to talk about Iraq, but now she was pleased that she had not. Now that he can bring up this idea himself, they can explore together how it affects him, and he can make representations of his perceptions.

Eduard

Eduard has had his hair cut very short, and is also wearing new glasses. Other children have made negative remarks about both, he says. He says that it is his birthday; T did not know this. On the one hand, Eduard says that T couldn't have known because he hadn't told her; on the other hand, he says that T might have had a look at his papers! The rest of the session is extremely laborious. Eduard doesn't know what he wants to do; he slumps down further and further in his chair. He does not allow any contact at all with T, and at one point she sighs, "No matter what I think up, I always get it wrong." The session passes in a sort of intellectual sparring on Eduard's part; he misunderstands the therapist or puts words into T's mouth. After having contained all the anger and disappointment, at the end of the session T makes one more attempt to restore contact simply by showing explicit interest in his birthday: *"So what else are you going to do on your birthday; some kids give a party?"* Almost for the first time, Eduard has a positive response to this show of interest. He says that three children are coming to his party and that they are going to do a treasure hunt. It is all planned for Good Friday, whereupon T makes the pun, "Good Friday, good birthday."

It was important for Eduard that the therapist took a different tack, taking the initiative to restore contact by explicitly showing an interest in an everyday and important event in his life.

Focusing on the child's qualities

This means pointing out to the child things he is good at. These will often be qualities that the child has not yet been able to think about in this way. Explicitly discussing the child's qualities is a way of justifying or confirming his sense of self.

Maartje

Maartje is playing with the castle. She is shouting out orders in a peremptory tone of voice and sometimes even shrieking. Several times she says, "Launch the attack!" She puts figures on the horse and fiddles with the saddles. She snarls at T that she is doing it all wrong. T says, *"You're the one who knows all about horses."* Maartje plays with horses a lot; she also rides, and riding is the link with her absent father. So horses play a big role in her self-perception.

Geert

Geert is quite pleased with his achievements in a game of Monopoly and says proudly, "I know how to do business." T: *"You sure do know how to do business, I can learn a lot from you."* Geert: "I could teach you, but my lessons are expensive, 100 Euros." T: "If I learn a lot from them, it's worth it." Geert: "Maybe you won't learn anything from them". T: "That depends on whether I understand it."

The therapist is happy with the clear affect in Geert, who often creates a deathly atmosphere during sessions. She gives reality value to a quality in the child, which also helps him to feel himself seen more clearly as a person.

In conclusion

The interventions described in this chapter are all intended to contribute to an experience of "being understood". Because a child knows that the therapist understands him and, more importantly, sees him as a person, a step has been taken towards a safe attachment relationship and towards strengthening the child's affective activity. For several of these children, their impulsiveness became somewhat regulated because their impulses were given a place in their contact with the therapist in the form of needs and wishes. Some children who were over-regulated became a bit more playful and showed more intersubjectivity. Because their attention has been regulated, they have gained a better tolerance for frustration, enabling the development of their capacity to mentalize.

CHAPTER EIGHT

Intervention techniques: affect regulation

Annelies J. E. Verheugt-Pleiter

The objective of Chapters 7, 8, and 9 is to demonstrate mentalization-based intervention techniques. In Chapter 7 we showed intervention techniques that have to do with attention regulation; in this chapter we discuss those that have to do with affect regulation: keeping play within boundaries, giving reality value to affect states, and deducing second-order affect representations. Examples of interventions illustrate the intervention technique.

Introduction

What is affect regulation? The affective experiences of a child take on their full meaning, their emotional quality, in the child's relationship with his primary caregivers. The way in which children can regulate their affects also has implications for the development of the self. According to Fonagy, Gergely, and colleagues (2002, p. 95), regulation of affects largely takes place outside consciousness. Affect regulation may refer to the type of emotion, to the moment when it occurs and when it subsides again, the style in which it is experienced, and the way in which it is expressed. Meurs, Vliegen, and Cluckers (2005) studied modes such as intensity, pleasantness, control, and frequency of occurrence. If affect regulation is faulty, it may be the result of difficulty in understanding affect states, in linking them to something, and in the ability to verbalize them. The marked and contingent recognition of a person's own affect in a significant other, an attachment figure, should serve as a crystallization point for the child in developing his own affect regulation (Fonagy, Gergely, et al., 2002).

An important aspect of affect regulation is giving reality value to the child's experiences: if the child and his experiences are taken seriously, they are more anchored in real life. The purpose is to make room for the deduction of second-order affect representations (see Chapter 4). If the parents have not really seen their child as a person in his own right, the child will have had too few opportunities to link inner experiences to a representation perceived as true or real. So in the therapy it is important to make the perception aspect explicit and to give it reality value. Then an inner world can be built, a representational structure with which to reflect about the primary affect states (Fonagy, Gergely, et al., 2002). From this mentalization process, children ultimately learn to interpret their own behaviour and that of others in terms of feelings, wishes, desires, and intentions. This is discussed further in Chapter 9.

In some therapies, a great deal of work needs to be done on attention regulation before there can be any kind of focus on feelings. Only after that will the child be able to show something in the way of a feeling. In working with children with a mental process disorder, it is sometimes extremely difficult to verbalize affect. If children are not ready for it, if they have too little mental scope, they often take a verbalization of feeling as an attack. If, for example, the therapist sympathizes with their feeling of fear, they often take it as an intrusion or an insult. So it is a delicate matter to decide when affects can be named and when they cannot. "Analyst-centered interpretations" (Steiner, 1994) work well with this group of children according to our experience. Steiner describes a group of adult psychotic and borderline patients who are not interested in understanding themselves, but who do attach a great deal of importance to being understood. If the analyst gives an interpretation of what the patient feels or thinks, it causes the contact to deteriorate, because the patient feels that projected elements are thrust back at him. Comments on the lines of what the patient thinks the analyst thinks are more appropriate to the patient's need to know what goes on in the analyst's mind. This refers to a type of intervention such as: "You are afraid that I. . . ." Or: "You see me as. . . ." If the therapist can contain the patient's or the child's projections in this way, it leads to integration and to the experience of being understood. Steiner is of the opinion that insight and coping with mental pain are necessary for genuine change. He may be underestimating the value of feeling understood and the consequences this has for the development of the sense of self and for mentalization.

The therapist must have a good idea of the most important affects. Sorting out the antecedents of an affect is an important technique. The therapist will help the child to describe the feelings that introduce or accompany the behavioural patterns identified. Another important technique in regulating affects is to discuss the consequences strong feelings on the part of the child can have for himself and for others (Bateman & Fonagy, 2004). The shared experience in the therapy can serve as the starting point for a child to start thinking about his own behaviour. The safety of the shared experience can form a bridge to communication about needs and feelings, so that they no longer need to be acted out. The ability to step back and to observe is a crucial skill in order to start mentalizing later. The interaction with the therapist and the interpersonal experience thus gained help the child to communicate with himself and to develop both a part of self that observes and a part that feels and experiences. Setting boundaries is helpful to this process because it helps to decrease the tendency to act out and encourages verbalization. The introduction of playfulness and markedness (see Chapter 2) lend the necessary scope for this.

It is always essential to keep an eye on the relationship to the child's real feeling, even when working in pretend mode. If there is no such connection, there may well be no point to the play situation—it may merely be cognitive chitchat. This is what Bateman and Fonagy (2006) have called "pseudo-mentalization". The therapist will therefore always need to remain alert and to validate whatever signals she can get about the child's genuine affective perception.

The following topics are discussed:

1. playing within boundaries;
2. giving reality value to affect states;
3. deducing second-order affect representations.

Playing within boundaries

Playing safely is an important form of affect regulation (see Chapter 4). Exaggeration and dramatization offer huge opportunities for children to get to know their emotional life and to experiment with boundaries: what is inside and what outside. The following aspects are considered:

a. introduction of fantasy to facilitate the pretend mode;
b. focus on separating fantasy and reality;
c. setting boundaries; and
d. joining in the pretend mode.

Introduction of fantasy to facilitate the pretend mode

Naming the possible presence of fantasy in nonverbal play is a therapeutic intervention, because pretend mode can be viewed as a vehicle for the representation of wishes, intentions, and feelings. A child's need for immediate action will be lessened if symbols can be used.

Paul

Paul is very busy with the water and the tap. He opens the tap to let the water run fast, closes it so that it runs slowly, fills a dish with water and watches the bubbles, throws pieces of chalk into the dish of water. The doll that was surfing on a self-devised surfboard just a minute ago is suddenly flung about the room like a football. T attempts to bring the play aspect to the foreground by saying, *"Did the girl on the surfboard turn into a football?"*

Focus on separating fantasy and reality

The therapists actively makes remarks on the difference between possible fantasies and reality.

> Ivo
>
> Ivo is fencing; on the one hand, he is attacking and being aggressive. On the other hand, he is encouraging the other to attack, and he seems to feel safer when he is on the defensive. Then T says, *"You're too close to my eyes, master."* He picks up on this and says, "Let's follow the etiquette", and thinks up a procedure that ends with *"en garde"*. But he becomes uninhibited again, until T says, *"You'll knock my head off. We mustn't really hurt each other."* "I'll be careful", Ivo promises. T clearly does not trust this completely and says, *"It's really supposed to be pretend."* And when, after this remark, he gets it right, she says, *"That was good pretending."*

Earlier, when they were playing Stratego, the therapist had noticed that Ivo fantasizes a lot about winning from the other with great bravado but is very uncertain when he has to attack. He becomes so involved in his fantasy world that its relationship with reality is sometimes very tenuous. On the one hand, he seems to be quite afraid of his aggression, because it feels too real; on the other hand, he does not regulate his aggression because it is too much fantasy. Explicitly introducing pretend thinking can help in dealing with both the reality aspects and the fantasy aspects.

Setting boundaries

Boundaries can be set actively or passively. It is only necessary to set boundaries if the rules and the structure of the therapeutic situation are under pressure. Boundaries need to be set because otherwise anxiety can mount very high. In principle, the therapist always responds by mentalizing, except here. First the boundary needs to be determined before any exploring can be done of what is taking place in the world of experience. Bleiberg (2001, p. 68) speaks of "reflective" limit setting of mentalizing caregivers in opposition to caregivers who react with a standard and automatic "no". This can help the child to use the reflections of the caregiver's and the therapist's minds in these matters as a model to establish their own limit-setting capacity.

Maartje

The session is over, and Maartje is having a difficult time leaving. She asks T to make her a clay strawberry, even though there isn't really any time for it. She wants to take the strawberry with her, but T says no. T tries to make this clear, but Maartje does not accept it and just goes on asking if she can take the strawberry home. T says, *"If you can't take it with you, how are we going to solve this?"* And Maartje laughs and says, "Then I'll take it anyway, or can I come to your house once?"

The therapist does not give in to her wish to take the clay home with her, but she feels uneasy about it, because she senses that a lot depends on this for Maartje. This is why she asks Maartje to help her to find a solution; she shares her position of power with her. The intervention was prompted by the previous game in which Maartje tried to take power and control, and had difficulty dealing with reality. By sharing the problem, there is more mental room to think.

Paul

Paul is very busy with the water and the tap. He fills the dish with water brimful: the water runs over the counter . . . in short, Paul is basically making a mess of things and not really playing at all. T: *"You know, we can play without making such a mess of things . . . you'd like it, wouldn't you, if you were allowed to do everything here that you're not allowed to do at home . . . you're not allowed to play football in the sitting room at home either, are you?"* Paul goes on throwing bits of chalk into the dish of water; he throws them so hard that they break. T: "That's enough with the chalk for a while, or else there won't be anything left. If you want to do it, try to throw the chalk carefully so that it doesn't break."

Introducing and naming the difference between playing and making a mess can draw his attention to the fact that there is such a difference, and also that making a mess is not only not allowed, but that it also spoils the game.

Joining in the pretend mode

Sometimes it is necessary to join in the pretend mode to bring about a transitional space. This will make it easier later to underscore the playful aspect in a way so that the two aspects can be integrated—for example, as a wish representation in the self. As an active commentator, the therapist can bring the drama to life more easily, and even be part of it now and then. She can help expand the child's behaviour—for example, by asking what the other should do in the game.

Paul

T and Paul are still playing football; T has to shoot the ball to Paul, who is the keeper. Paul does his very best to stop the ball. Clearly, he finds it of great importance to excel at this. He calls upon T to throw more difficult balls. She does. Paul falls and says he has hurt himself. T walks up to him and sympathizes. She says, *"This is injury time."* Paul turns over onto his stomach and his eyes glaze over. He asks when the time will be up. T shows him on the clock, and it is clear that Paul knows perfectly well. Then T asks, *"Is there a break in a football match?"* Paul wants to play a match; he explains what he wants, and he negotiates with T about who she will be (which football player). Once this has been accomplished and they can resume the game, T asks, *"So you've recovered from your injury?"* Paul: "Wait a minute." T: "Take your time . . . so, are you all right again?"

Xander

With a great deal of commotion, Xander is once again carrying on with his bean-bag chair. First it's a scooter, then it's a planet. He tears back and forth and runs around with it. He bangs it on the ground and is thoroughly enjoying himself. It is really a transitional object (TO) that he can turn into anything he wants. T puts this into words: "You can do just about anything with it, can't you. Now it's a scooter, now it's a planet", and there is a mutual understanding that this "doing just about anything with it" can give Xander a great sense of freedom. T is also enjoying the boy's fantasy, liveliness, and creativity, and she supports this verbally.

Giving reality value to affect states

Giving reality value to inner affective experiences is very important; it is sometimes even the first time that this happens for a child. If a child's anxious state is recognized and acknowledged by the therapist, it is an affective representation of the anxiety, a first-order affect representation. When the child can do it on his own, can recognize the fact that he is anxious and can put this into words, we speak of a second-order representation of the anxiety. The latter is the result of the former: if the relationship has become safe enough, the child can gradually start to internalize the function of the therapist as the representer of affects. How to further encourage this process is discussed in part three of this section and in Chapter 9.

The following aspects are considered:

a.   giving reality value to an affect state of a play figure; and

b.   giving reality value to an affect state of a child.

Giving reality value to an affect state of a play figure

In Chapter 7 it was discussed how complicated it can be for a child with a mental process disorder to understand and accept a verbalization of an affect. Many smaller steps need to be taken, and the connection with the child's perception is crucial. Sometimes a feeling can be named through an intermediary—a figure in the play situation—or as a feeling of the therapist. Exaggeration opens the door to a playful approach and makes it easier to start accepting difficult feelings.

Maartje

The kitty climbs up high on the roof, lets out high-pitched squeals, and is in danger of falling off. This game is repeated several times. T is playing the princess. T tries to discover the feelings of the kitty Maartje is playing with by asking questions during her play, such as, "What's the matter with the kitty?" or "What is the kitty doing on the tower, will it be able to get down?" or "Who will save the kitty? Will the poor pussycat fall? Will it land on its feet?" Then she has the princess say, "Kitty, don't do such dangerous things." Maartje tells her that the kitty can do extraordinary things. T asks, *"Do you suppose the kitty thinks it can do everything?"* Then she has the princess say, "It makes the princess feel frightened", and she adds, *"Do you suppose the kitty is afraid?"*

Because the child has made it clear in a nonverbal manner that fear is part of it, the therapist can carefully put it into words. Because it involves a play figure and not the child, the child is more accepting, and she can experiment a bit with the affects that have been put into words. In this example, she is encouraged to feel overconfident and fearful.

Maartje

Maartje is playing school. T has made a lot of mistakes. But it is also T's birthday, and she is allowed to choose her favourite colour; the teacher draws a flag and a balloon on the blackboard for her. Maartje looks in T's arithmetic book and tells her that she has all the sums wrong. T says, *"I feel so very unhappy that I made all those mistakes."* Maartje says, "Then you should do it right." T says, *"I don't always manage."* Maartje (putting a good face on it): "You didn't always know the right answer." T: *"I don't like it when I don't know, it makes me awfully unhappy."* (Figure 8.1)

Then the scene is repeated in a slightly different form. Maartje has written down very difficult sums on a sheet of paper, and T is supposed to solve them. T starts by saying, *"I hope I can get them right"*, and later, *"You make it awfully hard, Miss T"*. Maartje responds very gruffly as the teacher, saying, "Get to work! Or else you won't be allowed to go to the party or to go to school any more. Get to

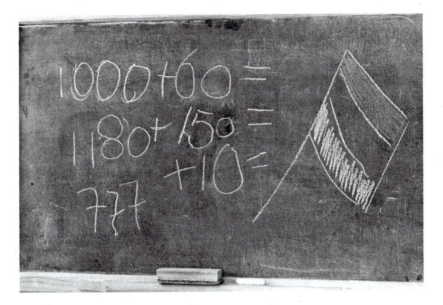

FIGURE 8.1. I feel so very unhappy that I made all those mistakes.

work!!" T does the sums, and Maartje says, "That's good." For her reward, T is allowed to do some drawing.

In the play situation, the therapist is the child who makes the mistakes. She verbalizes the fact that the child feels unhappy when she makes so many mistakes. Maartje does not mention unhappiness in her play, but as the teacher she does show a bit more leniency towards the child who makes mistakes. She has serious problems at school and cannot bear any talk about them. The therapist shows how you might deal with feelings of failure and feeling unhappy about it. This encourages the child to start feeling these feelings, as appears from the fact that she is able to deal with the play situation.

Geert

In a previous session, T and Geert introduced the play figure of Donald Duck as a metaphor for T, who always has to pretend to be the dull, awkward child. Now Geert asks T, "How do you like being Donald Duck?" T says, "Now I can imagine what it must feel like." Geert: "And? How does it feel?" And T says, *"I'm not sure if it is really so very much fun to be Donald Duck."*

The therapist is surprised and relieved that Geert has suddenly asked a question about the therapist and her feelings. It is one of the first times that Geert has asked the therapist a direct question, and straight away it is one about feelings. Apparently the introduction of a play figure was a good idea and a safe one for Geert; in this way, for the first time he can communicate something about an inner experience.

Paul

Paul has started playing darts and suggests a match. For this, they have to find a piece of paper on which to keep score in this room, which is not their usual therapy setting. T: "There you are, we have to hunt around again." Paul: "What a bore. It makes me feel quite horrid ." He refers to the observation room as a secret chamber. T: *". . . like someone is always keeping an eye on you?"* Paul: "Big Brother. . . ." T: "Will you be happy if it stops?!. . . *You're right, it's just like Big Brother.*"

The therapist feels how unpleasant and threatening it is for Paul to be observed. She too feels a bit uneasy when she is in a strange room; it makes her feel somewhat insecure, somewhat uncomfortable. By making use of her own feelings about this, she makes it possible to represent Paul's affect about being watched.

Giving reality value to an affect state of a child

This is about putting into words aspects of behaviour that cannot be discussed openly, usually a feeling or reaction in the course of the session. It involves identifying feelings that a child is perhaps not yet able to name, but which he clearly exhibits. Sometimes a feeling has to be described very concretely, in expressive terms, so that the child can understand it or is able to allow it. When an affect is identified and named, it takes on more reality. It is certainly essential to link it with the child's experience, behaviour, or mood. Therapists are so used to verbalizing affects that they sometimes make too many assumptions, and then they will have missed an opportunity. This intervention will only be successful if it is exactly linked to what the child presents.

Eduard

In a previous session, Eduard made it known that he has a hard time starting a therapy session. He doesn't know what to say; still, he thinks silences are really dreadful. Previously he has started sessions by talking non-stop, telling interminable detailed, technical tales about computer programs and the robot he is making. Now, too, something similar happens, about arithmetic sums in class, and the tops that he collects and swaps with other children. Then he falls silent and does not know what to say; there is nothing in particular to tell. He says, "If something in particular has happened, then it's easy", and then, emphatically and a bit sarcastically, "And I do have to start somehow." He pulls a face and sticks out his tongue. Then T says, *"And you think it's tiresome. . . . I saw it in your face . . . you don't like it one bit."* Eduard laughs and says, "Then I'll just start talking about the tops."

Clearly, Eduard has a fairly easy time accepting this cautious and generalized representation of his affect ("you think it's tiresome"). He can even laugh about it and admit that he is trying to get out of it. In principle, the therapist can now go on to explore with him what happens inside him when he thinks something is tiresome.

Eduard

Eduard tells a complicated story about a file that his cousin ("a loner just like me") had given to his uncle to give to him. This file can do whatever it wants; it can even go against the will of the computer. When Eduard wanted to look at it just before the therapy session, suddenly almost all the software disappeared. "We don't know why." It has all his attention, and he uses it to rationalize. T's intervention: *"It only just happened, it's still foremost in your mind, maybe it gave you a bit of a shock that it all just disappeared"*, proves to be spot on. Eduard falls silent, is calm, and replies, "It did a little."

It seemed as though this was genuine, and intensely felt. Eduard had been babbling. The therapist had felt rendered quite helpless and wanted to linger for a moment on this point, to be able to feel together with Eduard that it was on his mind. Verbalizing a feeling in a concrete and lively, almost expressive manner created room for something of a response.

Eduard

Eduard has been on holiday to the Dutch seacoast with his father. When T asks what it was like, he talks about it indifferently, tells about flying a kite on the beach and watching illegal surfers and stuntmen. Then T asks, "And how did it go, being with your father and his girlfriend and your brother for a whole week?" Eduard: "It was all right, but I really would have liked to go home a little sooner." T: *"Did you miss being at home, was that it, or was it just not really so much fun?"* Eduard says that he missed his mother and couldn't call her because she was on holiday abroad. He could leave a message on her voicemail, but his mother was unable to listen to the message. T asks whether his mother could reach him, and says, "Your Mum didn't know that you just wanted to chat with her", then asks, "What did you miss, exactly? Perhaps that's a difficult question—perhaps you just wanted to know she was there?" Eduard nods.

On the one hand, the therapist tries to investigate Eduard's feeling together with him; on the other hand, he tries to let Eduard see something of his vulnerable feelings (uncertainty, anxiety, feeling alone). Eduard sits quite relaxed and responds positively to the invitation to talk more about feelings and persons; with help, he comes more and more to the point.

Deducing second-order affect representations

Once the child feels sufficiently recognized in his primary affect states, it is time to start working on the deduction of secondary affect representations. Chapter 9, on mentalization, focuses specifically on this. In this section we are talking about a sort of preliminary stage, although in practice it cannot be clearly distinguished from the interventions that come in Chapter 9. This section discusses primarily interventions that focus on containment of a variety of projections. As the sense of being understood increases with this containment, the therapist will sooner be able to make more explicit comments, such as those elaborated in Chapter 9.

Here we look at:

a.   guiding and differentiating affect;

b.   looking for your own share in enactments.

Guiding and differentiating affect

This comes under the heading of "Giving back to the baby the baby's own self" (Winnicott, 1971). These interventions are more complex than giving reality value to inner experiences: they involve a special type of support to the child's "true" or "real" self. By speaking in two different intonations, for example, a dimension of containment is added. The therapist really shares in the feeling, especially in its intensity, and adds an incompatible affect to it, such as comfort or reassurance, thus making it easier to accept the affects.

Maartje

Maartje's playing with the swords is growing in intensity, with shrieking and stamping and hitting hard, when T says, *"We're just pretending, take it easy!"* Then T asks, "Am I wounded?" Maartje says, "I didn't hit you." The game stops, and Maartje goes back to the darts. She starts throwing darts into the linoleum, and T says, *"I don't think that's all right."* Maartje is growing wilder and wilder, and T says, *"Enough."* The dart game stops, and Maartje goes over to the dolls' house. At the end of the session, when T has said three times that they will stop (the first time after 40 minutes have passed), Maartje is so frustrated that, when she goes out the door, she smacks T. To this, T says, *"You're going to smack me just a little, that's how angry you are."*

Maartje grows more and more excited about the darts game; however, her motor skills are not so well developed, and the therapist has to intervene, because otherwise she may literally hurt herself. It is still a game, but just barely: it is on the edge, so it is not easy to decide where the boundary is. But when the boundary is drawn, Maartje responds very well; she accepts it readily in the dart game situation. At the end of the session, when she has to stop, she crosses the boundary and really hits the therapist.

The therapist mirrors her perception and feeling about Maartje, acting like a child who has to hit someone when she feels so angry. The way it is worded also expresses containment of the difficulty this child has in controlling her impulses. The therapist can recognize and acknowledge affect and at the same time give it back in a form that the child can accept more readily.

Maartje

Maartje spilled a bit too much glitter on her card, and she is not happy about this. Disappointed, she says, "Completely spoiled." T says, "It's not exactly the way you planned it." Maartje says, "You're better at it." She swaps their cards; satisfied, she goes on working on T's card. T says, *"Sometimes you have an idea in your head, but it's hard to make it look exactly the way you want it to. You know exactly how you want it to look."*

The therapist has no trouble giving up her nice-looking card to Maartje. She lets it happen. By doing so, she shows that Maartje is the child who is making something pretty, and the therapist is the adult who gives her room to do so. Although the therapist mentions Maartje's feeling of dissatisfaction, she adds something to it: indirectly, she puts the sense of being powerless into words. She does so while not stepping on Maartje's narcissism by not referring to her failure (for example: what a shame, you've spoiled your card), but by naming the competence instead: it's in your head, you know exactly what you want, now all it has to do is come out that way.

Xander

Several times, Xander has given T rather difficult sums with Roman numerals. She has been working on them for a while, and Xander is getting a great deal of enjoyment from this, especially when T has been working for a long time; he says to her, "It's not right, do it over." At a certain point, T asks, "Can I just write something down?" Xander: "No", and he laughs. Then T says, *"Oh, is this supposed to be a bit of a bully game?"* in a tone of voice that is at first surprised, later laughing. Xander laughs even harder and says, "Yes it is."

From the beginning the atmosphere has been one of cheerful excitement, as he enjoys the teasing that he has thought up. There is something euphoric, overactive, about it all, with a lot of running back and forth. The therapist feels tremendously called upon to respond quickly, but has a difficult time finding a moment of peace and quiet for herself. This interaction shows very clearly the somewhat sado-masochistic manner Xander has of making contact, which has been evident for some time. The containment offered by the way in which the therapist makes her intervention will also encourage Xander to recognize his need to bait and badger others.

Looking for your own share in enactments

The child situates his alien self, the non-responsiveness, in the therapist and keeps it there by being manipulative and controlling. This causes the child to feel more coherent and thus better, but it places the therapeutic relationship under great pressure. It is an enactment, because there are no mental contents to speak of. The child is functioning in the equivalent mode, which is to say that his perception of the other is the same as reality: this is how it is. The therapist tries to come into contact with the child's primary perception and confirms that she is aware that this is *reality* from the child's point of view. Because the child actually perceives the therapist as someone who doesn't understand at all, it is helpful to formulate this from the child's perspective. This is, in fact, giving reality value to feelings taken one step further; it is now concentrated on the therapist's feelings, which the child does not understand, from the child's perspective. If the therapist can contain the child's projections, then what takes place in the contact between them can be given a place in the child's mind. This makes the attachment relationship safer, which again supports the child's affective activity.

Paul

Paul immediately starts this session by throwing the darts about wildly. T: "First I am going to hold the darts." Paul protests vehemently. T: "Here, I'm always the one who has to take control of things. I think that you can control things yourself . . . that you are pretty good at that yourself." Paul, cross: "Yeah . . . you bet." He makes it clear that he thinks this is a lot of hogwash and that he can indeed do it himself. In the next few minutes, T makes several attempts to make contact with Paul, which elicit one-sentence replies from him. He is not throwing the darts very well. He becomes crosser and more irritated about the fact that he can't manage to throw them properly. Then Paul says, "If someone's watching me, then I don't do well, or if there's someone around." T responds with empathy: *"So it won't help if I just turn around."* Paul: "No, then I still know you're here. I don't know why that is." T: *"If no one were in the room, you would throw the darts a whole lot better."* Together, they are in agreement: isn't it strange. . . .

Initially Paul responds with anger. And yet he reacts well to the therapist's attempts to translate his inability into something interactive. She actively looks for the aspect of their contact that gives him a sense of failure. The fact that she takes it seriously when he feels like this is valuable to him. A bit later, it even means that he can confide to the therapist what goes on inside him.

Paul

Paul is lying under the sofa. T is sitting on a chair next to it. T asks herself out loud, "I'm just wondering . . . whatever could be the matter." Paul: "Why aren't I allowed to do those things?" T: "That's exactly what's so unclear, isn't it." P: "I think you're tiresome." T: "You think I'm tiresome, yes." Silence. T: "The camera can't see you. You're sick and tired of the camera." P: "Yes." T: "I can imagine. Anyhow, now you've found a place where you can't be seen." Silence. Paul knocks on the bottom of the divan. T: "Hey, someone's knocking." It gets louder and louder, becomes rhythmic. T: "Did that really sound like music, or is it just knocking?" Paul knocks very hard. T: "It's knocking." Paul: "Gosh, you are so annoying." T: "*You think I'm very annoying today. Would you rather that I keep my mouth shut?*" P: "Yes". T: "Okay." This is followed by three minutes of silence. Then the time is up. T: "Was it better that I kept my mouth shut?" P: "Yes." T: "It's not working so well between us today. . . ." P: "No, I'll go downstairs by myself." T: "Aren't I even allowed to come with you . . . ?" They walk down the stairs together.

Because the therapist looks at the interaction from his own perspective, peace descends on the therapist and Paul. It may seem that their contact was broken, but it was not really.

Maartje

Maartje and T are sitting at the table and painting a plaster cast of a dog. At first, Maartje is busy mixing the paint to get just the right colour. T is helping her. When Maartje tells T to squirt a colour onto the dish at the same time she does, T says, "We're really working together, aren't we." After this Maartje becomes a bit commanding, critical, and strict with T. When T wants to stir the paint, Maartje says, "I'll stir." Then T says, "You're the boss of the paint." Then Maartje starts giving T even more commands: "Some white! No, not the right colour, red, red, re–e–e–e–d (impatient, commanding)." T goes along in the game and says, "*Yes boss.*" Then Maartje says, "No" (she means, don't say that). T says, "*I'm not allowed to say it, just do it, is that right? Is that the way you want it?*"

As in previous sessions, Maartje is being bossy, and the therapist is the one who has to carry out her orders. So the therapist is used to being given orders in the course of play, used to carrying them out and being scolded. During play, when she says "yes, boss", this apparently does not tally with Maartje's perception. Perhaps it was too unmodulated, too directly mirrored. Maartje does not feel recognized, and so the therapist says, "I'm not allowed to say it, just to do what you want!" She gives reality value to a feeling in Maartje, who feels misunderstood by the therapist. Because the therapist very seriously placed the child's perspective first and foremost in her representation, contact was restored.

Maartje

Maartje and T are making cars out of clay. T makes a remark about an attractive car, which Maartje—strangely enough—takes to be abusive of horses (her favourite means of transport). Maartje says, "That is name-calling." T says, "You don't like me to call your horses names." T and Maartje go on working. A bit later, T goes back to the name-calling. T says, "*Do you know, I didn't notice that you felt that way about it.*" T and Maartje are still working on the garage for the car. At a certain point Maartje says, "If you decorate something, you can. . . .". T finishes the sentence, "take it home with you." Maartje says, "No." T says, "Here you are, busy thinking about what you can take home with you, so that other kids can't play with it." Maartje does not respond, and so T says, "*Did I guess wrong?*" Maartje says, "No." After this, Maartje says that T is making a nicer garage than hers. T says, "Am I not supposed to?" They swap garages. Maartje becomes very strict with T, and T says, "You are strict with me." "No", says Maartje, "the car is strict with you." T says light-heartedly, "*I'm not listening, that's what you mean, isn't it?*" (Figure 8.2).

When the therapist draws the miscommunication to herself, the child feels that she is understood better. Maartje is tuned in to the idea that another person will not understand her. When the therapist showed that she did understand this feeling of hers—without disqualifying herself—she showed that the child had affective activity of her own, that her "no" could be received. This opens possibilities for further exploration.

In conclusion

In the here and now of the treatment relationship, the therapist can work at the child's level of mental functioning by relating to the child's affects. She gives them reality value and adds a play dimension or an incompatible affect, thus giving the child more scope to discover that his affects exist and can be acknowledged. If the therapist takes responsibility for the affect states externalized by the

FIGURE 8.2.   Do you know, I didn't notice that you felt that way about it.

child, it creates space in which to become familiar with them and to assimilate them. Through this "benign split" (Bateman & Fonagy, 2004) within the therapist, she contains the often vehement affects of the child and gives them back in a digestible form. This is only possible if the therapist allows herself to be borne along in the projective identifications of the child while remaining open to their nature, intensity and colour.

CHAPTER NINE

Intervention techniques: mentalization

Annelies J. E. Verheugt-Pleiter

In discussing what mentalization-based intervention techniques look like, Chapters 7 and 8 were devoted to attention regulation and affect regulation, respectively. This chapter is about interventions that are intended to promote thinking about mental states and mental processes, and about interactive mental processes, with examples of interventions to illustrate the intervention technique.

Introduction

It will be clear that the regulation of affects changes once children have learned to mentalize—that is, when they are able to start from the fact that not only they themselves, but others, too, have an internal world, with feelings, thoughts, and desires. In normal development a child can mentalize reasonably at around age 4, which means that he also uses affects to regulate the self. The most mature form of affect regulation is termed "mentalized affectivity" by Fonagy, Gergely, and colleagues (2002, p. 5). This refers to the capacity to discover the subjective meanings of a person's own affect states. Mentalized affectivity implies the ability to think about your own affects while you are affectively involved, not talking about yourself from a distance. Fonagy, Gergely, and colleagues (2002, p. 435) consider mentalized affectivity to be a form of affect regulation that is particularly important for adults: "Mentalized affectivity is a sophisticated kind of affect regulation that denotes how affects are experienced through the lens of self-reflexivity".

Although this is the highest achievable goal in psychoanalytic work with adults, in working with children this advanced form of affect regulation is not the ultimate goal. As stated previously, non-clinical children just start to develop their ability to mentalize and—relatedly—an "autobiographical self" at around age 4 (Fonagy, Gergely, et al., 2002, p. 245). An autobiographical self refers to the ability to have multiple representations of themselves with a historic causal concept of self integrated into an autobiographical self-representation. Mentalization-based child therapy is focused on getting the child back on its developmental track.

Therapists can help children with a mental process disorder to improve their ability to mentalize and to obtain a representational structure by:

▷ giving their affects and their world of mental equivalence reality value, thus making it a first-order representation (see Chapter 8);

▷ helping them to create second-order representations that are congruent with the first-order representations, which basically gives them the ability to see representations as separate from reality and from others;

▷ helping them to understand the gaps in the self that used to correspond to non-contingent behaviour of the attachment figures and the alien self: "The inability to think about mental states removes the possibility of "narrative smoothing" of the basic gaps in the self-structure, and the alien self emerges in a manner much clearer for the therapist to see and experience" (Fonagy, Gergely, et al., 2002, p. 13).

Not all forms of mentalization have to do with affective experiences, but in a therapy affective experiences are quite central. This chapter discusses interventions intended to encourage thinking about mental states and mental processes. This includes all interventions that attempt to give a representation of internal experiences so that they can be communicated and interpreted. If a child can use mental representations about real inner experiences, we may speak of mentalization, which gives the child an important instrument for self-regulation and for integration of the self in relationships.

This main group of interventions can be divided into three types:

1. comments on mental contents;
2. comments on mental processes;
3. comments on interactive mental processes.

Comments on mental contents

Commenting on mental contents means making remarks on the child's fantasies, thoughts, wishes, or interests. The therapist follows the child and makes comments, thus creating an interactive experience. The therapist helps the child to relate to her in a way that clearly differentiates various aspects of the experience. The focus may be on the problem areas—for example, with a narcissistic child, on the difficulties he has in putting himself in another person's place; or with a child who is unable to think in triads, on the resulting limitations. This would be the case, for example, if the therapist is late, and the child seems to think that the therapist does not like him. Perhaps the idea does not occur to the child that there may be something the matter in the therapist's private life. The therapist then tries to unravel, together with the child, how the child gets the idea that the therapist does not like him by tracing the antecedents of this thought (see Chapter 7). The therapist comments on this mental content, so that the child can think about alternatives. In this way the child acquires more interactive experiences that create or strengthen his ability to structure self.

The following aspects are considered:

a. making comments on mental content in pretend mode;
b. discussing thoughts and feelings with respect to attachment figures;

c. commenting on mental contents of the child;

d. additions of positive content.

Making comments on mental content in pretend mode

Altering the context of play so that playing can take on greater emotional and mental content—for example, helping the child to think about psychological traits of play figures.

Xander

Xander is drawing; he no longer wishes to discuss school with T. He says it's no fun. In his drawing, two people are fighting. First it is good against bad, but pretty soon they both turn out to be bad guys. Suddenly he draws a cannon behind them: it is the good guy's cannon and is a serious threat to both of them. Then T says, *"They don't really see that there is a bigger danger."* (Figure 9.1)

Here the therapist verbalizes a theme that is very important to

FIGURE 9.1.   They don't really see that there is a bigger danger (Xander).

Xander: the theme of feeling threatened and being attacked. In this way the therapist lets him know that she sees it is actually about the whole rather than about the two people fighting. It is likely that Xander identifies himself with the good guys, and the link between threatening and being threatened is represented in this way.

Ivo

Ivo starts to order the play figures belonging to the castle. He calls one of them brave, and one a noble knight; another one he calls Sir Lancelittle. Then T says, "*You're naming different types of men.*" Ivo finds a princess, but he can't do anything with her dress; she doesn't fit on a horse. T gives him a prince, which results in a differentiation between two sons of the king, the elder of whom is worthless and is called "Nobody" and the younger one "Top Dog". The younger one is taken hostage because he is so valuable: he is the one with brains. At a certain point, Ivo asks T if she knows a name for the castle. But when T hesitates, he suggests his own—"Wolfenstein or something like that"—and finally the clever son is given the name "Wolfenstein the second". (Figure 9.2)

Naming was important during this peaceful session. Ivo seems to be busy defining personalities; this was why the therapist was reticent about making up a name. Names stand for character: Nobody, Lancelittle. Ivo is very much occupied with his identity. The intervention underscores the fact that there are different kinds of men, thus implicitly indicating that he can become his own sort of man, can develop his own identity. The therapist encourages him to investigate the differences.

Discussing thoughts and feelings with respect to attachment figures

Discussing thoughts and feelings about the person of the attachment figure and, for example, promoting differentiation between attachment figures also contributes to creating object relations. When the

FIGURE 9.2.   *You're naming different types of men.*

child is able to give more thought to others and what motivates them, mentalization can develop.

Ivo

While playing darts, Ivo introduces the text: "De Cock (famous TV series) and the murder of T." T says, "Goodness, the murder of T, what aggressive fantasies!" "They come from school", says Ivo, and he continues, "That's what you hear there: De Cock and the murder of the Easter Bunny and that sort of thing. I watch police series a lot." A bit later, T asks him, "Do I have 17 or 11?" Apparently she cannot make it out on the dartboard. Ivo more or less harasses her: "What do *you* think; what does it look like?" "It looks the most like a 7", T answers rather timidly. Then it suddenly occurs to Ivo that it's just like his father always says. He always says, what does it look like to you, or something like that. T: "Does he think you're asking just for the sake of asking? Or does he think you're stupid?" "Well, usually both", says Ivo and laughs. T says, "Not really nice, is it?" but there is no reaction.

When playing darts, Ivo throws them so hard that he almost can't pull them out of the board. And so he says, "Now, that is really a world record." Then T responds, *"Now you're being just as sarcastic as your father!"*

It is the first time that Ivo has spontaneously brought up a feeling about his father. He seems to have built up more self-confidence in the therapy. He no longer needs to practise throwing and quickly feels up to a match. So he feels safer, and because of this he can talk about a feeling about his father and about himself as a person who sometimes resembles his father. The therapist can even elaborate this point if he makes another remark along the same lines. Then she can make the statement that he is just as sarcastic as his father. In this way she stresses his affective activity.

Ivo

In the previous session, Ivo had himself observed that he makes certain sarcastic remarks the same way his father does. At the time, his struggle with the dartboard also seemed to have something to do with his relationship with his father. In this session, Ivo once again says, "I act just like my Dad!" He says things like that too, like, "Come on, do it ri–yi–yi–yight!" T asks him, "What do you think of that?" Kind of funny, Ivo replies. *"Which father are you talking about?"* T asks. And Ivo says, "Um, how to put it, my real father." Then T says, *"We talked about your father last time too. About his sarcasm. Who was that about?"* "That was my real father too", says Ivo. "My stepfather doesn't say very much." A bit later, Ivo says to T in a commanding tone of voice, "Throw!" T says, *"You sound just like your Dad!"* And she asks him, *"Is your Dad not easily pleased?"* "Oh sure", says Ivo—then, defiantly, "He's more often pleased than cross."

The therapist thinks it is striking that Ivo does not have specific names for his two fathers. He seems rather undifferentiated in this respect: as if he doesn't want to make a distinction. And so she is pleased that now and then he makes a remark about a father. She tries to differentiate it a bit. Promoting the differentiation between the fathers will also help him to differentiate between himself and others and will hopefully lead to more such questions as, "And who am I, am I just like father number 1, or not? In what ways do I resemble father number 2?"

Eduard

Eduard says that he has been to the eye doctor and the optician for a pair of glasses. T shows that she is interested, both in the glasses themselves—Eduard shows their exact colour via the tops that he has also brought along and has now set out on the table—and in how Eduard feels about having to wear glasses. Eduard says he doesn't know what it will be like to go to school with glasses; he won't know until he does it. But it startles him to see his Dad without glasses; he almost doesn't recognize him. Mum usually wears lenses. Spontaneously, he suddenly says that he is precisely in-between his parents; his Mum got her first glasses at the age of 7, his Dad at 13. Then T says, " *You could say: you're really a lot like your parents.*" "Yes", says Eduard, and goes on with his tops.

Precisely in Eduard's case, this was a very appropriate point for the therapist to let him know, by making a neutral remark, that he does not need to choose between his parents, to be loyal to just one of them, but that he is linked to both of them.

Comments on mental content of the child

In the chapter on affect regulation, a category similar to this one was discussed: giving reality value to inner experiences. That was about putting into words aspects of behaviour that cannot be discussed openly, usually a feeling or reaction in the course of the session. It involved identifying feelings that a child is perhaps not yet able to name, but which he clearly exhibits. Commenting on mental content implies that the feelings are present with reasonable clarity. It is assumed that the child already has certain affect categories. Making comments on the content of what the child shows in the way of affects is intended to strengthen the secondary structure in the form of second-order affect representations. The intervention by the therapist thus makes it possible to look at the primary experience from a different point of view, and to make different attributions to affect representations.

Xander

T is talking with Xander while he is sitting on his throne. He has made a throne in which he can curl up on a pillow. It is an enjoyable conversation. It is about the dog they will get shortly. Last time he had mentioned that they would get a dog. From his answer to the question whether he had helped choose, T gathered that it was the last puppy in the litter; but, he added quickly, it was really the very cuddliest one. To which T said, *"You thought it was the very cuddliest one, did you? It was the last one to be picked, but you think it's the cutest one of all!"* Xander had to laugh in recognition and nod firmly.

However, this exchange also seems to be about his wish to be perceived as the best-liked child. Xander's reaction is one of increasing intimacy. He can't help laughing. He relaxes even more, and a bit later he tells the therapist that he wants to bring the dog along and show it to her. He seems to find it important that people treat his feelings and experiences sensitively and that they remember how he feels.

Geert

T and Geert are still playing Monopoly. Geert had to pay a huge amount on houses and rent, and this obviously occupies his mind. He makes almost no eye contact. He is entirely absorbed in how to get his money back and how to be able to turn over the houses on his streets again. He keeps repeating, "I've turned them all over again." After T's intervention, *"Yes, I could tell you were worried, you were completely occupied with it"*, he sighs deeply. He seems to feel understood and says, "Luckily, I got out of it." The relief is palpable.

The therapist is continually seeking ways to gain access to this child. When talking to this boy, it is difficult to speak in an animated manner or to have lively facial expressions. Because of this, it may be that less of the outside world is mirrored to him, thus increasing his isolation. He seems to assume that no one will understand him anyway. He does not make contact, nor does he seem to expect any. The therapist is always looking for ways to come into contact with him and his experiences. Particularly when a great deal of affect is involved, such as here when he loses a lot of money, Geert shuts himself off completely from the rest of the world.

Additions of positive content

There is no point in asking the child for associations on what is externalized to the therapist. If the child is in a non-mentalizing process, in addition to discovering her own share, the therapist can sometimes also offer different mental content, in this case positive. But it must be related to the child's context. Mentalization presumes a good link between the emotional experience as it is perceived and the attribution of a certain state of mind to be formulated, a secondary affect representation. These interventions only make sense if the child is almost able to uncouple representation from reality. He must almost be able to evaluate an emotion. The therapist will thus try to correct mistaken connections between experience and affect representations and to put forward new affect representations or alternative explanations for rigid views.

Ivo

Once he has practised throwing darts for a bit, Ivo wants to play a match: now he involves T, who is also allowed to throw the darts. His behaviour when she does so is quite remarkable. He holds his arm in front of his eyes, and first of all T asks, "You don't want to watch?" "No", says Ivo, "I'm protecting my own head." Then T says, *"Are you afraid that I'll throw the darts at your head?"* And she adds, *"I don't have such awful feelings towards you!"* When it is her turn again, Ivo takes cover on the sofa, and T verbalizes this as follows: "Are you so frightened? Do you have to take cover?" When the next round comes, Ivo stands behind T, to which T says with a laugh, *"You don't trust me one bit!"*, to which Ivo replies, "That's allowed, isn't it?" T confirms that this "is allowed" and adds, "What's important is how you feel!" "Here I feel safe", says Ivo and continues, "At other times of day. . . ." T says, "Then you feel less safe?" Ivo does not respond to this.

The therapist decides not to suggest a transference interpretation, but in the first place to stress the safety aspect and to palliate: she indicates that she does not have such feelings.

Paul

T and Paul are playing armies. They set up their armies opposite each other. Paul makes some remarks to the effect that T has made a foolish arrangement. T alters her arrangement, saying that she will put his good ideas to use. T: "Now let's see whether my arrangement is any good." Paul, indignantly, "You just copied mine." T: "*It was you who gave me the bright idea to put my soldiers behind barbed wire.*" Shortly afterwards, Paul spontaneously remarks that, when he gets home, he will call a friend to come over and play. He has never before spontaneously said anything like this.

It is becoming increasingly clear that, before she knows it, the therapist will find herself in the role of persecuting bad object. Although their interaction here was not heated or unpleasant, it is evident in the tiniest details. The therapist counteracts the intention attributed to her by labelling it differently.

Xander

Just before the end of the session, Xander's mother brings in the puppy; although it happens fairly suddenly, Xander had said she would come. T is very enthusiastic about the dog and the good bond Xander has with it. Petting the puppy, Xander says, "Yes, you get a little bit frightened when you're at school, with all those kids." T: "Is that right, is he a little bit frightened?" Xander: "Yes, but he's also very popular!" Then T says, "*Maybe it gives you the feeling, that makes me more popular? That you are the popular Xander with the popular dog?*"

Xander made it easy for the therapist to say something about his tendency (at school and in therapy) to create a place for himself using all manner of attributes to improve his sense of self. It shows that the interaction between Xander and the therapist is becoming easier. In a more relaxed manner, they can talk about difficult matters such as school, and Xander can respond not with resistance, but positively, by letting the therapist briefly pet the dog.

Comments on mental processes of the child

This is about things like remembering, forgetting, fantasizing, wanting, and the relations between them. The therapist will help the child to make the links between different affects, themes, and representational areas—for example, the link between loss and aggression or between dependence and withdrawal. In mentalization-based child therapy, the therapist will look for the areas where the child does not make such connections and will encourage the child to do so. The therapist should resist the temptation to explain the link. Once a certain level of affect regulation and mentalization has been achieved, the child can be challenged to see perspectives different from his own, often rigid, views. "Playing with reality" starts to become an option. The timing is important. If the therapist makes such remarks too soon, it may be taken as an attack.

The following aspects are considered:

a. making comments on mental processes of the child such as re-membering, asking, wanting, fantasizing, and making connections;
b. verbalization of wish and/or intention in the pretend mode;
c. verbalization of wish and/or intention of the child;
d. verbalization of thoughts about the mental life of others/objects;
e. stressing the individual character of the child's mental world.

Making comments on mental processes of the child such as remembering, asking, wanting, fantasizing, and making connections

Mentalization acts like a buffer. If the behaviour of others or something that takes place is unexpected or incomprehensible, mentalizing helps us to have more than one hypothesis about what can be the matter. Children who are not good at mentalizing often have the idea that others have bad intentions. The therapist can help them to "play" with reality.

Paul

T and Paul are talking about a dream of Paul's and his fear that this dream could really happen. In the dream, suddenly there was a man on the balcony. This man said a number of things unclearly, including something that sounded like "going to die", and then he fell off the balcony and was dead. Paul woke up in a cold sweat, very frightened, especially because he didn't know whether it had really happened or was just a dream. It was also very frightening that his friend had had exactly the same dream. Paul remained frightened for most of the day—so frightened that he even had to be careful about what he said, because you never know. Because of the way T responds, Paul alters position a bit during their conversation: at first he is firmly convinced that such a dream can really happen, that it is a prediction. Thanks to T's interventions, emphasis comes to lie more on the fear and the effect that fear can have on you: it causes you to doubt, and sometimes makes you think that something might really happen. Paul responds well to this. He even puts forward the example that if you dream a lot about monsters—while you know that there is no such thing—you nevertheless start to doubt and think that they do exist. T lets Paul know she thinks he has put this very well. Together they agree that the hardest part is that you can never be completely certain. T tells him that she sometimes still thinks about it: *"That in fact there are two thoughts side by side in your mind: the one in which you know it's a dream, and the other in which you doubt that and become uncertain because it can seem so very real."*

The therapist feels that there are very many layers in what Paul brings up—fear of losing control, fear on account of the imperfect distinction between "fantasy" and reality, the imperfect distinction between "self" and "other": Paul mentions that a friend of his had exactly the same dream and that this also made him, Paul, very frightened.

Xander

Xander has just been talking about a boy in his class who is mean to him. Suddenly he rediscovers the camera and shouts to the camera that Olivier is very stupid. But at the same time Xander mentions things at which Olivier is better than he is. At a certain point T says, *"Are you perhaps a bit jealous of him?"*

Last time, too, Xander talked about this boy. He perceives him as a threat, and next year they will be in the same class. To make matters worse, he has been assigned to a much higher hockey team than Xander.

Geert

Geert is winning at Monopoly; he is triumphant, but he still keeps a careful watch on the balance in the relationship. He has just acquired a whole street, and he is building hotels. T makes a remark about his "clever plan". Geert: "I would be even stronger if I had eaten some sweets." Initially, T is surprised, doesn't know what this is about. Geert then pulls out a lollipop. Then T says, *"So you're asking me a question?"* Geert nods. T: *"You're asking me if I mind if you eat your sweet?"* Geert sticks the lollipop in his mouth.

The therapist has a strong feeling that Geert does not really believe that another person can keep the contact in place. To the therapist's mind, Geert is very fearful of losing touch with the therapist; a depressive mood then makes itself felt. He seems to overregulate himself at the expense of his relationship with another person. What the therapist in fact did was to translate an implicit sign, or clue, of Geert's into a question in their relationship. It is also a form of modelling: showing how people can get along with each other.

Eduard

Eduard is talking about acting up in class, something that he did not take part in but for which he—and the entire class—was nevertheless punished. He talks about being bullied; he plays it down, saying that it used to happen a lot more, but that it doesn't bother him much now, because it has always been like that, and so on. The therapist says, *"So in fact it has become something completely normal for you . . . it's just part of life . . . but even so, maybe it's still extremely tiresome every time it happens."* Eduard responds to this immediately, "Even if you're used to it, it can still be pretty awful", and he goes on, with much emotion in his voice: "Just like when my little brother acts stupid; he can be a real bore . . . but I'm used to it, you just have to ignore it."

Once more, the therapist tried to bring up his playing down of bullying. Eduard responded surprisingly well. Not only did he immediately agree, he also proffered new material.

Verbalization of wish and/or intention in the pretend mode

Giving words to a wish and/or intention of a fantasy or play figure when it is not yet possible (would be experienced as an intrusion, for example) to link the wish and/or intention to the child.

Maartje

Maartje and T are playing with the four horses (two mothers and two children) in the castle. At Maartje's request, T is playing the two mothers, Sniff and Sniffle, and Maartje is playing the two babies. The babies are locked up in the castle, and they cry and shout for help. The mothers want to save the babies and have to find the key. Then a baby jumps up high in the air and falls. T says in the game, *"Oh my, sometimes they jump just a little too high."* When the baby goes on jumping, T says, *"She really likes to do crazy things sometimes."*

The remark *a little too* (high) is an interpretation of the feeling of excitement that is aroused by doing something dangerous, but it is an interpretation that remains very close to the material. If Maartje can accept this intervention, the therapist can go one step further. She now puts into words the feeling of excitement, into which she also builds in its acceptance: "She really likes to do crazy things sometimes." The therapist refrains from linking this remark to Maartje, who likes to do crazy things and stir things up. The result of the intervention is that, in the game, Maartje lets the babies act very chummy and cheerful, creating a pleasant atmosphere. Because the excitement and the stirring up were accepted, Maartje apparently feels confirmed in her sense of self; in the game, she changes from an excited toddler into a toddler who says, "Me do it myself."

Eduard

T and Eduard are playing Battleships for the first time. They talk about the various types of ships and how easy or hard it is to find them. Eduard says, "You can never hit my submarine, it's so far under water", to which T replies, "*It must defend itself very well like that, when you can hardly see it . . . sometimes people are sort of like that too.*" Eduard goes on talking and ignores this.

The therapist felt that the picture Eduard gave of his submarine fit his own picture of Eduard quite precisely.

Verbalization of wish and/or intention of the child

The therapist puts into words a wish and/or intention of the child that the child does not actually name, but which is present in play or in behaviour, and then links it with another affect or thought.

Maartje

Maartje is sitting at the table with T. In the previous session, Maartje made a dog out of plaster of Paris, and this time she wants to paint it. Maartje has been whispering since they started. Then T asks, "Is something wrong with your voice?" Maartje does not reply, but goes on whispering. Then T says, "*No one can hear you, but I can, can't I*". Maartje says yes and keeps on whispering. After two minutes, she starts to talk in her normal tone of voice and continues to do so for the rest of the session.

At first the therapist is unable to place the whispering, probably because Maartje's voice is somewhat hoarse. But Maartje often speaks in a slightly hoarse voice, probably because she uses her voice incorrectly and does a lot of shrieking. Because Maartje did not reply to the question: "Is there something wrong with your voice?" and continued to whisper, the therapist hit on the idea that her whispering had to do with her wish to exclude the observer and to be alone with the therapist. The therapist decides to say *no one* can hear you, and not *the observer* can't hear you. In this way, she intends to emphasize the fact that it is a wish, and she also sidesteps the problem of Maartje's loyalty to the observer. Like this, she makes it easier for Maartje to express her need to be alone together with the therapist. When the therapist adds, "But I can, can't I", it puts Maartje's wish to be alone with the therapist into words somewhat more explicitly. The fact that the therapist's intervention was correct becomes apparent from what happens after that. Maartje and the therapist work together as a team on the task at hand.

Maartje

Maartje and T are working on the drawing for her father, which is in its final phases. She has said before that it looks like a Christmas drawing. When the drawing is almost finished, T says, *"An especially beautiful drawing for a very special person!"* Maartje says, "You know who it's for? For someone who can ride horseback without a saddle!" T says, *"You'd like to see him at Christmas?"* Maartje says, "No I wouldn't", and immediately gets up and starts talking with the observer through the screen window. Then T says, *"Sometimes you want to talk with someone else, and then I just don't understand you properly, do I?"* (Figure 9.3).

The therapist assumes that Maartje's relationship with her father is of a highly wishful nature. The therapist is cautious about giving her interpretation that Maartje would like to see her father and paves the way for it by first saying that the drawing is for a special person. What probably also plays a role is the fact that Maartje did not get a present from her father for St Nicholas, and so she did not want to talk about St Nicholas's Day. The therapist senses very strongly Maartje's vulnerability in her feeling for her father, and so she manoeuvres with great care. By using the word "special", the therapist

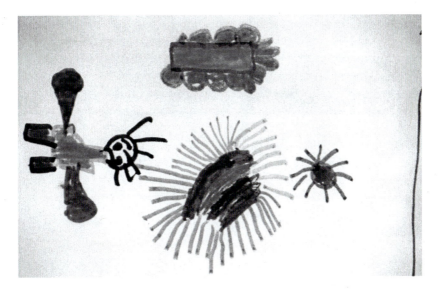

FIGURE 9.3.   A special drawing for a very special person! (Maartje)

intends to evoke Maartje's feeling of love for her father, and this is quite successful. After this the therapist can verbalize her feeling of loss in the form of her wish to see her father at Christmas.

Maartje

Maartje and T are busy making a Christmas tree. She comes back to the theme of wanting to take things home with her. Maartje asks if she can take the Christmas tree home. She says, "I put my hand up first." She says, "Let's use everything up." T finishes the sentence: "So that there's nothing left for other children." Maartje says, "They won't play with it anyway." Maartje thinks that she can make a top for the Christmas tree out of clay, and then she can take both the pipe cleaners and the clay home (which isn't allowed). Maartje says, "Everything that is on this tree you can take home with you." Then T says, *"You want to take something home with you, and you don't want other children to play with it."* And a bit later, T says, *"Then you'd have things at home from the therapy; you'd like that."*

The therapist does not directly refer to acquiring the therapist's love or the jealousy of the other children in therapy. She stays very close to Maartje's actions in the therapy and links them to an intention, giving Maartje some insight. It is worthy of note that the therapist does not use the word *because* between "You want to take something home with you" and "You don't want other children to play with it." This has to do both with Maartje's cognitive abilities and with her emotional ones. By splitting up the reasoning into smaller pieces, it becomes digestible for Maartje. In the end, the therapist nevertheless arrives where she wants to be, which is the wish: to have things from the therapy at home. By not saying that Maartje would then also have the therapist at home, she leaves room for Maartje to colour in this feeling herself.

Verbalization of thoughts about the mental life of others/objects

The therapist mentalizes about things in relation to the inner life of others, people the child talks about and who apparently have significance for the child. They may also be fantasy figures. This can be an important intermediate step in discovering their meaning for the child, and it also helps the child learn to put himself in another's place.

Xander

T and Xander are talking to each other, with the toy dog between them. They are talking about the dog that has just come to live with Xander, a young puppy that needs a great deal of care. After hearing his account, T says, "*It makes me think that Mum has just as much work with it as with a little baby.*" Xander responds, "It is a little baby. The dog acts just like a baby; you know, it doesn't finish its dinner." And that while Xander always has to clean his plate.

The arrival of the dog makes it easy for the therapist to take a preparatory step towards the moment when Xander's problems started: the birth of his younger brother. Moreover, the therapist really has the impression that it almost seems as if a fourth child has joined the family instead of a dog. It is an important subject for Xander, the fact that his mother's care goes to another person or thing.

Xander

In the therapy, Xander talks about using poison to defend the shack against the other children. At a certain point, T says, *"Are you all agreed about your choice of weapons (poison)? Or do the other children have other ideas about weapons?"* Once again, Xander replies from the point of view of his perception of the poison: it's the best weapon, any way you look at it.

In this way, the therapist shows indirectly that there is another world apart from Xander's, to whom poison is clearly the best and deadliest of weapons. But he doesn't ask himself how other children see it. By saying: "The meaning of poison is very strong in your world, but there are other possible worlds", she seems to be making a suggestion to Xander. As so often, Xander just rattles on in his own fantasy world. He is completely convinced that he and the other shack dwellers are invincible thanks to the good poison and the antitoxin that he has invented. Because the therapist suspects that he will have misunderstandings with both friend and foe on this account, she tries to find out whether he has any idea of how the other children feel about it. The interventions and their contact have so far been focused on what took place in his inner world within the therapy, but now the inner world of others takes on meaning because of the therapist.

Eduard

Eduard is talking some more about the tops. They have been banned at school because there was too much rowing about them. Then T says, *"There's a saying: Trading, here today and gone tomorrow."* At first, Eduard seems to ignore T's remark, but he comes back to it later, and this leads to a discussion of how younger children are more likely to regret a trade and cry than older ones, but that at school you need to have a general rule that applies to everyone.

Quoting a saying has a playful aspect, and it is less confrontational; together, you can try to figure out why people come up with such sayings. This is very important, particularly for a boy who rationalizes, like Eduard.

Eduard

Eduard first says that he has been ill all week. It was boring. He is acting a little standoffish, perhaps a bit cocky. After ten minutes, he wants to show something: tiny tops, very "in" at school at the moment. He talks about trading them. Some children, he scoffs, trade two or even three tops for one. He always trades one for one. Then T says, *"Other children apparently have a different system, and they think the blue ones are worth more than the orange ones"*, to which Eduard replies, "If you ask me, it's completely daft, but I take advantage of it."

The therapist felt some irritation and wanted to point out to Eduard that his manner of trading, which he considers to be better and cleverer, is also the reason that he is so isolated. Here, Eduard's rigidity is crystal-clear; he is completely unable to imagine that tops might have a different value in the eyes of other children. The therapist makes an attempt to get him to think about other children.

Stressing the individual character of the child's mental world

Stressing the fact that a child can do things, want things, and invent things himself, can be his own and independent person—indeed, the therapist is often focused on confirming the child's self—for example, with affect regulation—but the difference here is that the therapist can also do this very explicitly.

Eduard

Eduard has started to play with the tops; he is explaining all about them to T: the various names, their purpose, the series. He shows the series he is saving together with his younger brother. He talks with a certain enthusiasm; he wants T to come into the closet and look at the tops that glow in the dark. This is the first time that he has moved freely about the playroom. Later he sits and plays, very relaxed; he includes T in it, explains. At a certain point, he says, "Maybe it will stay fun" with the tops. To which T replies, *"One reason it's so much fun is that you keep on thinking up new things."*

The therapist wants to stress the fact that the boy has an active part in making play fun and keeping it fun, that the creativity comes from within him, and that he does not need to feel dependent on another person's initiative.

Comments on interactive mental processes

This revolves around interventions such as: "You think I didn't notice that you were laughing at me." These interventions move in the direction of reciprocity in the contact. The objective of therapy is for the child to learn to communicate instinctively. Communicating affects also implies that a feeling is expressed, and that this goes along with an expectation of how the other person will receive it. This reciprocity, and the ability to reflect about it, is the goal. Ultimately the objective is "mentalized affectivity" (Fonagy, Gergely, et al., 2002), but for many children this will probably only be possible once they have matured cognitively during adolescence.

The therapist offers himself as a development object. He will try to discover what significance he has (whether as a transference object or otherwise) in the child's life. Is he seen as a differentiated person or as an extension of the child? If the therapist knows something about this, he can usefully communicate about it. If the child becomes entangled in his own associations, he helps by saying, "I've lost the thread", thus inviting the child to differentiate actively. When children cannot differentiate the therapist from their parents, they are not yet ready to explore dynamic contents (Greenspan, 1997). First the structural basis needs to be strengthened. Because the transference is usually a fairly undifferentiated experience but does have great intensity, there is a lot that can be learned here. The various patterns of relationships come clearly into focus and can be investigated. If the therapist is truly neutral, the child can give up old patterns and start practising with new ones. Structure is thus formed not by resolving conflicts, but by learning on the basis of the present relationship (Greenspan, 1997). At the same time, it can at times be better to work "in displacement" because of the fact that the therapeutic relationship triggers the disorganized attachment system. Too much proximity can be too disturbing, whereas too much distance can give the impression of indifference. In play there are usually a lot of possibilities to work "in displacement ".

Ivo

While playing darts, Ivo was being quite coercive. He threw the darts in a particular way, and T had to do the same. She went along in this, in the meantime verbalizing that they had to do it his way and that she found this difficult to do. Then T gets a high score on the dartboard. Ivo whistles in admiration and tells her to throw the next dart the other way. Indeed, the next dart misses. Then T says, *"You got exactly what you asked for."* Ivo says that other people seem to find this a problem too. Then T asks, *"Who would that be?"* "Oh", says Ivo, "my parents." T: *"Do they give you exactly what you ask for?"* "Sometimes", says Ivo. T: *"Oh yes? How then?"* But then Ivo has had enough. He goes back to fiddling with the darts in the dartboard.

Twice Ivo makes a spontaneous remark about his parents. This is unusual. The parent counsellor informs his colleagues that there has been a big change in the relationship at home. Ivo is suddenly interested in his parents. He asks them how their day was, whether they slept well. And his contact with his stepfather in particular is warm and cordial. In the therapy, he is now quieter, and he draws a distinction between his fathers. The therapist can clearly feel that he does not yet give her much room to say anything about it. He can accept it only briefly, but it is better than nothing, and he is also developing something of a sense of humour. Now that his need for love and understanding has become evident (presumably along with a lot of anger about what he has not had), the way he is indulged and pampered can be discussed. More inner structure seems to be emerging, allowing him to differentiate more clearly between love and permissiveness.

Xander

Throughout the session, Xander is very active and tears around the room. He keeps looking at T with a questioning look. He continuously makes jokes, and the session is not very peaceful. *"It's as if you have no idea of what you want from me today"*; "you want to make me laugh". Xander: "No." "You want to tease me?" Xander: "No." "I can't really think of anything else." Xander: "That's odd." T: *"Maybe you can help me? You know best how you feel?"*

In this intervention, the therapist states her own thoughts about Xander. Both for herself and for him, the therapist tries to get a grip on the atmosphere, which is one of cheerful, pesky excitement and his activity, his tearing around, running out the room. She is mentalizing about him, and she makes it clear that she does not know what he is thinking. Their relationship is one in which Xander can freely indicate what he wants, and so he says, "No, no!", implicitly confirming that he does, indeed have a mind of his own.

Xander

Xander is still teasing, and each time he laughs in T's face. He is having great fun and tells her she's stupid. Then T says, *"You really enjoy taking the mickey out of me. You like me, but you show it by being mischievous."* After the intervention, Xander's hilarity fades, and some more serious material is forthcoming.

This merriment has been going on for quite some time; it doesn't seem to change. Obviously, it includes several dimensions, and at this point the therapist perceives it primarily as Xander's not really knowing how to deal with the intimacy and the positive feelings. The fact that they are able to talk about positive feelings, and especially the way in which Xander shows it, is positive. The mischief is very clearly present.

Geert

Geert is concentrating on controlling the situation and the game. The game gives him something to concentrate on. At the same time, it allows him to avoid contact, as it apparently makes him very anxious. He is very much occupied with keeping his contact with T in equilibrium. One way he does this, when it looks as if T will get less money and he will get more, is by giving money to T. Once more, Geert wins some money and once more, he gives money to T. Then T says, "*You embarrass me like this. . . .*" Geert says, "I have plenty, you know." T: "Then it's easy for you to share?" Geert says, "Yes." T: "Or do you feel sorry for me?" Geert: "No." Then T says, "*You're really keeping an eye on how things are going with me.*"

The therapist tries to bring their contact to a different level without causing tension to rise. The comments on what the child thinks about the therapist can encourage him to mentalize.

Maartje

Maartje and T are sitting at a low table and have gone back to painting the Indian. Maartje again gives T the role of the helper: Maartje is the one who gives the orders. She says, "I'll tell you what to do", or "Get some water", and then immediately after this "More water!" and "Throw this water out." The role ascribed to T, that of the helper who is commanded, has been brought up several times. When T has brought Maartje fresh water, she is immediately sent off in a stern tone to get more water; T giggles, saying in a disbelieving voice, "*Really?*" And later, "*It certainly makes things easy when you have a helper.*" She elaborates the contents of her helping, first by saying, "*I'm at your beck and call!*" With her intervention "*Pretty nice, isn't it, that I do everything you ask*", T summarizes what went before. For Maartje this is reason to say, "My sister never does that." T picks up on Maartje's sense of injury: after Maartje has barked a few more commands at her, T says, "*Your sister ought to do that too, she ought to be at your beck and call too!*", which Maartje confirms in full. She says that her sister doesn't do anything for her, while she does something for her sister if she asks her to.

T expresses the intensity of Maartje's controlling behaviour in her reaction: "Really?" With the word "easy" in the intervention "It certainly makes things easy when you have a helper", the therapist indicates that she accepts the role of helper. Implicit in this remark

is that Maartje cannot wait, but the therapist does not put this negative aspect into words. She simply says that Maartje enjoys being
helped. This is the first time that Maartje has made a reference to a
person in her family—in this case, her sister. The result of verbalizing the feelings expressed towards the therapist by Maartje in
her playing is that the therapist can finally make an intervention in
which Maartje's relationship with an important person (her sister)
can be commented on.

In conclusion

In this chapter we have discussed the interventions that are meant to
encourage mentalization. Mentalizing can be regarded as the creation
of a representational structure to understand, within an attachment
relationship, what can take place between people in the way of communication and miscommunication. Mentalizing interventions are
only useful if there is first a foundation of attention regulation and
affect regulation. The therapist must be able to meet the child's level
of mental functioning. In the here and now of a new attachment relationship, the therapist can offer a form of containment for whatever
comes up in their contact. The therapist will encourage mentalization
by mirroring the child's mental states and processes in a manner that
is contingent, congruent, and marked (see Chapter 2).

One disadvantage of the material we have collected (see Chapter
6) is that it comes largely from therapies in the early phases. For
this reason, it is possible that we made more interventions in the
categories of attention regulation and affect regulation. On the other
hand, every therapy always involves a blend of several levels. Some
children can mentalize better than others at the start of therapy. And
every child can revert to an earlier manner of mental functioning in
a certain area.

It may be important to clarify here that I am not necessarily describing stages or phases of linear development. Instead, what I
am suggesting is that there are cycles that can be detected within
a given session or a particular segment of an analysis, related
to the working through of certain pathological constellations or
states of mind, and leading into the development of the capacity

to experience and to think about specific situations as they arise. [Mitrani, 2001, p. 1102]

As described in Chapter 4, the process always takes precedence over the technique. Once a child can mentalize and is capable of interpretative self-regulation, in principle he has the capacity to postpone, modulate, and regulate emotional reactions and also has a coherent sense of self with a feeling of agency. Having mental representations of oneself and of others generates a subjective conviction that a person's behaviour belongs to that person, in contrast to the passive feeling derived from prescribed procedures that are activated by concrete, context-dependent cues. Behaviour is no longer something that comes over a child: the child is its owner (Bleiberg, 2001, p. 49). The coherency and organization that a child then has makes it possible to tell autobiographical stories.

CHAPTER TEN

Treatment in practice

Froukje M. E. Slijper

A number of elements in the practice of mentalization-based child therapy require specific attention. This chapter discusses the practical aspects of treatment and the practical agreements to be made. This refers to becoming acquainted with the treatment and the setting—for instance, the frequency, the therapy room, and the toys and play material available. The various stages of treatment are described as well. What can you expect at the end of mentalization-based child therapy?

Introduction

Mentalization-based child therapy is not possible unless the parents also receive guidance (see Chapter 5). If the child's therapy is to progress and be successful, it is important that the parents support the treatment. They are asked to make a considerable investment: they need to take part in parent guidance, they will have to bring the child to therapy and pick the child up afterwards, they need to motivate the child and offer support. Parents have a certain perception of their child, their own feelings about the child, and a more or less fixed reaction pattern to this. Moreover, parents may have several very different perceptions of their child. This is often clearly the case with divorced parents. First and foremost, it is necessary that the parent counsellor and the child's therapist reach agreement, together with the parents, both about the child's issues and about the objective of treatment. Unless both parents support the treatment, there is no point in starting. A child must be able to feel that she has the permission of both parents to entrust herself to the therapist. If this is not the case, the child will intentionally or unintentionally be burdened with a conflict, which often expresses itself in loyalty problems. Divorced parents often use their disagreement with respect to their child's needs assessment to fight their own feuds. It is sometimes helpful to work with the parents, together or separately, to make them aware of this and able to talk about it.

It is important that parents become acquainted with their child's therapist, that they can ask questions and tell the therapist about their doubts and fears so that further work can be done on this in the parent guidance sessions. The first step is a meeting of the parents with the parent counsellor and the child therapist at which the latter explain mentalization-based child therapy. Parents have many questions, one of which is always how long the therapy will take. Only a rough estimate can be made of this aspect. It is important that the parents agree to the frequency of treatment. It is certainly not easy, either in an emotional or in a practical sense, to entrust a child to another person one or more times a week. In this meeting with the parents, it is also advisable to talk about the fact that whatever the child discusses with the therapist is confidential, and how they should respond if the child shows resistance to the therapy.

Children with a disorder in their ability to mentalize need certainty and continuity. To achieve this, firm agreements must be made with the parents about the more practical aspects of the therapy such as payment, the length of a therapy session (45 minutes), how to deal with holidays and illness, and how the child will be returned to the parents. When it comes to informing a child about the proposed therapy, parents are the obvious choice. If they do so, the child knows that they stand behind it emotionally. So parents need to know how to go about this, and for this they will need the formulations of the therapist.

Finally, the child must also have a chance to meet the therapist to hear why he will undergo therapy and what the therapy involves. Although most parents inform their child adequately, it is better not to simply assume that this is the case. The child also needs to be informed of the practical agreements and be given a voice in deciding on suitable appointment times. Some children prefer to go to therapy after school, because they are not yet ready to tell their classmates that they are in therapy. They may find it shameful, but they may also simply not want to be different. Some children do not want to go to therapy at times when they would usually play with friends.

The setting

Frequency

Mentalization-based child therapy is an entirely new field of treatment, and there is as yet no international agreement about the indicated frequency. If treatment advice points to mentalization-based child therapy, this means children who primarily have difficulty with attachment issues, and so a high frequency is needed to be able to work on their disturbed manner of forming relationships. The therapist will act as a new attachment object. However, another problem is that some of these children have such difficulty in regulating their anxiety and anger that they soon become overwhelmed by this new relationship. These children respond better if therapy starts with less frequent sessions—for example, once a week—which are gradually stepped up, based on what the child can cope with.

Therapy room, toys

The setting must make it possible for a child to feel safe and comfortable. This physical aspect is part of the holding that the therapist must be able to offer (Sandler, 2004; Sandler, Kennedy, & Tyson, 1980). Children with a disorder in their ability to mentalize can be very inhibited and withdrawn, but they can also be impulsive and may quickly become uninhibited. In general, they are children who soon feel anxious. The therapy room must not be so big that a child feels lost in it. It must be furnished in a child-friendly manner, and be neither too personal nor too neutral. If the room is too personal—for instance, with products made by other children, or pictures of the therapist's children, on display—it can evoke anxiety or feelings of rivalry. But a room that is too impersonal can also evoke anxiety: something of the style and the person of the therapist must be there in the room for the child to find. The carpet and the upholstery must be suitable for heavy-duty play, spills and other accidents, playing ball games, and other such activities. If the therapist is too concerned about the furnishings, this can have an inhibiting effect on the child's expression of feelings.

Children must have the feeling that what they show about themselves in the therapy remains between themselves and the therapist, which means it is important that the room is sufficiently soundproof. Noises from outside that can be heard in the therapy room, such as a screaming child or a person making a telephone call in the hall-way, can sometimes be frightening for a child. The waiting room for the parents and for brothers or sisters who come along must be far enough from the playroom to give the child a sense of privacy.

The time children spend sitting in the waiting room waiting for the therapist to arrive is a difficult time, particularly for impulsive children (Slijper, 1998). They are often extremely active and rowdy, and when the therapist comes, they may run off or hide. Parents often have no idea of how to react. Are they supposed to run after the child and correct him, or is this up to the therapist? In such a situation they often feel the implicit criticism of the therapist, which causes them to be either too lenient or overly strict. It is important to make firm agreements with the parents about how to deal with this: that their responsibility ends only when the child is walking to the therapy room with the therapist.

Playing

The room must make it possible for the child to sit down and talk or to play. In mentalization-based child therapy, play is not an end but a means—a means of communication, but also a means to en-courage the pretend mode. This means that the toys must stimulate imaginative play: puppets, a doll's house, Play Mobil people, animals, coloured pencils, drawing paper, clay, materials for painting, cutting, pasting, and so on. However, children with a disorder in the autistic spectrum will often need more cognitively oriented things to play with such as board games, because they are not yet ready for imaginative play at the start of their therapy. But then, too, a game is primarily used by the therapist as a means of communication, as will be clear from the following example.

Ivo

Ivo is a 12-year-old boy with narcissistic problems. In the early phases of the therapy, he has a hard time losing at board games, and T needs to spare his sense of self by offering him the opportunity to correct himself. For example, she says, "Do you really want to make that move?" As this helps Ivo start to feel more certain, he begins attacking and pursues T relentlessly in the game; when he wins, he gloats over his triumph. T shows him what losing does to her feelings. For example, she says despairingly, "Oh no, I lost another piece", or "Sniff, sniff, another one bites the dust."

By thus dramatizing, the pretend nature of the game is stressed, which makes it clear that the therapist is not really upset. The pretend nature inspires Ivo to show something more of his own feelings. In this way reciprocity is built into the relationship, as is pleasure in the activity.

The first therapy session

A child who starts therapy has first undergone an assessment to determine his specific needs. Often the person who does the assessment is not the same person as the therapist. This means that the child is confronted with different people, which can evoke feelings of anxiety, distrust, anger, or distress. Children who are not good at mentalizing are unable to name these feelings because they still largely function in the equivalent mode. The therapist will have to reassure the child by making an intervention in which the physical experience of the situation here and now is foremost. For example, in the first therapy session, the therapist can say to a child who sits down hesitantly, "You're used to a completely different chair, but how does this one feel?" With this, the therapist wants to indicate that the child has emotions about the therapist and that he will need to become accustomed to the therapist and the new situation.

Moreover, the assessment setting is more structured, which also makes it different from the therapy setting, which is less restricted. Children in mentalization-based child therapy often have difficulty making such a switch. For some children, such as those with Asperger's syndrome, the assessment situation offers more to go on. So it is important to discuss the newness of the therapy setting with the child. But sometimes the transition from structured to less restricted will have to be more gradual—for example, by going back to activities the child carried out during the assessment. Drawing together or playing a board game may also be good alternatives.

At the start of the therapy, the therapist and the child have to become acquainted, and there will be exploration on both sides. Some children plunge eagerly into therapy; for them, the beginning is a sort of honeymoon phase. For others, starting out evokes much tension and anxiety; for them, the beginning is awkward, and they do much testing and sounding out. Narcissistic children may try to maintain their omnipotent feelings by presenting themselves with great bravado as children who need no one, who can do it all by themselves, and who always know better. But they can also present themselves as pleasant, clever children who understand everything and who seemingly show good cooperation and much insight. But all children approach the therapist with their own mental picture of their parents as a guide. The picture may be one of incapable, unreliable, or inconsistent parents with whom the child has learned to deal by relying solely on his own strength, so as to retain an illusion of control and interpersonal relations. We see an example of this in Maartje, a 7-year-old girl who, playing in her first therapy session, barks out orders to the therapist in a loud, commanding voice and sometimes even shrieks. She simply assumes that the therapist will not listen to her and will not do what she asks, so she will have to coerce compliance. We see another example in Ivo, who projects the picture of his intrusive, overprotective mother on the therapist when, in his first session, he stands in front of the games cupboard and asks the therapist, "What game do you think I want to play?"

The initial stages

Mentalization-based child therapy starts from the assumption that a child has insufficient mentalizing ability to allow feelings to be named, let alone interpreted (Fonagy, Gergely, et al., 2002). This type of therapy is intended to improve mentalization and build bridges between affects and their representations so as to arrive at better affect regulation and finally at a better attachment representation. The therapy works with existing mental states, and consideration is given to the child's deficiencies. Mentalization-based child therapy works with a hierarchy of interventions, from attention regulation to affect regulation and, finally, to mentalization (see Chapters 7, 8, and 9). This should not be taken as a recipe: it must become clear in the relationship what is at stake for the child (see further Chapter 4). The therapist will gear her interventions to the seriousness of the disorder in the child's ability to mentalize. This means that if the disorder is serious and the child functions in equivalent mode, the therapist will start with the first step in the hierarchy: interventions to regulate attention. If the child has a certain degree of mentalizing ability, then in addition to attention-regulating interventions, interventions can also be made to regulate affect. However, the child's level of mentalization is not always clear; it can shift a great deal in a single session, depending on the affects that are addressed. The child's ability can also be affected by the tension of the beginning of therapy, and thus remain low throughout an entire session. The reverse is also possible: as a result of vehement emotions that develop later in therapy, a child who initially seemed able to handle interventions of a high level may revert to lower levels.

The therapeutic relationship

Throughout the therapy, in the course of each session the therapist will constantly need to adapt her interventions to what the child can handle. In any case, it is a prerequisite that the therapist creates an affectively safe climate in which feelings can be explored, expressed, and experienced so that a therapeutic relationship can develop. Offering holding and support is important in this. From the beginning, the therapist will communicate to the child the fact that she is interested in the child's inner world. We see this in the previous example from Ivo's first therapy session, when the therapist makes it clear that she would like to know which game Ivo has in mind. She says, "Can I guess, do I know you well enough for that?" Laughing, he says, "Why don't you just try." She says, "You need to tell me something about yourself; I can't see inside your head." In this way she tries to focus his attention on his own mentalizing, but also on hers.

The therapist can use various intervention techniques to make it clear that she is concentrating on the child's inner world. There are, for instance, attention-regulating interventions in which contact is maintained with the child during play without naming a behaviour or the feeling—for example, describing what the therapist sees ("I see the kitty falling") or taking part by proffering toys ("Is this the kitty you were looking for?"). Another possibility is nonverbal mirroring: by means of posture, facial expressions, and intonation, the therapist magnifies feelings or slows them down to mirror enthusiasm, pleasure, or disappointment. We saw the latter in the example with Ivo, when the therapist mirrors her feelings when she loses.

The therapist can also introduce her own person a bit more by saying, "I understand that you are saying . . .—is that right?" or "Do I understand you correctly; you said . . . didn't you?" Meting out understanding and feeling for the child and gearing this to what the child can handle is essential. Seeking a balance between showing too much empathy, which could cause the child to feel overwhelmed, and too little, which could cause the child to feel rejected or left out in the cold, is a process of constant adjustment. If the therapist shows too much empathy, a child's concealed vulnerabilities can come to the fore too quickly, thus overwhelming the child (Bleiberg, 2001). But showing too little empathy can give the child a sense of desperation and strengthen his belief that the relationship with the therapist leads to pain and frustration. In the beginning, the child will show undifferentiated feelings; then holding and containment are important.

A therapeutic relationship is starting to develop if the child can use the therapist as an audience for what he knows, or is able to do. For example, if a child says, "Do you know, I've got a book about planets and you have Mars and Venus. . . ." The therapeutic relationship has evolved if the child is able to let the therapist share in his experiences. We can see this in play situations—for example, if the child can allow the therapist to join in the playing, and the therapist no longer needs to adhere to a script rigidly prescribed by the child.

Midway

Transference, development object, and countertransference

According to Bateman and Fonagy (2004), the therapist needs to maintain a "mentalizing stance" in order to develop a person's ability to mentalize. By this, they mean that the therapist must be able to ask herself continually which mental states, both in the child and in the therapist, can explain what is happening. For example: why does the child say this now, why is the child behaving like this; but also, why do I feel the way I do, what has happened recently in the therapy or in our relationship that can account for the present state? Since the child is not yet able to perceive the therapist as a person with wishes, desires, thoughts, and motives, the child does not experience the therapist as a real person. In the relationship with the child, the therapist serves as a development object—an object that mentalizes about the child and in this way attempts to arouse mentalization in the child. Transference is seen not as a manifestation of unconscious mental forces, but as the coming forward of latent meanings and beliefs aroused by the vehemence of the therapeutic relationship. Bateman and Fonagy (2004) say that transference is a means by which the inner drama is "played out" in the therapy. It is a new experience, and although it is influenced by the past, it does not repeat it. The therapist must create conditions in the therapy to allow the transference to develop. An important prerequisite is containment of both the positive and the negative feelings. Many beginning therapists find it difficult to realize that they are important for a child, and because of their reticence towards the positive feelings expressed by the child, they may try to hold the transference in check. Some also find the negative transference difficult to accept, so that they tend to suppress expressions of anger and destruction.

In mentalization-based child therapy, the countertransference feelings are also seen as broader, as empathic answers that arise as the therapist moves along with the child. However, mental representations of relationships from the therapist's past can also play a role. For example, the child can evoke feelings in the therapist that belong with a deceased younger brother of whom she was very fond, so that the therapist starts to idealize the child. It is important that the therapist is aware of feelings of countertransference; her personal therapy and supervision can be helpful in this respect. Entering into a therapeutic relationship evokes anxiety in the child and a tendency to withdraw into a coercive, non-reflective manner of functioning. This can also affect the therapist's ability to mentalize. We see this, for example, in therapists who compete with the parents of the child and who appoint themselves as the child's saviour. But conversely, we also sometimes see therapists become the parents' saviours, wanting to protect them from the aggressive or destructive behaviour of their child.

A difficult aspect of the treatment is dealing with projective identification. The child can ascribe to the therapist feelings that the therapist does not have (projective identification) but that do affect him or her very directly, thus endangering the therapist's own mentalization. It is then important to be able to work with a benign split between the role imposed on the therapist and her mentalization about it.

Setting boundaries

Views on the rule of abstinence—not imposing standards or values and not simply giving in to the needs of the child—no longer apply in classical psychoanalytic therapy, in psychoanalysis, or in mentalization-based child therapy. However, the reasoning behind this rule is still important: in a therapy, it is not advisable to satisfy the child's wishes, because this makes it impossible to talk about them and, more particularly, to feel them. However, satisfaction of needs is often part of the way we normally deal with children. For example, when a child is thirsty and has just arrived from a long journey or has just come home from school, it is common practice to give the child something to drink; but if a child who lives just around the corner is always asking for a drink, it is better to find out about the feelings and fantasies underlying this need before complying with it (Slijper, 2001). However, it is important to keep an eye on whether the child is able to accept the frustration of not getting a drink and to deal with the fantasies. If a child who has a poor ability to mentalize lives very close by and is always thirsty, he may see the withholding of a drink as a direct rejection, because he is still functioning in equivalent mode. In such a case, the need should be complied with, but an intervention can be linked to it, along the lines of making interaction explicit: "Every time you're here, you want me to give you something to drink." With this the child's attention is focused on his own desire, but also on the therapist's intention. So it involves making a accurate estimate of what will and what will not be fruitful in a therapeutic sense, in which good timing and attunement to the child's capacities are essential aspects. Setting boundaries is only necessary if the child seems to challenge the rules of the therapy in order to avoid too much anxiety.

A good example of how the therapist's thinking can be clouded by vehement emotions in the child is the example of 6-year-old Maartje, who gives a great many conflicting orders to her therapist (Deben-Mager & Verheugt-Pleiter, 2004, p. 27). When the therapist says, "You know, I really can't keep it up, I'm confused; I really try to do what you want, but I just can't manage", the child relaxes. Then the therapist can say, "It seems like we are both afraid of losing each other." By using the benign split between feelings of the child and of herself, the therapist is again able to mentalize.

Interruptions

For children who have difficulty with mentalizing, interruptions, even in the form of having to end the session, are often difficult to accept, because when the therapist is no longer there, the child has the feeling that there is no longer anyone to give words to his experiences. Anxiety is often expressed in the form of anger. It is only possible to put both anxiety and anger into words if the child is able to mentalize. Until this level has been achieved, if such feelings are named, it only thrusts them upon the child and encourages the development of the alien self. Mentalization-based child therapy is intended to emphasize the reality value of the child's feelings, whether they are anxiety, anger, or sadness (missing something). Even using the least threatening form—"You probably missed coming here for these sessions"—the therapist can do quite some damage.

Shifting the level of interventions

Midway through the therapy, more and more affect-regulating interventions will be made. Initially, this means giving reality value to primary affect states (see Chapter 8). This is because affects of the child in the form of sensations from within have not been adequately mirrored by the parents. Too often, parents will have mirrored affects together with their own affects, so that the child no longer knows what feeling is his own and what belongs to another person. It is of great importance that the therapist does not make the same mistake in the therapy by putting forward her own feelings instead of the child's. The therapist must not tell the child what he is feeling, but should let the child explore this and ultimately put it into his own words.

> Ivo
>
> After a few months, when it looks like T is going to win from Ivo in their board game, he says, "I can't win this game; next time I'll go back on the defensive." She tells him how impressed she has been by his strategy of attacking and adds, "You shouldn't give up so quickly, even if losing makes you feel bad." Then he replies, "Napoleon is completely defeated." And T says, "Yes, you're right that you are defeated, but you're still Napoleon", and he laughs with relief.

There are various techniques with which to regulate affect. The playful aspect of these interventions is particularly helpful in promoting affect regulation, as can be seen in the following example.

> Ivo
>
> A game unfolds between Ivo and T as they bat a bouncy ball back and forth between them. At first the game is in the nature of a competition—one that Ivo has to win—and T spares his sense of self. But as Ivo continually adjusts the rules in his favour, T makes it clear to him what feelings this evokes in her. For example, irritation and anger: "Hey, listen, I'm getting confused", or "Come on, you just won't let me win" or "It makes me really cross." She expresses her desperation: "How am I supposed to figure this out,

you keep on changing things!" And her distress: "If you keep on like this, I'm going to cry."

Her interventions have both a real and a pretend quality, and are meant to arouse in Ivo awareness both of his own feelings and those of the therapist. This encourages reciprocity in their relationship, and the therapist shows Ivo that you can play with reality, that you are not simply at its mercy.

In the therapeutic relationship, mirroring is an important technique: it means giving something back to the child in a slightly different form. This process causes the child to consciously feel his own feelings (self-states) and, later, those of others (other-states) as well. It is important for the therapist to stay close to the child's mental state.

The final stages

In the final stages, mentalizing will come more and more to fruition. Once the child can use symbolic representations, we may speak of mentalization, and this gives the child an important instrument with which to regulate his relationships as well as his inner self. Then the therapist can give interventions that give meaning to the child's internal state, so that it can be communicated and interpreted (see Chapter 9).

Paul

Paul has related a bad dream that he had the previous night. T asks Paul if he is afraid to go to sleep again tonight, and if he has told his mother about the dream. Paul says he is indeed afraid to go to sleep tonight. T: "What could help you to be less afraid?" Paul says he doesn't know. T asks about his bedtime ritual, if he has a lamp, whether his Mum puts him to bed. Paul says that the night-light is broken. And he says, "I'm not afraid of the dark, but I'm afraid of what might happen." T: "You're not afraid of the dark, but you are afraid of your own thoughts . . . and that's why I'm wondering what might help." Together they start thinking about strategies that might help. Paul reports, "I'm thinking hard." T: "Yes, me too, I'm thinking hard. . . ." The outcome is that Paul thinks it might help if he could fall asleep in his Mum's bed . . . or, in fact, that it would be best if he could sleep next to his Mum all night. Then it turns out that Paul is afraid to tell his mother this, because he thinks she won't take it seriously and will just make a joke out of it. Together, they decide that it will help if T goes with him to tell his Mum that Paul has something very serious to say.

This is an example of an intervention in which comments are made about the mental processes such as thinking, remembering, being afraid.

Criteria for termination

Achievement of the goals of mentalization-based child therapy can be taken as the guideline for termination of therapy. Four—to some extent overlapping—objectives have been hierarchically formulated by Bateman and Fonagy (2004):

▷ identifying and adequately expressing feelings (affect);
▷ developing stable internal representations;
▷ forming a coherent sense of self;
▷ developing a capacity to enter into safe relationships.

But how do we see whether the objectives have been achieved in practice? As mentalization is set into motion, the child can start to experience someone else as a person with intentions, desires, motives, and mental constructs. This enables the child to enter into and to maintain friendships, because he is able to reach compromises and resolve conflicts. As the child can rely more on his own feelings and can separate them from the feelings of others, he can come to perceive parents and other caregivers as sources of protection, comfort, and regulation. Then others can also serve as identification models. Because the improved affect regulation allows children to regulate their own impulses better, relationships with caregivers and peers can be more positive, and the children will start to feel happier. Symptoms will decrease, and maladjusted behaviour can disappear or greatly diminish. Ideally, in the end phase of treatment the therapist has become an important real person because she is someone who has had access to the child's inner world and has helped the child to identify and accept anxiety, frustration, anger, and sadness. Once the therapist has become more of a real figure for the child, the child will also be able to turn to other significant others. So in the final stages, mourning the loss of the therapist may be an important theme, but so is also anger at the therapist's limitations. Now it is possible for the child to mentalize on this theme.

But old problems and conflicts that had temporarily obstructed mentalization may crop up again in the final stages. The idea of termination of the treatment calls up the fear of not being able to manage alone, or the fear of disappointing the therapist. Often it will then be necessary for the therapist to go back to attention-regulating or affect-regulating interventions until the mentalization block has been lifted. Since mentalization is only temporarily limited, these problems can be discussed later in relation to the newly learned methods of solving them.

Within the therapy setting it is not easy to tell whether the objectives have been achieved. Because of countertransference feelings, the therapist may take too optimistic or too sombre a view of the sequence of events. Moreover, the opinion of the parents is not always parallel to that of the therapist or that of the child. Parents may insist on termination too soon; or they may press to prolong the therapy. To arrive at a more objective evaluation, it is advisable to administer a few tests—such as attachment stories (see Chapter 3)—before starting therapy to test the child's capacity for mentalization, and to repeat these tests at the end. In the end phase, the therapist and the child will together look back at how the child felt and how he responded in the initial and middle stages. During this evaluation, it is important to point out the limitations that are almost always there, but to include a discussion of how the child has learned to deal with them. The sense of disappointment at not having achieved everything will need to be discussed as well.

Not all children who start out on mentalization-based child therapy are capable of reaching the level of mentalization required if they are to go without therapy for a longer period. There are children whose capacity to mentalize remains low, or in whom the process towards development of mentalization stagnates. This may be due to limitations either in the child or in the parents. Sometimes the parents are no longer up to it, or the therapist encounters limitations in the development of mentalization in the parents. In such cases it is advisable to wind up the treatment and to suggest to the child that treatment can be recommenced at some later point (the multiple-entry ticket, see also Chapter 4). If the therapist runs into limitations in the child, it is sometimes advisable to suggest forms of treatment that are more physical, such as psychomotor therapy or manual therapy, or that are more active, such as drama therapy or creative therapy. But often it is also a good strategy to suspend treatment and wait to see how the child develops: here, too, the child can be offered the option of coming back if he feels the need to do so. In such cases, it is not advisable to prolong the therapy, because it may increase resistance and may stop the child from entering treatment again later.

CHAPTER ELEVEN

Research strategy

Jolien Zevalkink

Empirical research into the effectiveness of mentalization-based child therapy is a next step after having identified therapeutic interventions and having constructed a manual that can be used to train new therapists in this method. Such an endeavour is subject to a number of specific considerations. Following Kazdin (2002), a six-step procedure is presented in this chapter, highlighting a number of general and methodological factors that play a role in setting up this kind of research.

The first step is to include the theoretical background of the treatment programme in the research question. If the treatment is aimed at promoting the ability to mentalize, then it is important that the research investigates whether this was indeed attempted. In addition, a research design must be chosen that includes aspects such as setting up a comparison group. At each step, specific research questions aimed at clarifying and assessing the effectiveness of mentalization-based child therapy as a treatment method are formulated.

Research in child and adolescent psychotherapy

A survey article by Kazdin (2002) shows that many effect studies have been conducted within child psychotherapy. The general conclusion from these studies is that "children who undergo a therapeutic treatment are considerably better off than children who are left untreated"(Kazdin, 2002, p. 220). However, the outcomes of the research cannot be unconditionally generalized to clinical treatment in actual practice. First of all, the research was done under controlled conditions and did not include empirical study of the most common treatment methods. Second, the research population was generally different from the group of children who find their way to a clinical practice. The research group was recruited via channels such as advertisements; the children were not referred after having registered with a mental health organization. Moreover, children in the research groups had less serious and less chronic symptoms, and there was little or no co-morbidity—that is, when a child has problems in several areas, such as anxiety and personality problems—compared to children in a regular clinical practice. Furthermore, the parents of the children in the research group had fewer psychiatric complaints, stress, and social handicaps (Kazdin, 2002). Research on psychotherapy among children and adolescents seems to find itself in a complicated and somewhat paradoxic situation. Most treatment methods that have been studied are applied in practice only to a limited extent, while the effectiveness of forms of treatment that are frequently used have not been empirically studied. For example, therapists often use psychoanalytic psychotherapy in treating children with anxiety problems, but few attempts have been made to study the effectiveness of this form of treatment (Fonagy, Target, Cottrell, Phillips, & Kurtz, 2002). Kazdin (2002) names another important limitation of the research in psychotherapy: its limited perspective. If research looks into the effectiveness of a treatment method only to the extent that symptoms have decreased after treatment is terminated and does not investigate why and how the treatment works, then no insight is gained into the effectiveness of psychotherapy.

The above-mentioned objections can be met by setting up an effectiveness study along different lines. In developing an effective treatment, Kazdin (2002) distinguishes six steps, each of which includes systematically carrying out empirical research. These steps do not necessarily have to be taken in chronological order, and there is some overlap between them. The steps are the guiding principle for this chapter in relation to the mentalization-based child therapy project. The rest of the chapter is devoted to elaborating each step into concrete research proposals.

Step 1: Theory and research
on the nature of the clinical disorder

Kazdin's first step is "theory and research on the nature of the clinical disorder". In Chapter 2 we formulate an extensive theory about how problems arise in developing mental processes, and in Chapter 3 we describe the clinical group to which this disorder seems to be related. Research is needed to investigate whether the treatment indicators formulated and the presumed target group can indeed be identified. There is no lack of theory formation on mental process disorders and the borderline personality organization. This also means that clear-cut hypotheses have been put forward about factors that lead to the clinical problem or pattern of functioning, about the processes behind it, and about how these processes show up and how they work (Kazdin, 2002). In the theory of mental process disorders, three types of children can be distinguished based on the way in which they deal with their problems: primarily in the equivalent mode, primarily in the pretend mode, and alternately in equivalent or pretend mode without integrating the two. These children have sometimes been described as children with a borderline personality, and they can also be said to have a disorganized or disoriented attachment representation. For research, it is important to operationalize the concept of mentalization.

Much empirical research has been done of the origins of disorganized attachment representations. Children with this attachment representation seem to be highly vulnerable to attachment-related stress. Under such circumstances they exhibit role reversal and anxious or aggressive behaviour in an attempt to lessen the tension. Both externalizing and internalizing of behavioural problems are possible. In these children, affect regulation is quite radically disordered (Bradley, 2000; Verheugt-Pleiter & Zevalkink, 2005; Zevalkink, 2005). It has been demonstrated that a disorganized attachment representation is closely related to the circumstances in which a child has grown up and/or is still growing up. The presence of risk factors increases the chance of such a representation developing. The presence of an insecure attachment representation in the caregiver, in combination with a loss or trauma that has not been worked through, is of decisive importance in the development of a disorganized representation (Fonagy, Steele, & Steele, 1991; Van IJzendoorn, 1995). Attachment research has found sufficient empirical proof for this and—at least equally important—has yielded a wide range of research instruments that can be enlisted in research on mentalization-based child therapy. The disorganized attachment representation can be subdivided into children who are D–controlling/hostile, D–helpless/fearful, or disoriented (Hesse & Main, 2000; Lyons-Ruth, et al., 2004). Perhaps other subtypes can be distinguished as well in relation to the theorized descriptions of children with different mental process disorders.

Relevant research questions

⊳ Can the three groups of children with theoretically distinguished mentalization problems be empirically identified? Which types of disorganized attachment representations can be distinguished, and are they related to the three mentalization problems distinguished by the theory?

⊳ Is it possible to identify protective and risk factors that can explain the development of various subtypes of mental process disorders?

Step 2: Theory and research on change processes and treatment mechanisms

As the second step, Kazdin identifies "theory and research on the change processes of treatment mechanisms". A mentalization-based child therapy is intended to promote mentalization. Chapter 4 describes the strategy behind choosing to discover how the therapy works and the corresponding principles of mentalization-based child therapy. This step includes research on the operationalization of the concept of mentalization and the effect of the intervention techniques distinguished. Research on the effects of the psychoanalytic treatment of children is much more scanty than research within intervention projects, while intervention projects do use many elements that have been developed in treatments (Cummings, Davies, & Campbell, 2000). Such projects have studied effective factors shown by clinical experience to bring about positive changes, such as promoting sensitivity and respect for the autonomy of the caregiver. Intervention projects have studied these mechanisms, and there they have often proved to work, while they have seldom been seriously studied in clinical research. The promotion of mentalization is the objective of mentalization-based child therapy. How can this be made measurable? There are two sides to this: first, the child and the change processes in him and, second, the therapist and the intervention techniques used.

It is possible to study the change processes in the child by using constructs that have already been operationalized and that are theoretically related to mentalization, such as security/autonomy of the attachment representation, quality of play, and empathy. By following the child's development in these areas, it can be inferred whether his ability to mentalize has improved. For instance, mentalization may be related to the development of empathy (Slijper, 1997). Or by observing the child during therapy sessions and perhaps outside therapy as well, play methods can be used to investigate whether the child is able to use pretend play and to integrate it with reality. Perhaps it is possible to develop an instrument that can measure mentalization more directly (e.g. Meins, Fernyhough, Russel, & Clark-Carter, 1998). Research on overlap and uniqueness of the concept of mentalization is important.

Research into the treatment mechanisms used by the therapist can be and has been approached from several angles. According to Strupp (1973), psychotherapy aims to achieve changes in a person whose development has come to a standstill by giving him more self-control—or, as Freud put it: *"Wo Es war, soll Ich werden!"* [Where id was, there ego shall be!] But there are different forms of treatment, each with its own specific objective, focus, and techniques. How can it be decided which form of treatment works better than others for a particular problem ? And how can one form of treatment be compared to another if the criteria for change are very different? Behavioural therapy, for example, is aimed at changing certain behaviours, whereas mentalization-based child therapy is aimed at promoting mentalization. In addition, the fact that the child receives attention may be an important factor in achieving change, but every therapist can give the child attention, irrespective of the therapeutic direction. As formulated by Frank (as cited in Strupp, 1973, p. 106): "The patient's trust in the therapist's healing powers and a parallel belief on the therapist's part that his technical operations are effective encompass the substance of therapeutic outcomes."

Obviously, we are talking about positive attention. Earlier research has already established that the treatment outcome is inferior if the therapist shows little empathy, is not warm, and does not come across as genuine (Truax & Mitchell, 1971). In addition to such non-specific effects, specific effects of a form of treatment can also be distinguished. Research on mentalization-based child therapy explicitly aims to study the specific effects and not the non-specific effects of psychotherapy. According to Strupp (1973), the specific effects can best be measured in psychotherapeutic treatments of somewhat longer duration, because shorter treatments primarily focus on giving attention, support, and hope.

To measure specific effects, it is necessary to have a specific problem and techniques intended to correct it. Chapter 4 describes five therapeutic principles that are presumed to promote mentalization. These guidelines form the background to the observation system, but they can also be operationalized separately. Using the observation system, it can be studied whether, in the course of a therapy, a shift in the techniques occurs, thus pointing to an improvement in the child's ability to mentalize. It is hypothesized that a therapist who starts mentalization-based child therapy will make many attention-regulating interventions; as time goes on, she will more often use affect regulation and later, in the best case, will also start to make mentalizing remarks. The process of transference–countertransference is important here, and changes in the use of the techniques will be relative rather than linear. This may require a long period of time, and a treatment could even stop to give the child some time for the next developmental step.

Relevant research questions

▷ Can changes in the child's ability to mentalize be operationalized, or will this continue to be inferred from constructs?

▷ Is the use of the therapeutic principles related to presumed changes in mentalization in the child?

▷ In the course of a treatment, can shifts be observed in the intervention techniques used, from more attention regulation to more affect
regulation and then to more mentalizing interventions?

Step 3: Specification of the treatment

Kazdin's third step is "specification of the treatment". Other researchers have also stressed the need to systematically write down
the form of treatment and the techniques in a manual (Cummings,
Davies, & Campbell, 2000; Fonagy, Target, et al., 2002, p. 384). This
book is intended as a sort of scenario for initiating and carrying out
mentalization-based child therapy, and Chapters 4, 7, 8, 9, and 10
focus specifically on the actual treatment. Intervention techniques
have been identified by observing mentalization-based child therapy
sessions. In developing a protocol, the horizon of the therapy, what
the therapist actually does with the child during a therapy session,
needs to be made more specific. The book is not a "recipe—or a cook-
book". Just like the guidebook for mentalization-based therapy for
adult patients with a borderline personality disorder, so this book is
meant as a framework for therapeutic interventions in this group of
children (Bateman & Fonagy, 2004).

In fact, we must, rather, ask ourselves whether the therapist sets
to work according to the techniques proposed here, because clinical
practice has shown that people often work very flexibly with elements
from different forms of treatment (Cummings, Davies, & Campbell,
2000). If the therapist uses a variety of techniques from other forms
of treatment at the same time, then it cannot be assumed that an effect of therapy can be ascribed to better insight into mentalization
and the use of the principles of mentalization-based child therapy.
During the project on mentalization-based child therapy, regular peer
review meetings were held to keep everyone working with the same
principles as much as possible during treatment. We have learned
that advance training coupled with simultaneous peer review are
needed to carry out mentalization-based child therapy. In order to
study the effectiveness of this type of therapy, it is necessary to investigate to what extent the therapist actually used mentalization-based

child therapy techniques. This is referred to as "treatment adherence" (e.g. Trijsburg, 2003, pp. 217–218). Bateman and Fonagy (2004, pp. 315–318) drew up an assessment list for mentalization-based therapy with adults on the basis of which it can be investigated to what extent the therapist follows the techniques and how well she does so. This list will be adapted for working with children. Having decided to work with mentalization-based child therapy, the question must still be answered whether mentalization-based child therapy can be adequately distinguished from other forms of treatment. Once this has been studied, actual effectiveness research can get under way, using other forms of treatment as a basis for comparison.

Relevant research questions

> Did the therapist use enough mentalization-based child therapy techniques to be able to speak of mentalization-based child therapy?
> Can mentalization-based child therapy be distinguished from other forms of treatment?

Step 4: Assessment of the treatment results

The fourth step is "assessment of treatment results". This step involves choosing a research design and the research instruments. Chapter 3 describes what instruments can be used that are both theoretically and clinically relevant. Assessing the effectiveness of a treatment is crucial to developing the treatment further and to substantiate the treatment indicators. There are a variety of research designs, such as naturalistic research, fully elaborated randomized clinical studies, and quasi-experiments. Using these assessment methods or research designs, it might be possible to demonstrate that a change was brought about and that the therapy is responsible for this (Kazdin, 2002). The choice of the research design depends on choices made with respect to methodological issues, such as the minimum size of the research group, the formation of a comparison group, criteria for working with age differences within the group, decisions with respect to the simultaneous occurrence of several diagnosable disorders, categorizing factors in the family situation, and the generalizability of treatment effect over setting and time. An assessment of the treatment results often primarily means evaluating changes in the child. The therapist's work is then considered an independent variable, because the therapist is trained in the use of a certain method of treatment. This starts from the assumption that, after having been trained, therapists give more or less the same treatment, and that changes in the child should then primarily be attributed to the method used. Alternatively, therapist behaviour may be viewed as a non-stable factor, on account of different theoretical interests or a difference in training background, for example. The therapists who carry out mentalization-based child therapies within the present project all had similar training backgrounds. But in replicating research, it is important to think about possible therapist effects.

Measuring outcomes in the child will require the administration of a set of tests prior to treatment and once again at termination. It is also possible to carry out a number of outcome measurements during the course of treatment, but this is not common practice and primarily serves to measure the actual change process. Measuring the process was discussed under Step 2, and the instruments selected are listed in Chapter 3. Change refers to improvements in the indicator criteria, such as disorganized attachment representations (ASCT), anxiety and depression (CDI, MASC), impulse control, and affect regulation (Rorschach: CS). The child's parents and teacher also play a role in the outcome measurements, since they can describe the intensity of behavioural problems in the family situation and at school (CBCL, TRF). The choice of instruments here is prompted by clinical and scientific relevance (Zevalkink, 2003).

Many decisions need to be made in choosing a research design. The size of the research group is a good guide. A number of designs can be discounted if it is not possible to study large groups of children because of circumstances such as a small number of treatment assignments over the period of a year, too few therapists, or highly intensive treatment. A cohort study or a naturalistic study cannot be used, for example, because they are based on identifying group differences. The next choice involves the question whether the research should make statements about cause and effect. To draw this type of conclusion, an experimental research design is needed. This means that systematic process measurements must be added to the baseline measurement and post-measurement. A possible research design is an $N = 1$ (single-case) experimental design, in which various setups can be used: for example, an Alternating Treatments Design (ATD), in which a child has 10 sessions with no treatment, 10 sessions with treatment Method 1, 10 sessions with Method 2, and 10 sessions with no treatment, while the intended effect, such as less pulling out of hair, is continually measured (Barlow & Hersen, 1984). Single-case studies basically consist of a good baseline measurement during the first ten sessions and repeated measurements during treatment. Manipulation of the circumstances as in an ATD design is not possible with mentalization-based child therapy because it is not aimed at such clearly measurable behavioural changes. But an alternative for this type of experimental design is to watch out for changing circumstances and to incorporate them in the single-case results. This might include holiday periods, which can be deemed to be periods of no treatment, or times when home circumstances have clearly changed, such as when a father moves out after a divorce or a new partner joins the household. Although these circumstances cannot be manipulated, it is possible that their effect may be seen in the treatment. By systematically replicating the same design with several children, important change mechanisms will emerge, and it will become clear why mentalization-based child therapy works better for one child than for another (Barlow & Hersen, 1984; Hoyle, 1999; Kazdin, 1982). A systematic replication of an $N = 1$ design with several children in the same form of treatment can be expanded by replicating it with children who receive an alternative treatment. Then it is important that the children exhibit comparable problems. The therapists must be sure to carry out the treatment methods in accordance with the agreed guidelines (see Point 3). This is a group design with small numbers (Barlow & Hersen, 1984). Yin (1988) gives several pointers when setting up such a design. One of them is that, in following the case, the researcher should constantly keep an eye on the quality of the design.

Relevant research questions

 ▷ Is mentalization-based child therapy effective, as can be concluded from an improvement in outcome indicators in comparison with baseline measurements?

> Is mentalization-based child therapy effective, as can be concluded from process indicators over time?

> Is mentalization-based child therapy just as effective as, or more effective than, an alternative method of treatment with a comparable group of children?

Step 5: Assessment of the moderating factors

The fifth step involves an "assessment of moderating factors". The fact that characteristics of both child and parent play an important role is described in Chapters 2 and 5. Parent guidance seems to be important for this group of children, not only to carry out treatment but also for the presumed effectiveness, although further study is needed to substantiate this. In addition, research will need to devote attention to other factors that may influence the outcome of treatment. In clinical practice, it is difficult for a therapist to influence who comes in for treatment and when. Around 80% of children with problems do not wind up in clinical practice (Cummings, Davies, & Campbell, 2000). The children who do come in contact with a mental health agency constitute an a specific group. In addition, children come to treatment for a variety of reasons. The problem may have existed for some time, but when the child is registered for treatment, it is because a crisis situation has been reached. This means that it is often difficult to discover how the problem came about. These factors moderate the effect of treatment. Moreover, a wide range of child-specific characteristics, such as congenital traits, act as mediating factors. Rutter (2000) has stated that certain negative experiences are not important to the same extent for everyone, and the interaction of risk factors and protective factors affects the development of psychopathology. In other words, two children may react entirely differently to the same circumstances. The research must therefore take into account a wide range of environmental factors as well as several possible outcomes and change mechanisms, because not all children react to treatment in the same way (Cummings, Davies, & Campbell, 2000).

Alongside child-specific characteristics and environmental factors, the parents are another important factor in determining the success of the treatment. It is assumed that parent guidance must accompany mentalization-based child therapy. The effect of parent guidance can also be the subject of research. It is possible that successful parent guidance is a relevant factor in distinguishing more effective mentalization-based child therapies.

Relevant research questions

▷ What child-specific characteristics and environmental factors can be distinguished that influence the effectiveness of mentalization-based child therapy?

▷ What contribution is made by parent guidance to progress in a mentalization-based child therapy?

Step 6:   Assessment of generalizability and applicability

Kazdin's sixth step is "assessment of generalizability and applicability". If the results of the foregoing steps are satisfactory, then research is also needed of the extent to which the treatment can be effectively applied with other samples in clinical settings different from the one in which the mentalization-based child therapy was developed. After the foregoing steps, research is needed of the replicability of mentalization-based child therapy as a form of treatment in other clinical practice settings. The effectiveness of a certain treatment can only be determined with greater certainty if data are available from at least two well-designed independent studies showing that the treatment was more effective than an alternative treatment or just as effective as an existing treatment.

Relevant research questions

▷ Can the use of mentalization-based child therapy techniques be transferred to other therapists?

▷ Can mentalization-based child therapy be used in other mental health practice settings outside the one where this form of treatment was introduced?

In conclusion

Within the mentalization-based child therapy project, we have worked on elements described in Kazdin's six different steps to design a treatment and do proper research. Although some things still need elaboration, the formulation of a theory and the description of the mentalization-based child therapy techniques in this book are a necessary foundation for research on the effectiveness of this treatment. What remains to be done essentially is to formulate a project in which the various steps are integrated into a research proposal. Conducting research in a practical treatment setting demands much effort and much preparation before it can actually be carried out. Thanks to the efforts of the participating therapists, the preparations for research into mentalization-based child therapy have been tackled thoroughly. It might be stated that these efforts have paved a "royal" road to the conscious process of conducting empirical effectiveness research.

APPENDIX A:
Intervention techniques

ATTENTION REGULATION			
	Accepting the child's regulation profile and attuning to the same level		
		Attention to the content of the child's play or activity/introducing structure in play or story	A-ct
		Naming/describing physical states	E-pst
		Naming/describing behaviour aimed at the naming of mental content (cognitions and feelings)	E-mct
		Naming/describing anxiety or feeling threatened	E-anx
		Naming/describing a state of animosity	E-ang
	Working on the ability to make contact		
		Maintaining contact and introducing continuity in contact	A-co
		Creating a safe environment	A-sf
		Naming/describing interactions	E-in
	Working on the basis for intentional behaviour		
		Joining into the child's activities visually and/or in gestures	A-vg
	Giving reality value to preverbal interactions by taking the child's own style seriously		
		Directing attention at describing behaviour	A-beh
		Focusing on the child's qualities	A-qual
AFFECT REGULATION			
	Playing within boundaries		
		Introduction of fantasy to facilitate the pretend mode	I-fapm
		Focus on separating fantasy and reality	I-fare
		Setting boundaries	I-limt
		Joining in the pretend mode	I-pm
	Giving reality value to affect states		
		Giving reality value to an affect state of a play figure	I-afpf
		Giving reality value to an affect state of a child	I-afch
	Deducing second-order affect representations		
		Guiding and differentiating affect	I-afdif
		Looking for your own share in enactments	I-enac
MENTALIZATION			
	Comments on mental contents		
		Making comments on mental content in pretend mode	M-pm
		Discussing thoughts and feelings with respect to attachment figures	M-att
		Comments on mental contents of the child	M-menc
		Additions to positive content	M-posc
	Comments on mental processes of the child		
		Making comments on mental processes of the child such as remembering, asking, wanting, fantasizing, and making connections	M-proc
		Verbalization of wish and/or intention in the pretend mode	V-wpm
		Verbalization of wish and/or intention of the child	V-wch
		Verbalization of thoughts about the mental life of others/objects	V-mcot
		Stressing the individual character of the child's mental world	V-indch
	Comments on interactive mental processes		
		Comments on what the child thinks about others, the therapist	M-oth

Category identifications: A = attention to; E = explaining; I = identifying; M = mentalizing; V = verbalizing mental states.

APPENDIX B
Glossary

Abstinence, rule of: According to this psychoanalytic principle, the therapist should try to remain neutral and may not assume the role of a substitute from whom the patient is able to obtain satisfaction or any other feelings (Stroeken, 2000).

Actual mode: *see* Mode.

Affect: Literally, the noun "affect" means something done to one; it emphasizes the passive aspect. It is an older word for feeling or emotion (Stroeken, 2000). We follow Damasio in the use of the term "affect" because he uses it to refer to both feelings (invisible inner states) and emotions (visible conduct) (Damasio, 2004).

Affect regulation: The capacity to modulate affect states. It is a precursor to mentalization. As soon as mentalization occurs, affect regulation can develop further, primarily thanks to the great influence of mentalization on the sense of self (Fonagy, Gergely, et al., 2002, pp. 4–5).

Affect representation: Mental structure used in thinking about affect, which may or may not be closely related to the affect state experienced.

Agency: *see* Self.

Alien self: *see* Self.

Attachment: The term for a relatively durable affective relationship between a child and one or more specific persons with whom the child regularly interacts (Van IJzendoorn, Tavecchio, Goossens, & Vergeer, 1982, p. 13).

    secure attachment: A pattern that allows the child to use the attachment person as a safe basis for exploration. Upon activation of the attachment system—when the child is sad, tired, tense, or anxious, for example—the child seeks to be near the attachment person and subsequently becomes less anxious.

    insecure attachment: Three insecure attachment patterns can be distinguished: avoidant, ambivalent, and disorganized. A child with avoidant or ambivalent attachment will exhibit a rigid attention pattern during attachment-related stress; the former avoids the relationship, while the latter clings to the relationship with the attachment person (Main, 2000). Disorganized or disoriented attachment is the temporary collapse (or absence) of strategies in relation to attention and behaviour in dealing with attachment-related stress (Hesse & Main, 2000).

Benign split: Situation in which the therapist becomes the figure the child thrusts upon himself (by means of projective identification), although not completely, but still remaining himself. Switching between these two positions demands flexibility in inner splitting.

Conflict model: The opposition of incompatible inner needs, such as two wishes or a wish and a prohibition. This is a central model in classical psychoanalysis. A well-known conflict is the Oedipus complex (Stroeken, 2000).

Congruent mirroring: *see* Mirroring.

Containment: The metaphor of the container forms a central theme in the work of Bion. It refers to the containment or toleration (by the mother) of sensory perceptions and emotions (of the infant), being able to absorb impressions, give them meanings, and develop thoughts about them. In a treatment, this amounts to an attempt to understand what initially seems impossible to understand (Berkouwer, 2004, p. 175).

Contingent mirroring: *see* Mirroring.

Countertransference: The therapist's unconscious reactions to the person in treatment, especially to that person's transference. By registering her own reactions, the therapist makes maximum use of countertransference (Stroeken, 2000).

Declarative memory: The memory consists of two relatively autonomous systems: whereas the procedural memory incorporates more implicit procedures, the declarative memory incorporates more autobiographical content (Fonagy, Gergely, et al., 2002, p. 41).

Defence: A defence is a way of keeping in the unconscious certain stimuli to which certain representations are linked and situations that evoke such stimuli (Stroeken, 2000).

Defence mechanisms: All means of which the ego avails itself in mental conflicts. Common defence mechanisms are: repression, reaction formation, sublimation, regression, and projection (Stroeken, 2000).

Depressive position: The position reached when a person becomes aware that the same person is the object of both their love and their hate. The concept comes from Melanie Klein (Stroeken, 2000). As long as love and hate can still be split, Klein speaks of the paranoid–schizoid position.

Disorganized attachment: *see* Attachment.

Ego: A central concept in Freud's thinking, which refers both to an experienced sense of self and to a hypothetical system that serves to organize and synthesize the personality.

Enactment: Acting out an original event without consciously remembering it. It primarily refers to the manners stored in the implicit, procedural memory of how to act and to interact with others (Stroeken, 2000).

Epistemological: relating to knowledge.

Equivalent mode or **psychic equivalent mode**, see Mode.

Externalization: A defence mechanism characterized by the tendency to place outside the self instinctual wishes, conflicts, moods, and ways of thinking, so that they are attributed to another person. To be distinguished from projection (Tyson & Tyson, 1990).

False self: *see* Self.

Holding: Originally, the picture of the mother holding her infant firmly to her, the concept was expanded by Winnicott to include the feeling of continuity of being over time. In psychoanalysis, the holding function refers to putting into words the fact that the analyst knows and understands the true or feared deepest anxiety of the patient (Winnicott, 1963, p. 240).

Insecure attachment: *see* Attachment.

Intentional position: In the intentional position, not only are the physical actions of another person decisive, but also the intention of the other person with these actions. By assuming that others have an intention, a child shows the first indication of being aware of a mental state in another person. It is the start of the ability to mentalize.

Intergenerational transference: The process by which a generation has a psychological influence—intentionally or unintentionally—on the attitudes and behaviour of the next generation (Van IJzendoorn, 1992).

Integration mode: *see* Mode.

Internalization: mechanism by which intersubjective facts become intrasubjective (Stroeken, 2000). This occurs, for example, when the child adopts certain aspects of the way the caregiver deals with him. The child looks to the caregiver or the therapist as an example and takes over certain things, which can then become part of the child's mental toolkit.

Interpretation: Discovering the latent meaning—and particularly the wish it comprises—of a person's words and behaviours (Stroeken, 2000).

Markedness: exaggerating the way in which a parent would normally express an emotion. The expression is sufficiently normal so that the child recognizes the emotion, and sufficiently exaggerated so that the child sees that it is not the parent's emotion, but that of the child (Fonagy, Gergely, et al., 2002, p. 178).

Mental process disorder: a group of disorders in which entire categories of mental representations are missing in the mental structure. It is assumed that a child uses this mental block to protect himself against certain overly painful representations thought to be the result of mental processes. Mental processes themselves are then inhibited. The difference between mental process and mental representation can be explained as follows: if a mental representation is a melody, then the mental process is the violin that brings forth the sound (Fonagy, Moran, et al., 1993).

Mental representation: Internalization (q.v.) allows a child to generate her own representations, just as the caregiver originally did. As a rule, mental representation refers to the process itself: the generation of representations. The process of mental representation is a *sine qua non* for mentalization.

Mental representation disorder: disorder in which isolated non-integrated incompatible mental representations exert a pathogenic influence; they can be harmonized by interpretations given during psychoanalytic treatment (Fonagy, Moran, et al., 1993). These are neurotic disorders with mental conflicts that are mainly nonconscious.

Mentalization: The process by which we realize that the fact we have a mind modifies the way we experience the world (Fonagy, Gergely, et al., 2002). It consists of: (1) thinking about thoughts and feelings as abstractions (as mental representations); (2) drawing on memory processes, such as remembering; (3) thinking about the fact that others have thoughts and feelings different from your own.

Mentalized affectivity: state in which the affects can be used to regulate the self. This refers to the capacity of a person to reflect upon the subjective meanings of his or her own affect states (Fonagy, Gergely, et al., 2002, p. 5).

Mirroring: Through the eyes of another person, one sees a picture of oneself as a whole, thus negating the idea of the body as consisting of separate parts (Stroeken, 2000).

contingent mirroring: at certain moments, the other person gives back the affects. The child can then see a relationship between his internal sensations and the way they are mirrored. This builds up an expectation pattern.

congruent mirroring: this occurs when another person gives back the correct affects.

Mode:

equivalent mode: Sometimes also termed "psychic equivalent mode" or "equation mode". What a thing seems to be and what it is are then equivalent. Thoughts are reality, reality is thoughts. The equivalent mode is sometimes called the "actual mode", in which reality and fantasy are the same.

integration mode: In normal development, the integration of the two previous manners of thinking leads at the age of around 3 or 4 to the capacity to mentalize (Fonagy, Gergely, et al., 2002).

pretend mode: This is the phase in which fantasy play comes to full development. The child pretends, and the playful nature of being is easily recognizable. The boundary between external reality and the pretend world needs to be strictly observed in this phase.

Neural plasticity: a specific feature characteristic of the brain: it can develop, react, and adapt to internal and external environmental changes (Trojan & Pokorny, 1999).

Object: In psychoanalysis, this term refers to a person or partial object, which may be real or imagined (Stroeken, 2000).

Omnipotent fantasy: The omnipotent fantasy is the result of a normal mother–infant interaction. If a mother is "good enough", she will adapt to the baby's needs in such a way that the child seems to get everything he wants as if by magic. In normal development, the child gradually discovers that this fantasy is an illusion (Winnicott, 1963, p. 146).

Pre-representational: A level of functioning at which the capacity to form relationships is very limited and merely instrumental (Greenspan, 1997, p. 145).

Pretend mode: *see* Mode.

Procedural memory: The implicit, non-declarative, and non-reflective memory that primarily comprises "how" a wide range of behavioural sequences are carried out—motor skills, for example, but also attachment styles.

Projective identification: The person under treatment imagines a split-off part of himself inside the therapist and attempts to control this, according to Melanie Klein often quite aggressively (Stroeken, 2000). The aggression may also be turned upon the self together with feelings of being pursued (Tyson & Tyson, 1990). Cf. Projection.

Projection: A defence mechanism characterized by attributing to an external object unacceptable impulses and feelings that the person denies or rejects in himself (Stroeken, 2000). Projection is only a defence mechanism, while projective identification comprises a fantasized object relationship (Moore & Fine, 1990).

Proprioceptive data: Data concerning the receiving and processing of stimuli that arise in the nervous system.

Representational mismatch: This occurs when external reality challenges or contradicts the expectations generated by the internal models of the patient. It can be created if caregivers and therapists show effectiveness and consistency where it is not expected (Bleiberg, 2001).

Representational position: Around the age of 3 or 4, children begin to be aware of possible mental causality, allowing them to understand abstract constructs. Representations develop.

Resistance: The opposition of the person in treatment to making unconscious motives or fantasies conscious (Stroeken, 2000).

Second-order affect representation: Congruent and contingent mirroring by the primary caregiver, offering an affect representation for the primary unrefined experiences of the child, the so-called primary representations; thanks to the representations of the caregiver, the child also starts to represent second-order affects.

Self: This is an organization of the psyche or mind—a construct to be understood as a place—where an individual gains experiences with himself and his total surroundings. The self is also the place where a person's identity and awareness of the time dimension are located (Stroeken, 2000).

>   **alien self:** When mirroring is not accurate, the child internalizes representations of the parent's state rather than a useable version of the child's own experiences (Bateman & Fonagy, 2004, p. 88). This creates an alien sense within the self: ideas or feelings are experienced as part of the self, but not belonging to the self.

>   **false self:** When the child's primary caregiver cannot adjust "well enough" to the child's needs, the child is tempted to adapt to this mother or environment and to set aside his true needs or "true self". In this sense, the false self is a defence.

>   **self as agent:** Recognition of one's own affective activity. The concept of self as intentional mental organizer.

Transference: Emotions from the childhood years are repeated and relived with great intensity but endowed on the therapist. They are emotions that originally belonged with other persons (Stroeken, 2000).

Teleological position: In the teleological position, the reaction of the infant is determined by all that is visible, audible, or tangible for him. In order to read the intention of another person, the infant focuses on the physical world. This is in contrast to the intentional position, in which the intention another person has with actions is what decides the child's reaction.

Theory of Mind: A mutually cohesive set of views and desires that are ascribed to a person's behaviour. To investigate whether a child has a TOM, false-belief tasks are used (Steerneman, Meesters, & Muris, 2000). Many theories on the development of a TOM in a child examine how and when a child learns about the minds of others in an abstract sense. The contribution by Fonagy, Gergely, and colleagues (2002) is the link they make between this development in the child and the child's emotional bond with the parents.

Transitional space: Winnicott wrote an article in 1951 on transitional objects and transitional phenomena. It examined the first object—for instance, a blanket or a teddy bear—described by Winnicott as the first "not-me possession": an object that is not part of the body but not entirely external either. The illusionary space between the first bodily ego and the outside world is called transitional space, a term that is also often used to describe the characteristics of the analytic situation.

Unconscious: The mental contents and processes that are outside conscious attention (Tyson & Tyson, 1990). The unconscious knows no negation, no doubt, no degrees of certainty or uncertainty; it is not concerned with reality (Stroeken, 2000). Psychoanalysis is usually focused on the dynamic unconscious, in the sense of contents that are not known due to the strength of the repression. Mental process disorders often revolve around contents that are not conscious because they are underdeveloped.

Unmentalized exchange: If mentalization collapses under the influence of trauma, for example, the awareness of the difference between fantasy and reality is lost. Functioning in equivalent mode or withdrawing into pretend mode then leads to an unmentalized manner of getting along with others.

REFERENCES

AFC & UCL (1999). *The Child Therapy "Manual"*. Unpublished manuscript, Anna Freud Centre/University College London.

Ainsworth, M. D. S., Blehar, M. C., Waters, E., & Wall, E. (1978). *Patterns of Attachment: A Psychological Study of the Strange Situation*. Hillsdale, NJ: Erlbaum.

Allen, J. G. (2000). *Traumatic Attachments*. New York: Wiley.

Allen, J. G. (2006). Mentalizing in practice. In: J. G. Allen, & P. Fonagy (Eds.), *Handbook of Mentalization-based Treatment* (pp. 3–30). Chichester: Wiley.

Alvarez, A. (1992). *Live Company: Psychotherapy with Autistic, Borderline, Deprived and Abused Children*. London: Routledge.

APA (1997). *Diagnostic and Statistical Manual of Mental Disorders, DSM–IV*. Arlington, VA: American Psychiatric Publishers.

Argyle, M. (1975). *De psychologie van het intermenselijk gedrag* [Psychology of interhuman behavior]. Alphen aan den Rijn: Samson.

Barlow, D. H., & Hersen, M. (1984). *Single Case Experimental Designs: Strategies for Studying Behavior Change*. New York: Pergamon Press.

Baron-Cohen, S. (1991). Precursors to a Theory of Mind: Understanding attention in others. In: A. Whiten (Ed.), *Natural Theories of Mind: The*

Evolution, Development, and Simulation of Second Order Mental Representations. Oxford: Blackwell.

Baron-Cohen, S., Tager-Flusberg, H., & Cohen, D. J. (2000). *Understanding Other Minds: Perspectives from Developmental Cognitive Neuroscience*. Oxford: Oxford University Press.

Bateman, A. (2002). "Van regionaal naar landelijk zorgprogramma?" Symposium, From a Regional to National Programme of Care, Amersfoort, The Netherlands, 9 December.

Bateman, A. W., & Fonagy, P. (2004). *Psychotherapy for Borderline Personality Disorder: Mentalization-based Treatment*. New York: Oxford University Press.

Bateman, A. W., & Fonagy, P. (2006). *Mentalization-based Treatment for Borderline Personality Disorder: A Practical Guide*. New York: Oxford University Press.

Beckwith, L. (2000). Prevention science and prevention programs. In: C. H. Zeanah (Ed.), *Handbook of Infant Mental Health* (pp. 439–457). New York: Guilford Press.

Beebe, B., & Lachmann, F. (1988). The contribution of mother–infant influence to the origins of self- and object relations. *Psychoanalytic Psychology, 5*: 305–337.

Beebe, B., Lachmann, F., & Jaffe, J. (1997). Mother–infant interaction structures and presymbolic self and object representations. *Psychoanalytic Dialogue, 7*: 133–182.

Berkouwer, A. Y. (2004). *Handboek de psychoanalytische setting: Anatomie van een plek* [Handbook on the psychoanalytic setting: Anatomy of a place]. Amsterdam: Boom.

Bickman, L., & Rog, D. J. (1998). *Handbook of Applied Social Research Methods*. Thousand Oaks, CA: Sage.

Bion, W. R. (1962). A theory of thinking. *International Journal of Psychoanalysis, 43*: 306–310.

Bion, W. R. (1967a). Notes on memory and desire. *Psychoanalytic Forum, 2* (3).

Bion, W. R. (1967b). *Second Thoughts*. London: Karnac.

Bleiberg, E. (1994). Borderline disorders in children and adolescents: The concept, the diagnosis, and the controversies. *Bulletin of the Menninger Clinic, 58* (2): 169–196.

Bleiberg, E. (2001). *Treating Personality Disorders in Children and Adolescents: A Relational Approach*. New York: Guilford Press.

Böszörményi-Nagy, I. (1987). *Foundations of Contextual Therapy*. New York: Brunner-Routledge.

Bradley, S. J. (2000). *Affect Regulation and the Development of Psychopathology*. New York: Guilford Press.

Bretherton, I., Ridgeway, D., & Cassidy, J. (1990). Assessing internal working models of the attachment relationship. An attachment story completion task for 3-year-olds. In: M. T. Greenberg, D. Cicchetti, & E. M. Cummings (Eds.), *Attachment in the Preschool Years: Theory, Research, and Intervention* (pp. 273–308). Chicago: University of Chicago Press.

Brisch, K. H. (1999). *Treating Attachment Disorders: From Theory to Therapy*. New York: Guilford Press.

Chethik, M. (1989). *Techniques of Child Psychotherapy: Psychodynamic Strategies*. New York: Guilford Press.

Chethik, M. (2000). *Techniques of Child Therapy: Psychodynamic Strategies* (2nd edition). New York: Guilford Press.

Cicchetti, D., & Cohen, D. J. (1995). Perspectives on developmental psychopathology. In: D. Cicchetti & D. J. Cohen (Eds.), *Developmental Psychopathology* (pp. 3–20). New York: Wiley.

Cluckers, G. (1986). *Steungevende kinderpsychotherapie: Een andere weg* [Supportive child psychotherapy: Another way]. Deventer: Van Loghum Slaterus.

Cummings, E. M., Davies, P. T., & Campbell, S. B. (2000). *Developmental Psychopathology and Family Process: Theory, Research, and Clinical Implications*. New York: Guilford Press.

Damasio, A. (2004). *Looking for Spinoza: Joy, Sorrow, and the Feeling Brain* (3rd edition). New York: Harcourt.

Dawson, G., Frey, K., Self, J., Panagiotides, H., Hessl, D., Yamada, E., & Rinaldi, J. (1999). Frontal brain electrical activity in infants of depressed and nondepressed mothers: Relation to variations in infant behavior. *Development and Psychopathology, 11*: 589–605.

Deben-Mager, M., & Verheugt-Pleiter, A. (2004). Enkele toepassingen van de gehechtheidstheorie op de psychoanalytische praktijk [Some applications of attachment theory to psychoanalytic practice]. *Tijdschrift voor Psychoanalyse, 10* (1): 18–30.

De Lange, G. (1991). *Hechtingsstoornissen. Orthopedagogische behandelingsstrategieën* [Attachment disorders: Orthopedagogic treatment strategies]. Assen: Dekker & van de Vegt.

de Ruiter, C., & Cohen, L. (1994). Persoonlijkheidsdiagnostiek met het Rorschach Comprehensive System. Relevantie voor de indicatiestelling bij psychotherapie [Personality diagnostics with the Rorschach Comprehensive System: Relevance for treatment assignments in psychotherapy]. *Tijdschrift Voor Psychotherapie, 20* (5): 307–321.

Fearon, P., Target, M., Sargent, J., Williams, L. L., McGregor, J., Bleiberg, E., & Fonagy, P. (2006). Short-term mentalization and relational therapy (SMART): An integrative family therapy for children and adolescents. In: J. G. Allen & P. Fonagy (Eds.), *Handbook of Mentalization-based Treatment* (pp. 201–222). Chichester: Wiley.

Fonagy, P. (1995). Playing with reality: The development of psychic reality and its malfunction in borderline personalities. *International Journal of Psychoanalysis, 76*: 39–45.

Fonagy, P. (2001a). *Attachment Theory and Psychoanalysis*. New York: Other Press.

Fonagy, P. (2001b). Changing ideas of change: The dual components of therapeutic action. In: J. Edwards (Ed.), *Being Alive: Building on the Work of Anne Alvarez*. New York: Brunner-Routledge.

Fonagy, P., Gergely, G., Jurist, E. L., & Target, M. (2002). *Affect Regulation, Mentalization, and the Development of the Self*. New York: Other Press.

Fonagy, P., Moran, G. S., Edgcumbe, R., Kennedy, H., & Target, M. (1993). The roles of mental representations and mental processes in therapeutic action. *Psychoanalytic Study of the Child, 48*: 9–48.

Fonagy, P., Steele, M., Moran, G. S., & Higgitt, A. (1993). Measuring the ghost in the nursery: An empirical study of the relationship between parents' mental representation of childhood experiences and their infant's security of attachment. *Journal of the American Psychoanalytic Association, 41*: 957–989.

Fonagy, P., Steele, H., Moran, G., Steele, M., & Higgitt, A. (1991). The capacity for understanding mental states: The reflective self in parent and child and its significance for security of attachment. *Infant Mental Health Journal, 13*: 200–217.

Fonagy, P., Steele, H., & Steele, M. (1991). Maternal representations of attachment during pregnancy predict the organization of infant–mother attachment at one year of age. *Child Development, 62*: 891–905.

Fonagy, P., Steele, M., Steele H., Leigh, T., Kennedy, R., Mattoon, G., & Target, M. (1995). Attachment, the reflective self, and borderline states. The predictive specificity of the Adult Attachment Interview and pathological emotional development. In: S. Goldberg, R. Muir,

& J. Kerr (Eds.), *Attachment Theory: Social, Developmental, and Clinical Perspectives*. Hillsdale, NJ: Analytic Press.

Fonagy, P., & Target, M. (1996a). Playing with reality: I. Theory of mind and the normal development of psychic reality. *International Journal of Psychoanalysis, 77*: 217–233.

Fonagy, P., & Target, M. (1996b). Predictors of outcome in child psychoanalysis: A retrospective study of 763 cases at the Anna Freud Centre. *Journal of the American Psychoanalytic Association, 44* (1): 27–77.

Fonagy, P., & Target, M. (1997). Attachment and reflective function: Their role in self-organization. *Development and Psychopathology, 9*: 679–700.

Fonagy, P., & Target, M. (2000). Playing with Reality: III. The persistence of dual psychic reality in borderline patients. *International Journal of Psychoanalysis, 81*: 853–874.

Fonagy, P., Target, M., Cottrell, D., Phillips, J., & Kurtz, Z. (2002). *What Works for Whom? A Critical Review of Treatments for Children and Adolescents*. New York: Guilford Press.

Fraiberg, S., Adelson, E., & Shapiro, W. (1980). Ghost in the nursery. In: S. Fraiberg (Ed.), *Clinical Studies in Infant Mental Health: The First Year* (pp. 164–194). New York: Basic Books.

Francis, D., Diorio, J., Liu, D., & Meaney, M. J. (1999). Nongenomic transmission across generations of maternal behavior and stress responses in the rat. *Science, 286* (5): 1155–1159.

Frijling-Schreuder, E. C. M. (1969). Borderline state in children. *Psychoanalytic Study of the Child, 24*: 307–327.

Frijling-Schreuder, E. C. M., Bakker, J. E. M., & Verhage, F. (1988). *Techniek van de psychoanalyse bij volwassenen en kinderen* [Techniques in psychoanalysis of adults and children]. Assen: Van Gorcum.

Fury, G., Carlson, E. A., & Sroufe, L. A. (1997). Children's representations of attachment relationships in family drawings. *Child Development, 68* (6): 1154–1164.

Galtung, J. (1973). *Theory and Methods of Social Research*. London: George Allen & Unwin.

Gergely, G., & Csibra, G. (1997). Teleological reasoning in infancy: The infant's naive theory of rational action. A reply to Premack and Premack. *Cognition, 63*: 227–233.

Gergely, G., & Watson, J. S. (1996). The social biofeedback theory of parental affect mirroring: The development of emotional self-awareness and self-control in infancy. *International Journal of Psychoanalysis, 77*: 1181–1212.

Gerritzen, H. M. J. A. (2000). Groei-, regulatie- en hechtingsstoornissen bij het jonge kind [Growth, regulation- and attachment disorders in the young child]. In: F. C. Verhulst & F. Verheij (Eds.), *Kinder- en jeugdpsychiatrie: Onderzoek en diagnostiek* (pp. 195–215). Assen: Van Gorcum.

Gerritzen, H. M. J. A. (2003). Nosologie en classificatie: Enkele opmerkingen over het indicatiegebied van psychoanalytische ontwikkelingstherapie [Nosology and classification: Some remarks on the assignment to psychoanalytic developmental therapy]. In: M. G. J. Schmeets & A. P. Schut (Eds.), *Anders en toch hetzelfde: Psychoanalytische ontwikkelingstherapie met kinderen* (pp. 22–40). Assen: Van Gorcum.

Gilmore, K. (2000). A psychoanalytic perspective on attention-deficit/hyperactivity disorder. *Journal of the American Psychoanalytic Association, 48* (4): 1259–1293.

Gilmore, K. (2002). Diagnosis, dynamics and development: Consideration in the psychoanalytic assesment of children with AD/HD. *Psychoanalytic Inquiry, 22* (3): 372–390.

Greenspan, S. I. (1997). *Developmentally Based Psychotherapy*. Madison, CT: International Universities Press.

Halberstadt-Freud, H. C. (1983). *Psychodiagnostiek met kinderen* [Psychodiagnostics with children]. Lisse: Swets & Zeitlinger.

Hamilton, V. (2001). Foreword. In: J. Edwards (Ed.), *Being Alive: Building on the Work of Anne Alvarez*. New York: Brunner-Routledge.

Hellendoorn, J., Groothoff, E., Mostert, P., & Harinck, F. (1992). *Beeldcommunicatie. Een vorm van kinderpsychotherapie (tweede druk)* [Communication via images: A form of child psychotherapy]. Houten: Bohn Stafleu Van Loghum.

Hesse, E., & Main, M. (2000). Disorganized infant, child, and adult attachment: Collapse in behavioral and attentional strategies. *Journal of the American Psychoanalytic Association, 48* (4): 1097–1127.

Hodges, J., & Steele, M. (2000). Effects of abuse on attachment representations: Narrative assessments of abused children. *Journal of Child Psychotherapy, 26* (3): 433–455.

Hoyle, R. H. (1999). *Statistical Strategies for Small Sample Research*. Thousand Oaks, CA: Sage.

Hurry, A. (1998a). Psychoanalysis and developmental therapy. In: A. Hurry (Ed.), *Psychoanalysis and Developmental Therapy* (pp. 32–73). London: Karnac.

Hurry, A. (Ed.) (1998b). *Psychoanalysis and Developmental Therapy*. London: Karnac.

Jones, E. E. (1996). Introduction to the special section on attachment and psychopathology: Part 1. *Journal of Consulting and Clinical Psychology, 64* (1): 5–7.

Kandel, E. R. (2001). The molecular biology of memory storage: A dialogue between genes and synapses. *Science, 294* (November): 1030–1038.

Kaplan-Solms, K., & Solms, M. (2000). *Clinical Studies in Neuro-Psychoanalysis: Introduction to a Depth Neuropsychology*. Madison, CT: International Universities Press.

Kazdin, A. E. (1982). *Single-case Research Designs: Methods for Clinical and Applied Settings*. New York: Oxford University Press.

Kazdin, A. E. (2002). The state of child and adolescent therapy research. *Child and Adolescent Mental Health, 7* (2): 53–59.

Kendall, P. C. (1994). Treating anxiety disorders in children: Results of a randomized clinical trial. *Journal of Consulting and Clinical Psychology, 62*: 100–110.

Leslie, A. (1987). Pretense and representation: The origins of "Theory of Mind". *Psychological Review, 94*: 412–426.

Lyons-Ruth, K., Melnick, S., Bronfman, E., Sherry, S., & Llanas, L. (2004). Hostile–helpless relational models and disorganized attachment patterns between parents and their young children: Review of research and implications for clinical work. In: L. Atkinson & S. Goldberg (Eds.), *Attachment Issues in Psychopathology and Intervention* (pp. 65–94). Mahwah, NJ: Erlbaum.

Main, M. (2000). The organized categories of infant, child, and adult attachment: Flexible vs. inflexible attention under attachment-related stress. *Journal of the American Psychoanalytic Association, 48* (4): 1055–1096.

Marcelis-Eerdmans, G. L. (1994). *Facetten van ouderschap* [Facets of parenthood]. Rotterdam: Sectie Ouderbegeleiding NVRG.

Marcelis-Eerdmans, G. L. (1999). Grenzen vanuit de ouders [Boundaries coming from parents]. In: H. Gerritsma & I. Mettrop-Würster (Eds.), *Kinderen en grenzen* (pp. 78–86). Assen: Van Gorcum, Reeks Nederlands Psychoanalytisch Instituut.

Marcelis-Eerdmans, G. L. (2000). "Over de ontwikkeling van het ouderschap" [About the development of parenthood]. Paper presented at the Netherlands Psychoanalytic Institute, Amsterdam.

March, J. S., Parker, J. D. A., Sullivan, K., Stallings, P., & Conners, K. (1997). The Multidimensional Anxiety Scale for Children (MASC): Factor structure, reliability, and validity. *Journal of the American Academy of Child and Adolescent Psychiatry, 36*: 554–565.

Meaney, M. J. (2001). Maternal care, gene expression, and the transmission of individual differences in stress reactivity across generations. *Annual Review of Neurosciences, 24*: 1161–1192.

Meins, E., Fernyhough, C., Russel, J., & Clark-Carter, D. (1998). Security of attachment as a predictor of symbolic and mentalizing abilities: A longitudinal study. *Social Development, 7*: 1–24.

Meurs, P., & Vliegen, N. (2004). Gedrag, een verhaal met betekenis. Gedragsstoornis en psychodynamisch model [Behavior, a story with meaning: Conduct disorders and a psychodynamic model]. In: N. Vliegen, L. Van Lier, S. Weytens, & G. Cluckers (Eds.), *Een verhaal met betekenis: Diagnostiek bij kinderen en adolescenten vanuit een psychodynamisch interpretatief model* (pp. 175–206). Leuven: ACCO.

Meurs, P., Vliegen, N., & Cluckers, G. (2005). *Affectinterpretatie als deelproces van affectregulatie* [Interpretation of affects as part of the process in affect regulation]. In: M. G. J. Schmeets & J. E. Verheugt-Pleiter (Eds.), *Affectregulatie*. Assen: Van Gorcum.

Mitrani, J. L. (2001). "Taking the transference": Some technical implications in three papers by Bion. *International Journal of Psychoanalysis, 82*: 1085–1104.

Moore, B. E., & Fine, B. D. (1990). *Psychoanalytic Terms and Concepts*. New Haven, CT: Yale University Press.

NPI (2002). *Jaarverslag 2002: Op koers en op stoom* [Report 2002: On the right track and under steam]. Internal report, Nederlands Psychoanalytisch Instituut.

Pally, R. (2000). *The Mind–Brain Relationship*. London: Karnac.

Pianta, R. C., Longmaid, K., & Ferguson, J. E. (1999). Attachment-based classifications of children's family drawings: Psychometric properties and relations with children's adjustment in kindergarten. *Journal of Clinical and Child Psychology, 28* (2): 244–255.

Pleiter, A. (1983). Een wonderlijke school [An amazing school]. Themanummer psychoanalyse en opvoeding. *Comenius, 3*, 338–348.

Reuling, A. (1987). *Data-verzameling en data-analyse* [Data-gathering and data-analysis]. Baarn: H. Nelissen.

Rexwinkel, M. (2003). Infant research en ontwikkelingstherapie [Infant research and developmental therapy]. In: M. G. J. Schmeets & A. P.

Schut (Eds.), *Anders en toch hetzelfde. Psychoanalytische ontwikkeling-stherapie met kinderen* (pp. 81–106). Assen: Van Gorcum.

Rothstein, A. (2002). Plea for a balanced conception of AD/HD and its diagnosis and treatment. *Psychoanalytic Inquiry, 22* (3): 391–412.

Rustin, M., & Quagliata, E. (2000). *Assessment in Child Psychotherapy*. London: Duckworth.

Rutter, M. (2000). Psychosocial influences: Critiques, findings, and research needs. *Development and Psychopathology, 12*: 375–405.

Sandler, A. (2004). On interpretation and holding. In: L. Rodriguez de la Sierra (Ed.), *Child Analysis Today* (pp. 95–111). London: Karnac.

Sandler, P., Kennedy H., & Tyson, R. L. (1980). *The Technique of Child Psychoanalysis*. Cambridge, MA: Harvard University Press.

Schmeets, M. G. J. (2003). Hetzelfde en toch anders. Over de theoretische grondslagen van developmental therapy [Similar, but also different: About the theoretical foundations of developmental therapy]. In: M. G. J. Schmeets & A. P. Schut, (Eds.), *Anders en toch hetzelfde. Psychoanalytische ontwikkelingstherapie met kinderen* (pp. 6–22). Assen: Van Gorcum.

Schore, A. N. (1994). *Affect Regulation and the Origin of the Self: The Neurobiology of Emotional Development*. Hillsdale, NJ: Erlbaum.

Sharp, C. (2006). Mentalizing problems in childhood disorders. In: J. G. Allen & P. Fonagy (Eds.), *Handbook of Mentalization-based Treatment* (pp. 101–121). Chichester: Wiley.

Slade, A. (2002). Keeping the baby in mind. *Bulletin of Zero To Three, 22* (6): 10–16.

Slijper, F. (1997). De ontwikkeling van empathie in een psychoanalytische behandeling [The development of empathy in a psychoanalytic treatment]. In: A. Komter (Ed.), *Het geschenk. Over de verschillende betekenissen van geven* (pp. 152–165). Amsterdam: Amsterdam University Press.

Slijper, F. M. E. (1998). De samenwerking van kinderanalyticus en ouders. Een "therapeutische relatie" [Collaboration between child psychoanalyst and parents: A "therapeutic" relationship]. *Tijdschrift voor Psychoanalyse, 4*: 86–100.

Slijper, F. M. E. (2000). Het psychodiagnostisch persoonlijkheidsonderzoek [The psychodiagnostic personality research]. In: F. C. Verhulst & F. Verheij (Eds.), *Kinder- en jeugdpsychiatrie: Onderzoek en diagnostiek* (pp. 146–156). Assen: Van Gorcum.

Slijper, F. M. E. (2001). Psychoanalytische kindertherapie [Psychoanalytic therapy for children]. In: J. Hermanns & M. Smit (Eds.), *Handboek Jeugdzorg*. Houten: Bohn Stafleu & Van Loghum.

Solomon, J., & George, C. (1999). The measurements of attachment security in infancy and childhood. In: J. Cassidy & P. R. Shaver (Eds.), *Handbook of Attachment* (pp. 287–316). New York: Guilford Press.

Steele, H., Steele, M., & Fonagy, P. (1996). Associations among attachment classifications of mothers, fathers, and their infants. *Child Development, 67*: 541–555.

Steerneman, P., Meesters, C., & Muris, P. (2000). *TOM-test*. Leuven: Garant.

Steiner, J. (1994). Patient-centered and analyst-centered interpretations: Some implications of containment and countertransference. *Psychoanalytic Inquiry, 14*: 406–422.

Stern, D. (1998). The process of therapeutic change involving implicit knowledge: Some implications of developmental observations for adult psychotherapy. *Infant Mental Health Journal, 19* (3): 300–308.

Stern, D. (2004). *The Present Moment in Psychotherapy and Everyday Life*. New York: W. W. Norton.

Stoker, J. (2005). *Some Guidelines for Mentalisation-based Interventions*. Unpublished teaching materials, Netherland Psychoanalytic Institute, Amsterdam.

Stroeken, H. (2000). *Psychoanalytisch woordenboek* [Psychoanalytic dictionary]. Amsterdam: Boom.

Strupp, H. H. (1973). *Psychotherapy: Clinical, Research, and Theoretical Issues*. New York: Jason Aronson.

Target, M., & Fonagy, P. (1996). Playing with reality: II. The development of psychic reality from a theoretical perpective. *International Journal of Psychoanalysis, 77*: 459–479.

Thoomes-Vreugdenhil, A. (2000). Differentiatietherapie en fasetherapie: Behandelwijzen voor verwaarlozingsproblematiek [Therapy of differentiation and phases: Treatment strategies for problems of neglect]. *Kinder en Jeugd Psychotherapie, 3*: 21–38.

Trijsburg, W. (2003). Therapeutische factoren en interventies [Therapeutic factors and interventions]. In: S. Colijn, H. Snijders, & W. Trijsburg (Eds.), *Leerboek integratieve psychotherapie* (pp. 211–249). Utrecht: De Tijdstroom.

Trojan, S., & Pokorny, J. (1999). Theoretical aspects of neural plasticity. *Physiological Reseach, 48* (2): 87–97.

Tronick, E. Z. (1998). Dyadically expanded states of consciousness and the process of therapeutic action. *Infant Mental Health Journal, 19* (3): 290–299.

Truax, C. B., & Mitchell, K. M. (1971). Research on certain therapist interpersonal skills in relation to process and outcome. In: A. E. Bergin & S. L. Garfield (Eds.), *Handbook of Psychotherapy and Behavior Change: An Empirical Analysis* (pp. 299–344). New York: Wiley.

Tyson, P. (2005). Affects, agency and self-regulation: Complexity theory in the treatment of children with anxiety and disruptive behavior disorders. *Journal of the American Psychoanalytic Association, 53* (1): 159–187.

Tyson, P., & Tyson, R. L. (1990). *Psychoanalytic Theories of Development: An Integration.* New Haven, CT: Yale University Press.

Utens, E. M. W. J. (2001). Instrumentarium voor het meten van angst bij kinderen en jeugdigen. Nieuwe ontwikkelingen [Instruments to measure anxiety in children and adolescents: New developments]. *TOKK, 26:* 171–181.

Utens, E. M. W. J., & Ferdinand, R. F. (2000). Nederlandse vertaling van de MASC (MASC–NL) [Dutch translation of the MASC.] Rotterdam: AZR–Sophia/Erasmus Universiteit.

Van Delsen, K., & Meurs, P. (2004). Op de rand. Borderline als diagnostische entiteit [At the edge: Borderline as a diagnostic entity]. In: N. Vliegen, L. Van Lier, S. Weytens, & G. Cluckers (Eds.), *Een verhaal met betekenis: Diagnostiek bij kinderen en adolescenten vanuit een psychodynamisch interpretatief model* (pp. 241–265). Leuven: ACCO.

van der Maas, J. J., & Tates, J. G. (1990). Oudertherapie: Methode en model [Parent therapy: Method and model]. In: P. A. de Ruyter & J. van der Ploeg (Eds.), *Handboek voor Orthopedagogiek* (pp. 1–22). Groningen: Wolters Noordhoff.

van der Pas, A. (1994). *Handboek methodische ouderbegeleiding I: Ouderbegeleiding als methodiek* [Handbook of methodical parent counselling I]. Rotterdam: Ad Donker.

van der Pas, A. (1996). *Handboek methodische ouderbegeleiding I: Naar een psychologie van ouderschap* [Handbook of methodical parent counselling I: Towards a psychology of parenthood]. Rotterdam: Ad Donker.

Van der Ree, W. E. (2006). Psychoanalytisch indiceren en onderzoek. De Rorschach-inktvlekkentest volgens het Comprehensive System nader bekeken [Psychoanalytic assignments and research: A closer look at the Rorschach inkblot method according to the Comprehensive System]. *Tijdschrift Voor Psychoanalyse, 11* (4): 262–279.

Van IJzendoorn, M. H. (1992). Intergenerational transmission of parenting: A review of studies in nonclinical populations. *Developmental Review, 12*: 76–99.

Van IJzendoorn, M. H. (1995). Adult attachment representations, parental responsiveness, and infant attachment: A meta-analysis on the predictive validity of the Adult Attachment Interview. *Psychological Bulletin, 117* (3): 387–403.

Van IJzendoorn, M. H., Tavecchio, L. W. C., Goossens, F. A., & Vergeer, M. M. (1982). *Opvoeden in geborgenheid: Een kritische analyse van Bowlby's attachmenttheorie* [Parenting in security: A critical analysis of Bowlby's attachment theory]. Deventer: Van Loghum Slaterus.

Verheugt-Pleiter, J. E. (2002). *Programma-ontwikkeling psychoanalytische ontwikkelingstherapie. Werkplan over het traject september 2002 tot mei 2003* [Psychoanalytic developmental therapy programme: Action plan from September 2002 until May 2003]. Internal report, Nederlands Psychoanalytisch Instituut.

Verheugt-Pleiter, J. E. (2003). Ik zie, ik zie wat jij niet ziet. Over de technische aspecten van psychoanalytische ontwikkelingstherapie [I spy with my little eye: About the technical aspects of psychoanalytic developmental therapy]. In: M. G. J.Schmeets & A. P. Schut (Eds.), *Anders en toch hetzelfde* (pp. 61–80). Assen: Van Gorcum.

Verheugt-Pleiter, A., & Deben-Mager, M. (2006). Transference-focused psychotherapy and mentalization-based tratment: Brother and sister? *Psychoanalytic Psychotherapy, 20* (4): 297–315.

Verheugt-Pleiter, J. E., & Zevalkink, J. (2005). Gehechtheidsverhalen van een Floddertje en een mevrouw Helderder: Theoretische vragen bij de diagnostiek van regulatiestoornissen [Attachment stories of Floddertje and Mrs Helderder: Theoretical issues in diagnostics of problems with affect regulation]. In: M. G. J. Schmeets & J. E. Verheugt (Eds.), *Affectregulatie*. Assen: Van Gorcum.

Verhofstadt-Denève, L. (1988). *Zelfreflectie en persoonsontwikkeling: Een handboek voor ontwikkelingsgerichte psychotherapie* [Reflection on self and development: A manual for developmentally oriented psychotherapy]. Leuven: ACCO.

Verhulst, F. C. (1981). Diagnostiek van borderline kinderen [Diagnostics of borderline children]. *Tijdschrift Voor Psychiatrie, 23*: 21–33.

Verhulst, F. C., Van der Ende, J., & Koot, H. M. (1996). *Handleiding voor de CBCL/4–18* [Manual for CBCL/4–18]. Rotterdam: Sophia Kinderziekenhuis/Academisch Ziekenhuis/Erasmus Universiteit.

Verhulst, F. C., Van der Ende, J., & Koot, H. M. (1997). *Handleiding voor de Teacher's Report Form (TRF)* [Manual for TRF]. Rotterdam: Sophia Kinderziekenhuis/Academisch Ziekenhuis/Erasmus Universiteit.

Verhulst, F. C., & Verheij, F. (Eds.) (2000). *Kinder- en jeugdpsychiatrie. Onderzoek en diagnostiek* [Child- and adolescent psychiatry: Research and diagnostics]. Assen: Van Gorcum.

VKJP (1994). *Nota ouderbegeleiding* [Report on parent guidance]. Unpublished manucript, the Society for Youth Psychotherapy, The Netherlands.

Weiner, I. B. (1998). *Principles of Rorschach Interpretation.* Mahwah, NJ: Erlbaum.

Winnicott, D. W. (1951). Transitional objects and transitional phenomena. In: *Through Paediatrics to Psychoanalysis.* London: Hogarth Press, 1958.

Winnicott, D. W. (1960). The theory of the parent–infant relationship. In: *The Maturational Processes and the Facilitating Enviroment* (pp. 37–55). London: Hogarth Press.

Winnicott, D. W. (1963). Psychiatric disorder in terms of infantile maturational processes. In: *The Maturational Processes and the Facilitating Enviroment* (pp. 230–241). London: Hogarth Press.

Winnicott, D. W. (1965). *The Maturational Processes and the Facilitating Environment.* London: Hogarth Press.

Winnicott, D. W. (1971) *Playing and Reality.* Harmondsworth: Penguin Books.

Yin, R. K. (1998). The abridged version of case study research: Design and method. In: L. Bickman & D. J. Rog (Eds.), *Handbook of Applied Social Research Methods* (pp. 229–259). Thousand Oaks, CA: Sage.

Zeanah, C. H. (1996). Beyond insecurity: A reconceptualization of attachment disorders of infancy. *Journal of Consulting and Clinical Psychology, 64* (1): 42–52.

Zevalkink, J. (2003). Klopt het? Wetenschappelijke onderzoeksbevindingen betreffende psychoanalytische ontwikkelingstherapie [Does it work? Empirical research findings regarding psychoanalytic developmental therapy]. In: M. G. J. Schmeets & A. P. Schut (Eds.), *Anders en toch hetzelfde. Psychoanalytische ontwikkelingstherapie met kinderen* (pp. 41–60). Assen: Van Gorcum.

Zevalkink, J. (2005). Het meten van gehechtheidsrepresentaties bij basisschoolleerlingen: Gehechtheidsverhalen in de klinische praktijk [Measuring attachment representations in children: Attachment stories in clinical practice]. *Kind En Adolescent, 26* (4): 352–367.

Zevalkink, J., & Verheugt-Pleiter, J. E. (2005). Gehechtheidsverhalen van een Floddertje en een mevrouw Helderder: De diagnostiek van gehechtheid en regulatiestoornissen bij latentiekinderen [Attachment stories of Floddertje and Mrs Helderder: Diagnostics of attachment and problems in affect regulation in latency children]. In: M. G. J. Schmeets & J. E. Verheugt (Eds.), *Affectregulatie*. Assen: Van Gorcum.

INDEX